The Girl with Special Knees

ORLA KELLY
PUBLISHING

Eleanor O'Kelly-Lynch

Orla Kelly Publishing
27 Kilbrody
Mount Oval
Rochestown
Cork
Ireland

Printed and bound in Ireland by
www.printmybook.com

For Lauren, Gary, Alannah, Sophia and Theo
And for my cousin, Irene.

The Stolen Child

Where dips the rocky highland
Of Sleuth Wood in the lake,
There lies a leafy island
Where flapping herons wake
The drowsy water rats;
There we've hid our faery vats,
Full of berrys
And of reddest stolen cherries.
Come away, O human child!
To the waters and the wild
With a faery, hand in hand,
For the world's more full of weeping
than you can understand.

William Butler Yeats, 1886

The Girl with Special Knees

Preface

A few years ago, I was watching television at home on my sofa. My daughter lay next to me, curled up, self-injuring her face. Lauren was born with a rare debilitating condition. Her life was a battle. She couldn't talk; she had frequent chest infections, recurring reflux, anxiety. As many readers will know, it is heart-breaking to watch someone you love suffer, especially when it's your child.

Later that evening, when Lauren had gone to bed and I voiced my despair, my sister said, 'Maybe, inside her head or in some far-off place across the universe, she's living another life, a wonderful life . . . in another dimension. Maybe there's a parallel world where she's having a ball.' The thought lifted me.

I'd read about parallel universes, where time can fork off into different realities – the multiverse. Other worlds where we live different versions of ourselves. Imagine if Lauren could escape her half-life, slip through a portal, take flight, live her dreams. And so, *The Girl with Special Knees* was born.

Through the book, I could give her wings. She would ride a horse, eat sweets, experience friendship, danger, adventure . . . and I could help free her spirit – the smart, funny, courageous girl who was there all the time, just buried under the rubble of despair.

While the book is written out of my lived experience, it is a work of fiction. The story follows the other family members too, the relationships inextricably connected. When I started out, I thought the book would be about escaping the bonds that hold us back, untangling the fallout of grief and loss. When I finished, I saw then that the book was really about how courage matters, how it comes in different guises and how – if we look long and hard enough – we find it within ourselves. Looking back now, I can see that this was the lesson I had to learn – and am still learning.

Eleanor O'Kelly-Lynch
October 2022

CHAPTER 1

DOLL

My name is Doll. I'm nearly eleven. You'd never think it though 'cos I'm so small. I have special knees. Not sure what it means. But everyone says it. I hear it every day: *Doll, she's special knees.* Maybe it's the way they stick out of my stick-thin legs?

I don't speak. Not because I don't want to. I can't, no matter how badly I need to say something. One night last week my granny floated in and sat on the end of my bed. It blew me away, just seeing her again. Though her face was in shadow, I could see her lips moving. But her voice was crumbly and blurred and I couldn't make out the words at all. I tried to call out to her to get her to stay, but I could only manage an *aaah* sound before she broke up into a million glittery pieces right before my eyes.

I cried then. I mean, I can cry, and to be honest, I often feel like crying. Sometimes I wail. The doctor says, 'She's just vocalising.' I don't like him, the doctor. He never looks me in the eye, just nods in my direction and shakes his head as he talks to my mother.

And my mother! Well, hello. She's another story. She knows I'm not bothered, but she keeps talking to me, trying to catch my eye. I know the colour of her every mood. I can see things others can't. She wears her mind on her face. I know the way her gaze goes off into the distance. I see the hollow smile, the way she purses her lips and pushes her tongue over her teeth. She rubs my back, but I know she is somewhere else entirely.

Look, I don't mind. I have my dreams. In my dreams, I'm skipping:

One, two, three O'Leary,
Four, five, six O'Leary . . .

But I can't skip in real life. Or draw. Or write. Or even feed myself. Imagine that, at nearly eleven! It's disgraceable.

1

Anyway, as I was saying, in my dreams I'm singing 'Raindrops Keep Falling on My Head.' I kind of know the melody; don't ask me how. And I'm dancing, clasping my hands over my head and twirling like a ballerina. When I get to the last line I take a bow, arms out, palms up – ta-da! Look at me! And everyone is clapping. All the family are smiling at me. Best of all, my dad is waving over at me, proud as punch.

But that's Dream-land. In Real-land, okay, I can walk. Just about. Big wow. But I can't dance at all. Or play football. And in Real-land no one is clapping. Instead, I see sad faces, pity-eyes, tinfoil smiles.

Hello? Is it something I said?

But of course not. Since I can't talk!

Look, if you don't mind, can we get back to my dreams?

Bed. It's so cosy. My fat duvet with yellow roses and cool matching curtains. The faint smell of tea tree oil. There's a picture above my bed of Goldilocks and the Three Bears. She's running away like lightning from the bears' house. Wish I could run away. It's the last thing I see before I go to sleep – her running like crazy . . . and me, hoping that someday I will too.

Every night the curtains swish together, barely meeting in the middle. Through the gap, I can just about see a piece of navy sky, a sliver of silver moon. And every night, every single night, my mother, like a robot, whispers, 'Sleep tight, love,' before the door clicks shut.

I turn to the wall then and pray to the pushy angel who chatters back to me but isn't coming up with the goods yet despite all her promises.

CHAPTER 2

SALLY

'Sleep tight, love.' I close the door on my wordless daughter.

As I do every night. Every bloody night.

I stop to gather myself at the top of the stairs and rest my elbows on the banister. Take a deep breath. Hold for four. Exhale. Like the book says. Breathe, inhale. Hold for four. *You must be strong,* I tell myself sharply. *You must not crumple. You must not, under any circumstances, scream. Screaming is weak, pointless, dramatic.*

I need to keep reminding myself of this. Remind myself not to be crying, unravelling; to get over myself. Not to give in to that scream in the pit of my stomach, the one that keeps trying to make a run for it, past the sentries in my throat.

I fold myself onto the top step, jam my palms over my face. Is it okay to say . . . ? Well, I am going to say it: *God, you're spiteful. The life you gave my girl. Are you proud of yourself up there in your towering mansion in the sky? Did you hum softly as you made my small, broken Doll?*

Breathe in. Breathe out. I must stop this nonsense. Other mothers are strong, capable, grounded. They don't howl, those other mothers. I don't hear them roar and spit and cry. They smile. I know. I've met them. And I don't see despair. Not at all. Like that woman on *The Late Late Show* the other night saying her special-needs son was a challenge and a blessing. 'He's made me a better mum,' she said, smiling. She was rising to the challenge. Not like me. *A useless mother. Admit it.*

Tears, get back inside.

Don't they ever feel it, those wonderful mothers? The desolation? Like a small child tugging at you. *Go away!* you tell it, but it won't. It catches you sideways and drags you by its teeth, along the floor, down, down, till you seep right through the tiles.

Get up, Sally. Keep moving.

Sometimes I feel that if I sit here too long, I'll never get up. Turned to salt like that woman in the Bible. A statue, caked and grimy. Can statues scream?

I pull myself up.

Despair. It's such a little word. The emotion is bound to spill out and leak between the letters onto the floor . . . and I just can't mop it all up. Actually, it's me spilling over. I'd want to get a grip before Dan sees me. I know what *he'd* say.

I march down the soft grey stairs. I'll tidy up, fill the dishwasher. Put the kettle on. Keep moving. *Don't think, move.*

A shout from the living room. 'Prime Time's starting, Sal. C'mon.'

Prime Time's starting, Sal. The empty distractions of life. I pull my sleeve across my eyes.

'Com-ing.' Sing-song voice. Nice and bright.

I head for the kitchen and stack the dishwasher. Run a J-cloth across the table. 'Give me two minutes,' I shout to Dan as I flick the kettle on. I line up two stripy mugs and a packet of Maltesers. Two minutes is all you need to drag your face into a crayon smile. That's the job: march on, regardless. Keep the lid on. Say nothing. Always look on the bright side.

CHAPTER 3

DOLL

Bed. It's like death, but warm. I often heard my granny talk about it – death, that is, not bed. She said you close your eyes and then there's only sweet oblivion.

'What's that?' my sister Andi asked her one night when she was minding us.

'Close your eyes,' Granny told her, closing hers and folding her glasses on her lap. 'Now pretend you're fading away into . . . everlasting peace.'

It sounded so beautiful, everlasting peace. I'd love that.

I loved my Granny, and I know she loved me. Look, she did. You always know. She would sit next to me on the couch, stroking my hair and pushing the stray bits out of my eyes. People would come to our house and say, 'Who's Doll like? Has she a look of Auntie Joan?' or 'She definitely has her granddad's eyes.' And Granny would butt in and say, 'She's like herself. She's Doll. One of a kind.'

I liked that. The way she said I was one of a kind.

I often heard her talk about Arthur. She'd sigh a lot when she spoke about him, rolling her eyes, tut-tutting, her mouth set straight as a pencil. 'What can you do?' she'd say. 'It hasn't been an easy road.' No, she said, she wouldn't wish Arthur-itis on anyone. Very painful, very tough. She used to be able to dance, she said, before Arthur. Not anymore. Only in her dreams she said – she danced and ran and swirled in her dreams.

Like me, Granny.

I never met him. Arthur. Never even saw his photo, but I would have buckarooed him if he ever walked in the door of my house.

My mom tells people I buckaroo anyone I don't like. And I do. It's really easy. I bend one of my (special) knees, and then, just as the target is passing by my couch, I straighten my leg and *pow!* It feels good. Especially when they're not looking. Sometimes they wobble. 'Jeez,' they might say, looking at me in mock horror as if to say, *What did I do to deserve that?* I wish I could tell them. But then someone says, 'Don't worry. Doll buckaroos anyone who gets in her space; it's not personal.'

Look, hello. *It actually is.*

Some people really annoy me. They lean close. 'And how are *you*, Doll?'

Like they care. But they feel they have to say something. Kids especially bug me. Take Ruby from next door (take her away, someone, pulease). She's five. She marches in, leans over me, pokes my shoulder with her chubby finger. I can see her red dotty dress up close, her curls bobbing around her silly face. She's wearing red shoes with bows. When she flashes a smile, I can smell wine gums off her.

'Ya having a good day, Doll? Are ya?'

She turns to my mother. 'She won't look at me, Sally. Why are her eyes closed?'

'Be careful, Ruby,' she's told. 'Doll is tired. Leave her be, pet.'

Ruby turns back to me, 'Hi, Doll. Are ya having . . .'

Did you hear what my mom just said, Ruby? I bend my knee and push forward, hitting her thigh sideways. She wobbles, hands out to save her from a fall. She straightens then. Moves back to a safer distance. Looks hurt. Palms up.

'What ya do that for, Doll?'

I'd love to jump up off my couch, put my hands on my hips, just like she does. And I'd love to say, *Ruby! Who do you think you are, coming in here with your pretty dress and your stupid red shoes, thinking you're great?* I'd say, *Look, will you stop singing 'Twinkle Twinkle'? Spare me, please. And . . . and you dancing to 'Shiny Happy People' is not funny!*

And I'd shout, *Why aren't you outside with the others playing hot-scotch? Get out of my house now, right this minute.*

I know. I know. She *is* sweet. And kind. She tries to give me a crisp. She taps my head. But I don't want her in my house. I wish I could buckaroo her again, but she's gone, into the kitchen. I can hear them all laughing; they think it's kinda funny. 'But she doesn't mean it, Ruby. She doesn't understand.'

Look, I understand plenty. I understand what the pushy angel is saying to me every night. She knows I'm a girl in a cage and she's trying to fix it so that I get out. And even though she gets cross with me sometimes, I get that she's trying to help. Once, a few weeks ago, she touched my hand – I think it was an accident – and I felt a gust of wind blow right through my heart, leaving a tunnel, a hollow space behind. She never said a word about it afterwards, but I can feel it, that airy channel in the middle of my heart. And I know it's there for a reason. I'm thinking it might be a space for dropping my dreams in. Like a post-box. A place where dreams turn real. It just takes time, that's all.

As Ruby reappears, I close my eyes and pull my tartan rug up around me. I can taste salt in my mouth. But I remind myself that soon, very soon, something amazing is going to happen. I know it in my heart. And I can hear it – my future – flapping its wings and swooping towards me. And you know, that sound, it keeps me going.

CHAPTER 4

ANDI

I hate school. I hate my life. I hate Ireland, and I hate this rain-drenched, godforsaken town of Glengarvan. I hate St Mary's. I hate my class. I hate my teachers. *Andrea, your work is so disappointing. Andrea, you used to show such promise. Andrea Redmond, what is wrong with you?*

School's over for the day. I clip my rucksack to my carrier and cycle across the yard, through the puddles and out onto the road that leads to the gravel path that skirts the Lainey River. It's bucketing down and I pull my hood up.

At school, I feel like an outsider. I *am* an outsider. I know I have Stacey Ryan – and we do have a laugh – but I miss Laura so much this year. She's just moved to Glasgow. Her father owned Clifton Life Insurance in Main Street and got an offer he couldn't refuse, Laura said. My dad said he was a crook who had to get out of town fast, but I didn't tell Laura that. We hung out together all the time . . .

I wait for a break in the traffic, but a car lets me through, and I wave my thanks. At least some people have manners.

It's hard to break into the other girls' groups in my class of swots. Not that I even want to. The Fennell twins are up their own arses, and they don't like me anyway. Niamh and Kate are nerds. And Lisa Kenny and her crew are a bunch of slappers. The last night out at the Rugby Club, they made a show of themselves dancing on tables, and I'm not talking Riverdance here – I'm talking down and dirty. Don't get me wrong, I'm not a prude, but Jesus, there was nothing left to the imagination. Wouldn't be seen dead with them. And if you met them? Fuck it, butter wouldn't melt—

There's Lisa now in her dad's car, the smug bitch, waving from the back seat like she's Kate Middleton.

Everyone else in the class is pretty boring. Study, study, study. Straight As are the goal. Shauna wants to do veterinary, and Nadine Cox has her sights set on Wall Street. Wall Street? Give me a break!

Wallflower, more like. I've another three years in this dump, then I'm definitely out of here. I can't wait.

It's quiet on the river path, a few kids from school shuffling along in groups, having a sneaky fag. This is the best time of the day. A breather. A chance to rate the day. And today was pretty much a disaster. A two out of ten. I mean, Crosby accuses me there of back-answering in geography. Back-answering? What the hell is that, anyway? If you're asked a question, then you must answer. Back. Or back-answer. What's the difference? I actually asked him. I said to him, 'Sorry, sir.' (Dunno why I was apologising; I did nothing wrong.) I said, 'Sorry, sir; I was answering you back. What's the problem there, like?'

Everyone giggled at that. No wonder. It's just logic, but teachers only like logic when it's their version of it.

Anyway, he looks at me and says he's having no more of it.

'Andrea, straight to the principal's office. Ms Trout can deal with you.'

I sigh.

'Sorry, Andrea, is there a problem?'

I roll my eyes. He's such an idiot. I gather up my books in slow motion (just to annoy him), pretending to rummage for stuff, dropping pens and pencils.

'Oops . . . sorry, sir.' Titters all round. They don't like me, really, but this is a diversion, and a diversion is always welcome, especially in geography class. Unless you're Nadine or Shauna. I can see them tut-tutting, shaking their heads. Not impressed.

'Move along, Andrea. Stop looking for attention. Smarten up, move along.'

I can see I've gotten under his skin. Good. Mission accomplished. I can't help one parting shot as I exit.

'Mr Crosby?'

He peers over his glasses. 'Yes, Andrea?'

'I think all this is very fishy . . .'

The class erupts in laughter.

'I'm only codding,' I say. 'I know my plaice . . .'

More laughter.

He points to the door. 'Out. Now.'

Ms Trout's name suits her to perfection, with her mottled skin and fish eyes.

9

I slam the door behind me. I don't care if I get detention . . . just as long as my mom doesn't find out. More drama – I couldn't cope!

Lucky for me, Ms Trout is away for the day, and the bell goes as I'm leaving the office. 'Come back tomorrow,' the secretary says, but I won't. I'll probably be in more trouble, but do I care?

Laura and me keep in touch, but WhatsApp and Voice Notes aren't the same. And at home, it's Doll this and Doll that. Do I get a look in? Do I hell. Doll can't eat, Doll's in pain, Doll has a cough again. Don't get me wrong; I think my sister has a crap life. But what about me? Oh, yes, I keep forgetting. I'm the lucky one. Lucky me, I have it all. Sometimes I feel like screaming . . .

Can you imagine it? They'd come running. *Are you okay, Andi?* And they'd look at each other, eyebrows raised, and they'd say, *Darling, what's wrong with you?*

Then the lecture would start. And they'd tell me how precious I am . . . but. *But.* There's always a *but.* I'm the lucky one. I need to re-member that. To remember that Doll hasn't got what I have. Doll would love to be me.

Yes, of course, how selfish am I? I'm sure she would, but it's not my bloody fault, is it, that she can't talk or go to a real school and have a real life? It's not my fault, is it, that she makes her face bleed? That she has a dead life? Is that my fault?

I veer off the path and shoot left up the hill, past the old watermill, and take a sharp right up through Bluebell Avenue and on to Bluebell Grove. The rain's stopped, and I shake back my hood as I lean my bike against the potting shed round the back of number 6. Mom is stirring soup on the Aga. For once she's in a good mood.

'Hi, love,' she says. 'Sit down there and eat this. Doll is asleep on the couch.'

I pull the rug up over Doll's shoulders, tuck it in around her. I wish I had a real sister. One I could share things with and talk to and have a laugh with . . . but I never will. My sister will always be a baby, and she'll never be my friend. And it makes me mad. But my mother says that's life, girl. And my father says – without even looking at me – thank your lucky stars. Thank your lucky stars; that's his fucking answer.

CHAPTER 5

DOLL

I know I'm broken. That's not news to me. And I can't be fixed. She keeps trying to fix me; how can't she see I'm unfixable? Like Humpty Dumpty. Damaged goods. Second rate. She thinks I should be happy. She'd like me to be like Ruby. *But Mom, I will never be like Ruby. Get over it.*

Let's be honest. I'm like a cracked cup. Or an old skirt. Tattered, torn, worn . . . worn out. My granny used to say she was worn out. I know what she meant. Worn is when you're rubbed and scrubbed and the edges of you begin to fray. Buttons come off, holes start appearing, threads unravel. If it's a skirt, you throw it out and buy a new one, right? Makes sense. You can't keep stitching and mending and covering up the stains and the grubby marks.

I want out. I heard a robber say that on the telly: *I want out.* I want to vanish into another life. *Poof!* But how? Is that what my granny came to tell me? Or was it a dream?

'What's it all about, Alfie?' Granny used to say that in a sing-song voice.

Andi asked her once, 'Who's Alfie, Granny? Is it someone you knew?'

But Granny laughed and said, 'No, just a song in a film.'

But it's a good question, isn't it? *What's it all about?* 'Cos I sure don't know. And I don't think Granny knew either.

I'm not being mean, but I can't stick it out here much longer. I want to sing and slide and swim. I want to ride a horse and chew toffees ('Soft food,' the doctor said; otherwise I'll choke). I want to have adventures. I want a friend to share jokes and a packet of Taytos with. I want to know what it's like to kick a ball into the net and hear the roar of the crowd. *Well done, Doll. Great score, Doll. You've done us proud, Doll. Three cheers for Doll. Hip hip hooray!* I'd jump in the air, and everyone would come up to me and hug me and high-five me, and I'd swing my fist and punch the air. *What a striker*, they'd say. *Isn't Doll Redmond something?*

11

Well, that'll never happen. Unless I can get out. Unless I can be another Doll in another life. Imagine!

I know this is weird, but I love the feel of my nails piercing my skin. It feels so good. The more I dig my face, the sharper the pain, the more alive I am. I feel alive when I'm hurting. I like the blood; it makes me feel like I'm somebody. And it's not like I have other stuff to do.

On the telly, everyone looks so happy and I watch all the fun baking shows. But I hate food. It sticks in my throat, makes my stomach sore, and sometimes it comes back down my nose and makes me gag. So I have tablets for that. I like my tea, though, and hot chocolate. The sweet, milky taste sloshes around my mouth and trickles down my throat. Woo. Feels good.

Still, I'd love to drift away with my granny. To float off my couch or use my tartan rug like a magic carpet. I saw it on the telly. The carpet will do what it's told and fly over blue hills to places where there's sun and wild horses and trees with long green hair and men with hoods and beards and girls in pink and yellow dresses. Look, it's all true. I've seen it.

And there's a castle on the telly with stars and fireworks fizzing all over the sky, and someone – probably an angel – is singing about wishing upon a star and she's saying it doesn't even make a difference who you are . . .

The song makes me excited. I think it's a message telling me I can escape and – and the best bit is that it *doesn't make any difference who you are*. So it doesn't matter if you're broken or worn; things will come to you if you wish and dream. Well, hello. They couldn't keep saying it if it wasn't true, could they? That'd be cruel. And anyway, angels don't lie.

CHAPTER 6

DAN

Another day done. Another candle snuffed out. Above, the sky is muddy, and rain is sweeping in on an east wind. Rory Gallagher is singing on the car radio. He wants to be a million miles away. I turn the volume right up and swing out into Main Street. *Rory, I know how you feel, man.*

I inch forward, growling at the evening traffic, but there's another part of me that wants to stay in this car-cave forever. A cosy glass membrane between me and the rest of the world. The wind lifts umbrella skirts, exposing their spindly legs. Dripping faces mouth swear words. A man with a plastic shopping bag slams his palm on my bonnet as if to say, *Hold your bloody horses – I'm drenched, you're dry, give us a break.* As I move, revving, a woman gives me the two fingers. *Jesus, woman, you won't melt.* I honk the horn in reply. The pure ignorance. The weather definitely brings out the worst in people.

A green light, and one car gets through. One car! I slam on the horn. What is going on up there, for Chrissake?

Calm, Dan; chill out. Rory is still singing the blues. I sit back and watch the people hurry past. You never know what's going on behind someone's eyes, do you? The jumble of fears and anxieties that play out inside someone's head.

I spot Johnny Blake, a good friend of mine, dashing into Centra. He's holding a soggy newspaper over his head. I remember he told me over a pint in Whelan's one night that he was bipolar. Manic depression; that was what they called it in his day, he said. He tried to top himself when he was twenty-six. 'I couldn't stand it,' he said, tapping the side of his head, jabbing it quite hard. I remember that – jabbing more than tapping. 'It's Las Vegas up here.' That's what he said. I never forgot that. Even when I see him now, I still think of that. *It's Las Vegas up here.*

I was there once. Las Vegas. Me and Sally, just after we were married. Before life got . . . messy. The city that never stops. Brash, flashy, full of noise. If it was a person, it'd be Donald Trump. Las Vegas in your head? Sounds like a bloody nightmare. And if you saw him, Johnny, that is – wool suit, silk tie, a precise sort of bloke – well, you'd never think it. That's all I'm saying. You'd never think there was a sleepless city in his head.

The thing is, people don't really think about anyone else's interior life. They're too busy fretting about their own. We're all like that.

On the radio, Sarah McInerney is interviewing an economist. I turn down the volume, let my thoughts drift. People would look at me and say, *He's got it all. Lovely wife. Beautiful house in Bluebell Grove. He's in the bank, a good number; you do know him, the spit of Kevin Bacon? Seriously,* they'd say. *Golf captain last year. She works for the paper. Three kids, the eldest in college in Africa – a scholarship. The little one has some rare condition; autistic, I think. God love us.* They'd whisper that last bit. Still, they'd say, *He did well.* But it's all optics, isn't it? That's all people see. How perfect your life is. Instagram perfect is the goal. It's an own goal, though. People haven't a clue.

We're moving at last. Through the lights, over the bridge. There's a truck broken down on Church Street, hazards flashing. A guard is directing traffic at the crossroads, adding to the mayhem.

Must stop for milk at the Murphy's Garage. Lactose-free . . . or is it semi-skimmed? All the same to me.

I know I should be grateful – and I don't like to dwell on this too much – but sometimes life can be a washed-out grey. The sameness of the days. Like smoke, it can steal in. Swirl and curl around you, drift inside your head. Like a morning river fog flattening out the colour. I try not to think about it. About life being grey with pops of colour.

The phone buzzes. Text from Sally. Don't forget the milk, Dan.

Don't forget the milk, Dan. The trivia of marriage. Me and Sally? I'm not even going to go there.

Heavy drops hammer on the roof like nails; cars glide past, lighting up the slanting rain. Everyone's heading home, figuring out their day, looking forward, looking back. Ten thousand thoughts between them.

That dumb guard is causing more chaos than the truck. The engine idles. Colbert's Bakery and Deli is on my left. Jars of homemade jams and pickles in the window. Empty baskets on chequered cloths. Rob Colbert is locking up, hooded head bent. He's one of my clients. A good guy. Set up the business about ten years ago. Tied into an expensive lease. Still up at four in the mornings, six days a week.

Today, when he was in with me, he broke down. I didn't expect it. It's hard to watch a man cry. The wife has been diagnosed with multiple sclerosis. Thirty-seven. Two small kids. I could hear the sound of his life slamming and sliding into a wall. Like a car on black ice. He's worried about the repayments. No health insurance. *I've been there, mate*, I think . . . but I don't say it.

Even thinking about him now, I can feel my palms dampen. I loosen my tie. God knows what he must be going through. People are breakable.

When he looked up at me eventually, he said, 'Sorry, Dan, I'm all over the place.'

'I'll get you a glass of water,' I said, and as I touched his shoulder, I could almost feel the hope leaking through the fabric. His distress snagged me, like barbed wire on my skin.

'Listen. I'm washed up. A beaten docket.'

'Don't think like that, Rob.'

He took a sip of water.

'The light in the tunnel is an oncoming train – did you ever hear that one, Dan?'

We stayed a long time talking. It was hard to tell him there wasn't a lot I could do without involving head office. He didn't want that. 'Maybe zero interest for a few months, Dan? Could you swing that for me?'

When he left, I felt a sort of desolation spider down my back. You never get used to it. It drags you down, like a terrier with its teeth in your ankle, hard to shake off . . .

I swing into 6 Bluebell Grove and kill the engine. I can feel the rush of warmth in the hallway as I open the door. The spicy smell of chicken korma; orange flames leaping up the chimney. John Denver's on the radio singing about leaving on a jet plane . . .

I hum as I slip off my shoes. A voice from the kitchen. 'Did you get the milk?'

I touch the heel of my palm to my forehead.

She puts her head round the door, rolls her eyes. 'Never mind, we'll manage. It's a filthy evening, isn't it?'

'Shocking. How's Doll?'

'Same. Not good.'

'Did she eat much?'

'Not much. I think she's coming down with something.'

'She'll have to have that feeding tube, Sal.'

'No way.' She disappears back into the kitchen. 'Want a beer before dinner?'

'Does a swim duck?'

She smiles at our in-joke. I sling my jacket over the banister and move towards the fire. Doll looks up from her couch. She's stretched out, leaning on her orange cushion, her tartan rug loose around her shoulders. I ruffle her hair. She doesn't smile, just closes her eyes.

My phone pings. It's Shirley Lovett. My heart lurches. Bank stuff. It can wait. I need to keep Shirley out of my head. And out of my office. I put the phone face-down on the mantelpiece. I know she's a flirt, but a woman like that can get inside your head.

I sink into the armchair, feel my bones loosen. I look out into the dusk. The rain's morphing into a ghostly drizzle.

I'm thinking about Rob Colbert. I'm thinking about Doll. And the unsettling Shirley. I'm thinking about a spicy chicken korma and a slow iced beer. A pop of colour against a grey day.

CHAPTER 7

SALLY

The alarm shrieks like an angry fox. Black morning, frost on glass. I click open Doll's bedroom door. She looks happy as she sleeps. I place my hand on her shoulder and she jumps, dismayed to be awake. I lift her out of bed; she resists, a dead weight. 'Come on, Doll, help me here. It's another day, another dollar.' My mother used to say that – *another day, another dollar*. Don't know where she got that one. I miss her a lot, my mother.

I walk her downstairs, holding her hand while she grips the rail with tiny fingers. Slow steps. 'C'mon, you can do it, Doll.'

She walks into the kitchen unaided.

The table is set out like a pretend surgery. Cotton wool, boiled water, tea tree oil. Adhesive strip, cotton socks, sticky tape, check.

Doll's face is contorted, pain and misery fighting it out between them. We stand against the table, and she struggles in my grip. I cup her chin with my left hand from behind and begin to dab the deep crimson-yellow wound on her right cheek. I take a deep breath. I need to clean the pus first, gently. I carefully dab the wound dry and then apply gauze and adhesive. The sticky residue of last night's plaster remains like a ghostly outline. It's a gaping cut, and I'm sure it stings. She flinches and pulls away. Misery, thy name is Doll.

I'm staying calm. 'Well,' I tell her, in a very practical tone, though does she understand a word? 'This is what happens . . . if you insist on digging your face. It will get sore, and . . . and . . . and so, what do you expect, Doll?'

She looks up at me. Tears spill through her long lashes and snake across her temples into her hairline.

Breathe in, hold, breathe out.

The cut is a mini crater gouged out of her skin. Torn and healed, torn and healed a hundred times. Her tears drip down.

'Nearly there, love. Nearly there.' *Remain detached.* I wrap her tiny fist in layers of coloured cotton socks, finishing with a long white sports sock that stretches up to her elbow. I secure it with tape.

One down, one to go.

Soon I have both 'boxing gloves' secured. They will give her cheeks a chance to heal while she's in school. I say 'school,' but it's really day-care. A dedicated bunch of women doing their best. My allies.

Here's the thing I can't face – knowing she only wants to climb onto her coffin-couch, close her eyes, and drift off into . . . sweet oblivion, as my mother used to say. Is she trying to carve a bloodied message across her face? *Leave me die.*

She moves towards her couch, and I give her a beaker of tea.

Every day she retreats a little further from us, backing away slowly, half crouching . . . like a cowboy saying, 'Don't follow me; I need to get outta here. Don't touch me; don't feed me. Please, Mom.'

I throw some berries and yoghurt into the blender and warm a bowl of Ready Brek. She resists. Spits out the milky mixture.

It takes twenty minutes. *Come on, Doll.* I count the spoons. *Seven, eight . . . one more spoon.* 'Just one. Just one. Please, Doll.'

Job done.

I grab her pink duffle coat and squeeze the gloves through the sleeves. 'Come on, a walk for ten minutes before your taxi arrives.' We wander down the drive, my hand resting on her shoulder. She cooper-ates, staring ahead, one small foot dutifully placed in front of the other. A dainty soldier. She leans forward into the breeze. She's calm now. No tears. For that, thank you, God.

The day-care taxi arrives, and I secure her in the back seat. The driver takes her Dora lunch box.

'Nice morning.' He smiles.

'Indeed it is.' I make sure to say it cheerfully. 'Lovely and bright for October.'

He waves and is gone.

I walk back to the empty house, put the kettle on. And then I kneel on the kitchen floor and scream. I'm not proud of it. You wouldn't want to make a habit out of it. It doesn't solve anything.

Afterwards, I feel faint. Not good for you, I'd say.

I sip my tea, butter some toast, take two paracetamol. Get ready for work.

My baby wants to die. She's my child, and I can't reach her. She's drifting away, and I can't . . .

Breathe. Hold. Exhale.

I can't . . . I can't fix her. And I'm her mother. I should be able to fix her.

The tea spills.

Soon she will disappear from view, over the horizon, melting into the air. Someday we will lift that tartan rug and there will be nothing there, only a Doll-shaped hollow and an orange cushion damp with tears.

I fix my hair, apply some face powder. I really *must* try harder. Keep looking for a solution, right?

But we've been there: doctors, tests, scans, bloods. *All clear, mum.* Psychologists. Medication. *We'll try Prozac, shall we? Kinesiology and cranial massage?* Why not? Holy medals. Novenas. Energy healers. *Mrs. Redmond, Padre Pio never let anyone down . . .*

No. Joy.

Here's the thing: everyone gives up sooner or later. Shaking their heads. It's complex, they say. Sooner or later, they give up. Next patient, please!

There was one doctor; his compassion shattered me. I remember he touched her head lightly, and he smiled and spoke to her. Like he cared.

'We'll take away your pain, Doll. We won't give up on you.'

He said he wouldn't give up on her. He wouldn't give up.

I wanted to reach out and squeeze his arm tight. *Thank you. Thank you so much.* But I couldn't speak; I was rooted and, to be honest, mortified. I really shouldn't have, but I cried, in front of a stranger – the shame of it, tears spilling down my face, and me only able to mouth my apology, shaking, unable to catch my breath. Caught off guard by someone who had a heart. Trust me; kindness can puncture you like nothing else.

The GP says, 'Sally, you might have to accept that she is where she is . . . with her condition.'

Her *condition*. It's like a vandal spraying her cells with his aerosol can of poison. A rainbow of misery. A child with a death wish. God, what were you thinking? *What were you bloody well thinking?*

I clear away the breakfast dishes.

When Doll was born they whisked her away quickly. I heard the nurse whisper that she was very small. So what? Lots of babies are small. No panic, woman!

I'd had an epidural, so maybe that explained why I felt so eerily detached. Though, come on – I should have noticed that Dan and me were left alone in the delivery room. He was ashen. I was upbeat . . . *what was I on?*

I remember the footsteps on the corridor, the paediatrician in the pinstripe suit swinging through the double doors. Hesitating. Grey eyes, steepled fingers, thumbs to his chest. He spoke quickly, as if speed would soften the hammer blow.

'Your daughter has a very rare condition . . . low birth weight . . .' *Sorry, come again?* 'She has severe respiratory complications' – *What is he saying?* – 'and some digestive abnormalities.' *Am I dreaming? I don't understand.* 'She has some difficulty in . . .' *What is he telling us?* 'I'm afraid her general condition suggests mental retardation.' *He's joking, surely? It's not happening.*

His words were ashes falling onto the delivery room floor. *It must be a mistake. He can't be serious. Turn the clock back. Turn it back. Rewind. Rewind.* 'We will run further tests, and that will tell us more.' *Ashes.* 'I'm sorry.'

'You're sorry?'

'Yes, it is unhappy news, I am sure.'

Unhappy news. Well, that was one way of putting it.

The silence between us was a pillow over my face. I remember I could read the time on his watch. Ten past four in the morning. And his cufflinks were gold and shaped like anchors. I remember the anchors. I remember thinking, *How ironic!* And I remember his hands. The blond hairs on tapered fingers.

'Mr. and Mrs. Redmond?'

Silence.

'I understand this must come as a great shock to you both . . .'

I felt something crawl from my stomach, slither up my throat, some slimy swamp-like primal creature with a tail and tongue and teeth.

'Will she live?' I asked it calmly.

'Oh, she'll live all right. She's a fighter.' Those were his exact words.

The nurses were wheeling me back to my room. The corridor swam. 'Her BP is low; keep her on her side,' they said. I felt sick. Dan held my hand. *Abnormal. Abnormal.*

'We'll get a second opinion,' Dan was saying.

When I got back to my room, I turned to the wall. It couldn't be true. It wasn't true.

Knock at the door. I'm back there now, eleven years ago. A blonde head. 'Congratulations, darling. I'm here with your complimentary Bounty Bag.' She smiles. 'I've got baby creams and lotions . . .' She places the pink bag sideways on the bed and as the baby stuff spills onto the blanket, the first tears crawl down my face and drip onto *The A to Z of Baby Care.*

'Ah, don't worry, love; it's just the baby blues.' She plucks a floral tissue from the box on the locker and hands it to me. 'That'll pass in no time, but you'll have your little baby forever.' A bell tolls in my head.

Later, a nurse tiptoes in. 'Would you like to see your baby?'

'No thank you.'

'Why not, dear?'

'I'm not ready, dear.'

She smiles. I know she pities me. She's glad it isn't her. 'Don't leave it for too long, pet. Sooner the better.'

*

I remember the Baby Care Unit. Hushed. The clatter of a trolley over tiles. A whoosh from medical machinery.

I remember fastening the blue surgical cap and gown hanging inside the door and very slowly, arms folded, following the nurse to cubicle three, where Doll lay in an incubator. She was lying on a sheepskin-like blanket with a tube in her nose and another attached to her tiny hand. Her eyes were open, and she was gazing at a picture of the Blessed Virgin Mary on the wall. Her face was pale, shadowed by long dark lashes.

I leaned forward, my hand shaking as I stroked her tiny foot. Her skin was as soft as duck down and warm, I remember, to the touch.

The nurse hovered. 'Do you want to hold her?'

'No. Thank you.'

'Are you sure, Mrs. Redmond?'

'I just said no thank you.'

But as I stood there, tears falling, I felt something inside me untangle, like a ball of thread unspooling and tying me to her forever. And I remember, as the sun rose in a pink sky that autumn morning, I thought that, within her tiny cry, I could hear the words – I know it sounds ridiculous now, looking back, but I did hear the words: *Mind me.*

'I will, I promise,' I said, whispering it over the incubator. 'I will. Of course I will. I'm your mother, aren't I?'

CHAPTER 8

ANDI

Crosby is droning on again. What a dose. I'm counting the cracks on the wall next to my desk. Boring business class. The only business class I'm interested in is the one on a flight to Africa. My brother Will is off studying anthropology in Ethiopia – the Jewel of Africa, so they say. Addis Ababa University. It's hot there now, he said in his email yesterday, mid-twenties most days. Perfect weather for white shorts and strappy silver sandals. I was thinking maybe after Christmas – a mad idea . . .

'Andrea, can you give us an example?'

I nearly jump out of my skin. What's he want now?

'Sorry, sir?' There I go apologising again.

'Andrea, we're saying if your new business venture has cash flow problems, what happens if you can't get money off the bank?'

What on earth is the old twit talking about?

'Okay, so if my business can't . . . ?'

'Yes, yes, when you can't get money off the bank, what are your options?'

I have to think fast.

'Well, for starters,' I say, 'it's *from*, not *off* . . .'

Silence. He leans forward, folds his arms. Rocks on his feet. Deck shoes. Ugh!

'Sorry?'

'Oh, you needn't apologise,' I say, 'but it's *from* the bank, not *off* the bank – it's bad grammar. You can't actually pluck money *off* a bank; it's *from* . . .'

I'm expecting a titter, a few suppressed giggles. But there's silence.

'You're correcting my grammar, is it?' He sits back in his chair, arms still folded.

I'm kinda sorry I started.

'You tell me; you're the teacher. What would I know, right?'

Long pause. I'm starting to feel uneasy. I can feel the tension in the room winding around me like cat-gut.

He glares at me.

'Look, I'm just saying, it should be *from*, not *off*. Simple as. No big deal. Forget it.'

Crosby rises; his chair clatters back against the whiteboard, rocks for a few seconds, steadies. Everyone looks at me. I'm thinking, *Whaaat? He's the one making a big deal, not me. Can't you see this is a tactic to humiliate me?*

Everyone seems to be holding their breath. Have I gone too far this time?

'You've gone too far this time, Andrea Redmond.' Then he crosses the room and closes the door quietly behind him.

I look around. 'Well, thanks to me, it's a free class for everyone in the audience. Lighten up, guys.'

There's a clamour of accusations.

Shauna's first in. Typical. 'You're such an idiot. What did you do that for?'

Lisa looks smug. 'You've pushed it this time, Andi. You're asking for trouble.'

'We'll all pay for this, guaranteed.' Nadine looks around the room. 'Andi, what are you playing at? Go after him and apologise.'

'Are you joking?' I say. That's just what he wants – me, crawling back. 'No way. I'm off.'

I march out of the classroom looking a lot more confident than I feel. What a bunch of morons.

I make for the school gates. My head is thumping. Fuck. I realise my bike key is still on my desk.

I walk along the river path, trying very hard not to cry. What an idiot I am. I should have apologised – who needs this? It feels like I'm always looking for a fight. Someone to tangle with. It only feels good for a few minutes, and then I just want to cry.

I sit on one of the metal benches facing the river and watch two swans on the far side of the water, gliding along the surface like ballet dancers sneaking off for a smoke.

A crunch of tyres on gravel. It's my Dad. He buzzes down the passenger window.

'Get in. Now.' I slope onto the leather seat.

'That was fast. I suppose they rang you with their side of the—'

'Stop it.'

He's livid.

'What do you think you're doing, Andi? I got a call from that trout, I mean Ms Trout. I had to leave a critical meeting because you're apparently missing in action. She wants to see me – us – now.'

He jams his foot on the brake to avoid a woman darting across the road, still swearing as he turns to go through the school gates.

'Mr Crosby refuses to teach your class because of your insolence, and now I have to sit across from that principal woman and listen to a list of complaints about your disruptive behaviour—'

'Dad, they're—'

'Don't *Dad* me. Don't you think we have enough problems? And don't blame the teacher; he's not the problem. You are. And well you know it. It's so disappointing – you're nearly sixteen, and you behave like you're ten.'

He glares at me. He always pulls that 'disappointing' card; he knows it gets to me.

We turn into the staff car park and make for the principal's office in silence. She beckons us inside.

'Thanks for coming, Mr. Redmond. I'm sorry about this, but we need to talk.'

He nods.

She gestures toward the three chairs in front of her desk. The office is cramped, files piled high behind her. Books are stacked floor to ceiling – huh, like she reads all this stuff! I focus on a spider plant slumped on the windowsill. She disappears for a moment, and we sit listening to a drift of faltering piano notes seeping through from the music room next door.

Trout reappears and collapses into her swivel chair. I watch her from under my lashes. Her mouth opens and closes as she reads the file in front of her. She pinches the bridge of her nose, like she's thinking about what she's going to say, but I reckon she has it all well rehearsed. Crosby arrives, extends his hand to my dad. Ignores me. Very bloody childish. He takes a seat.

Ms Trout coughs.

'Mr Redmond, you know why we're here.' She fixes her eyes on me. 'Andrea, there've been a number of incidents over the past while that suggest to me that you are not in earnest.'

She looks at Dad and back to me and pauses for effect.

'At St Mary's, respect and courtesy are core values.' She peers over her glasses. 'Andrea, you have let yourself down, you have shown disrespect, and today you deliberately undermined Mr Crosby's authority by attempting to correct a so-called grammatical error. It's your *attitude*, Andrea.'

She glances at my dad again.

'Other teachers have also commented that your work is slipping. It worries me. This is your junior cert. You're a very bright girl.'

Crosby stretches out his legs, folds his arms across his chest. 'I agree with Ms Trout. Andrea is slipping behind.'

Talk about stating the obvious. What a creep.

'Can you explain yourself, Andrea?' Ms Trout demands. 'I told you before, we're here to help if you have any . . . issues.'

I blink and stare straight ahead at the plant, thinking, *You'd be the last person I'd come to with 'issues'.*

'Andi!' My dad is seething. 'Have you anything to say?'

'Nope.'

He leans forward.

'You're not doing yourself any favours, you know. What's with the attitude?'

'Whatever.'

I stare ahead. I feel sorry for my dad. He's disappointed in me. And he's tired, like the fight is going out of him. He's not letting on, but I can see it in his face.

There was a time when you couldn't separate us. A time when my Dad was ten feet tall. Now, it's aggro twenty-four seven.

Ms Trout pronounces my sentence: a written apology for Mr Crosby and I can resume classes today. She'll be monitoring my behaviour *very closely* over the rest of the term. She checks her watch. It's one o'clock – feeding time at the zoo . . . or the aquarium. We are dismissed. Dad and I walk towards the car in silence.

'Wait till your mother hears about this.' Slam. Tyres screech as he steams off.

I want to run after him. I want to get ahead of the car and slap my palm on the windscreen.

Stop! Dad! Listen. I want to say, *I'm sorry, Dad. What was I thinking?* I want to prise open his door, fling my arms around his neck, and smooth out the lines on his forehead. I want to burrow into his jacket and inhale the familiar scent of Paco Rabanne. Feel his arms wrapping around me like a quilt. I want him to ruffle my hair like he used to and tell me everything is going to be just fine.

When I was little, I'd hide under the duvet as my dad would tell me stories about goblins and witches. And he'd laugh and say, 'Come out. The coast is clear now, baby.' Then he'd fix my hair behind my ears, and he'd remind me I had special powers to magic them away. And I believed him. Everything was possible when my dad was around. I was immune to danger.

I run after the car, but he's gone, through the gates, into the lunchtime traffic.

*

Later at home, I help myself to some ice-cream and a bag of Taytos. I crack open a Coke and a packet of chocolate chip cookies. I'm not hungry, but there's a hollowed-out hole in my stomach that needs filling in.

In my bedroom I sit on my bed and write my letter of apology to Mr Crosby – in green marker, just to annoy him.

CHAPTER 9

DOLL

I pull the covers over my head and start to pick at the plaster on my face. Black feathers nestle around my shoulders, fanning out over my duvet. I feel their sharpness tickling and scraping the back of my neck. Their weight pressing down on me, cosying up. I close my eyes. I've gotten used to them and think of them now as a cloak to protect me. Under the duvet, it's dungeon dark. My thoughts spill out over the pillow, black as blood.

As I'm drousing into sleep, I hear it. A quiet breathing. Is there someone in my room? My heart stumbles. The feathers rustle, not happy to be disturbed. I hold my breath, listening. Is that a faint sigh? Like a sad dream-ghost. I push back the covers and sit up slowly, my eyes trying to peel back the darkness. I wait. Nothing. Just the muffled sound of the telly downstairs.

No. There it is again, that peaceful breathing. I lean up towards the window and try to yank the curtain back. Through the gap, the moon is scurrying through a skyful of silver stars. The black feathers float off the bed and sulk off into the ceiling.

I can smell lavender.

And then I see her, sitting on the pink velvet stool just inside my bedroom door, her hands clasped on her lap. I blink. Last Christmas was the last time I kissed my granny. The next day my mom and dad had a party for her, and I still can't believe she never turned up for it. And everyone was there for her, missing her already, they said, and crying and blowing their noses and singing 'Danny Boy'. No, she never turned up, and I never found out why she had to vamoose in such a hurry. My dad said she went off to Heaven.

Why did she go and leave us? And not even ring us? Or kiss us goodbye? It was a bit rich, as she'd say herself.

I'm so happy to see her, hoping she won't disappear this time. I sit up straighter. My heart curls like a kitten when she smiles over at me. *Oh, Granny. Granny!*

'I know you're hurting, Doll.' She shakes her head slowly. 'And for such a long, long time.' She sighs and closes her eyes, and I'm wondering if she's gone off to sleep as she often did, sitting by the fire on a Saturday night after a glass of Guinness.

Tonight she looks different. Her hair is dark, and there's a white light flowing from her. I can feel it like a warm breeze drifting towards me and enfolding me.

'I'm breaking all the rules here,' she says, a flicker of panic moving across her face. 'I can't stay long.' Her hands fidget on her lap.

I want to ask her if she's been to Heaven. And how come my dad said you couldn't come back from Heaven? 'They wouldn't let you out,' he said to Ruby. 'And you wouldn't even want to leave anyway.' But now here Granny is, sitting in my bedroom, like a secret. Whispering to me. Maybe dreams come true, though; like the song said, no dream is too extreme. Imagine!

She leans forward, and her voice shimmies. 'You must keep dreaming, Doll. You can untether yourself from all this' – she waves her hand in a circle – 'if you hold on to those dreams.'

I reach my hand towards her. I want to touch her face and feel her worn hand in mine again. I want to tell her I know about wishing on a star and dreaming and believing. Didn't the angel say it, and didn't I hear the song on the telly saying anything your heart wants will come to you? *I'll keep at it, Granny. I swear.*

There's the sound of footsteps on the stairs, and she puts her finger to her lips. 'Not a sound, Doll.'

We both hold our breath till they pass and fade away downstairs again.

I'm so happy. My lovely granny is back again. She's going to rescue me. I can feel my heart glowing inside me like a candle.

She whispers, 'Doll, what I want to tell you is that . . .' She smooths her skirt and folds her hands on her lap again. 'That beyond this life, there are many worlds. I had to come back to let you know. To tell you to have hope, to not give up.' Her eyes dart around the room. 'Someday, you'll figure it out, and when you do, my, my, what adventures you'll have, Doll.'

Hurray! She's come to take me with her. But she doesn't move towards me, and her light is starting to flicker. She looks over at me, frowning. 'I don't care what they say; I just had to let you know.' Her voice is fading out, like someone turned her volume button down. 'Dream, child. Dream on . . .' And then her light putters out and her shadow melts off the stool and disappears.

I sink back against the pillow. Her lavender perfume still lingers in the air, and I breathe it in, remembering and grateful. *Oh, Granny.* I lie back, my head in a muddle. Was it real? It *felt* real. My heart feels like butter sizzling, and I can't stop smiling inside. The black feathers drift down from the ceiling, but I push them away. *Get off me.* They hover in mid-air, surprised, offended, but I don't want them pressing their dark wings on me right now, annoying me, pretending to be my friend. *Get away from me. Let me think.*

Downstairs, on the telly, someone is singing 'Danny Boy' and how the summer's gone and all the roses are dying. And I know this much: my granny came to me tonight. She came to tell me to keep dreaming and hoping.

Hope is a golden bird, and I try to stay awake, cupping my hands around her fluttering body, not wanting to let her slip away.

When morning comes, she's flown – just as I expected – and as I lie under my duvet, I can hear the rain beating, beating against the window, and the wind, howling like a mad dog.

CHAPTER 10

DAN

The boardroom wall of glass gives a bird's-eye view of the open-plan office below. When I have five minutes, I love to look down and observe all the busyness, the ordinariness of everyday bank life, interactions and transactions and money saved and spent and borrowed and lent. Customers waiting, standing in line at the cash machines, the older ones queuing for the tellers. Looking for a human face, some emotional connection, even if it's only *Hello* or *How are you today?* or *The weather is dreadful, all right, but at least it's dry.* There's comfort in crowds.

Shirley Lovett is sitting in the glassed-off cubicle on the far right. She's leaning forward, absently fixing her hair behind her ear. Her long legs are crossed to the side. Jim Moore, CEO of Moore Motors, is leaning forward too, his elbows on the desk between them. He shifts his large bulk every few minutes. He's doing a lot of talking, and Shirley is smiling and nodding and taking notes. I have to hand it to Shirley – she's a great operator, the best financial advisor I've come across. She's only been with us two months, but already she's broken all her targets, and that is very good news for me. Keeps Regional Office off my back.

'Dan?' Joe from IT puts his head around the boardroom door. He drops a file on the long, polished table. 'Just wanted to leave these reports with you.'

I nod my thanks. Joe and I are friends as well as colleagues. We play golf together at the weekends, though his handicap is way lower than mine. Over a pint, he'll always tell me he's lonely, looking for a good woman to put him straight, but I think he actually likes being a single bloke.

I gesture towards the floor below.

He follows my gaze.

'A good buzz down there today,' I say.

He folds his arms and nods towards the glass booth. 'She's good, Shirley, isn't she? She's got the Midas touch. Fine-looking woman, too.'

He smiles. 'It's an advantage. Especially with the likes of Jim Moore. Looks like she has him eating out of her hand. And you know how bloody difficult he is.'

'Fair play to her if she can get him onside.'

'She'll do it, I reckon.' Joe comes to stand next to me. 'She's the type who doesn't give up easily.' He nudges me with his elbow. 'You better watch out, mate.'

'Me?'

He gives me a sideways look. 'Jim isn't the only one she'd like to have onside, Dan.'

'How do you mean?' Is it that obvious?

'Ah, Jesus, Dan, she has you in her sights. Don't tell me you haven't noticed? Get off the stage, man.'

'Noticed what?'

He tilts his head. 'Come on! She always sits next to you at team meetings. She'll schedule her breaks to coincide with yours . . .'

'Maybe you should be writing romantic novels instead of IT, Joe. You're running away with yourself there. Anyway, I'm an old married man.'

'You're telling me you haven't seen her brown puppy-dog eyes following you around? You are kidding me.'

'That's your imagination, Joe. I think you might fancy her yourself, eh?'

He ignores me. 'And she's always the second key holder when it's your week to open and lock up.'

Two staff must be present to open and lock the doors every day. It's a safety protocol. We do it by rota. It just so happens that Shirley and I have found ourselves sharing that duty. Big deal.

'You're scraping the barrel there, Joe.'

He rolls his eyes.

There's an awkward silence.

I wouldn't admit it to Joe, I wouldn't admit it to anyone, but yes, okay, fair enough – I have noticed Shirley's attention. And who wouldn't be flattered? She has a sort of smoulder, something more than just charm. A woman who can make your pulses race.

'Women like Shirley flirt because they enjoy the buzz,' I say. 'It makes them feel powerful, puts them in control. With Shirley, it's just a bit of fun, and I don't take it too seriously.'

'I'm telling you, Dan, as a friend and a colleague, watch that space.' He furrows his brow. 'I'm being serious. People talk, staff talk, and my instinct would be to steer clear. She could spell trouble. That's all I'm saying.'

He holds his hands up in surrender when I try to cut in. 'Look, I know you wouldn't . . . I'm just saying. I've heard stories about when she was in Limerick. Remember, she's Lorraine's woman, so she's well in.'

Lorraine Keegan is the regional manager, and it was she who encouraged Shirley to go for the financial advisor job here in Glengarvan.

'You don't like Lorraine anyway, Joe. You never did.'

'Neither do you, Dan, admit it. You should have gotten that regional manager promotion last year. You had way more experience than Lorraine, but it's all about gender quotas now.' He shakes his head. 'I'm not anti-women, don't get me wrong, but that was a bad call. Lorraine Keegan is out of her depth, and she has no people skills.'

'I'm over it, Joe. You have to let these things go, and to be honest, with Doll and everything at home, I have enough on my plate.'

He nods. 'I know, Dan. But just . . . you know . . . it's easy to get hooked in.' He taps the file with his fingers. 'Anyway, let me know if you need anything else.' I take one last look at the scene below as Joe closes the door behind him. Shirley is talking now, running her tongue along crimson lips, smiling, saying something that makes Jim guffaw. The conversation with Joe has me thinking.

If I'm really honest, I'm more than flattered. Shirley Lovett is the kind of woman who . . . well, if I was a free man, say, I would definitely be attracted to her. Okay, I *am* attracted to her. I shove the thought right out of my mind and head back to my office. I need to get my head into some figures, concentrate on Joe's reports, clear my mind and focus. Shirley Lovett is the last thing I need right now, don't I know it.

Back in my office, my mobile rings. It's Sally. Jesus, not now. I turn it to silent. Five minutes later she's ringing again.

'Yeah?'

'Well, you could say hello.' She sounds in bad form. What's new?

'Sorry. I'm just in the middle of something, Sal.'

'It's about Andi.'

'Jesus, what has she done now?'

'Well, you tell me, Dan. I've just had a call from Ms Trout telling me that the meeting this week with yourself and Andi will be filed and she'll email the summary and please could we both sign off on what's been agreed.' I stare out the window at the grey canopy of hanging clouds.

'Oh, yes, I meant to tell you about that.' I know my voice sounds flat. 'Look, it was no big deal. Andi was stroppy with one of the teachers, and he complained about her and—'

'And when were you going to tell me?' Her voice is starting to rise. 'I had to pretend I knew what she was talking about. I was mortified. She must have thought I was some idiot of a parent.'

'Look, Sal. I didn't want to worry you. I would have told you. Jesus, woman, give me a break.'

I can hear the long, angry sigh. 'I'm her mother, Dan! I need to know if there are walk-outs and meetings. Hello?'

There's a welcome knock on the door. 'I have to go, Sal.'

'How very convenient.' She hangs up.

Shirley Lovett is standing in the doorway. I can smell her musky perfume from here. 'Sorry, Dan, is it a bad time?'

'Come in.' My heart flips, and I don't know if it's the unpleasant conversation with Sally or the thought of spending a few minutes with the fragrant Shirley.

She takes a seat and smiles. 'I wanted you to be the first to know, Dan.' She bites the side of her lip, keeping me waiting a beat. 'Jim Moore is in.' She rubs her palms together. 'It was tough, but . . . we did it. And I mean *we*. I have you to thank for the referral.'

Joe was right; she's got the Midas touch for sure. 'Forget the referral. You did all the work, Shirley. Well done. Congratulations. I was watching you in action earlier. Very impressive.'

She adopts a puzzled look. 'You were?'

I give a little laugh. 'No, I was just keeping an eye on the floor. I saw you talking with Jim. That is amazing. He's not an easy guy to deal with.'

'Tell me about it.' Her glossy lips part in a smile. 'And there's more.' She sits back in the leather chair and crosses her legs. 'Okay, so we got the leasing; but – wait for this – we've also secured the pension plans for Jim himself and his three directors.' She runs her tongue across her lips. 'And, Dan, all the staff pensions business too.'

'Serious, Shirley? Brilliant work. He must have thirty on the books at this stage.'

'Thirty-seven actually. Plus' – she waits a beat – 'plus, Dan, all the insurance is ours too.' She stops, fanning her face. Her voice is excited. 'I'm still on a high. I have to get everything written up and signed off, but it's a done deal, Dan.'

She brushes some imaginary speck of dust from the front of her white shirt. 'I did my research. I showed him what we could do for him,

33

how we'd do all the heavy lifting, make it easy on him. Seamless, you know.'

'That's just what clients want, Shirley. Sounds like you've certainly nailed it. The deal must be worth . . .'

'Almost sixty grand. Lorraine will be pleased.'

'It's very good news. I'll let her know. This is worth celebrating; it'll give everyone a lift.'

She leans forward, resting her chin in her palm.

'Did you know Jim's brother-in-law is related to Nathan Power of the Powerhouse Group?'

I shake my head, smiling. 'How did you find that out?'

She taps the side of her nose and winks. 'I ask the right questions, Dan. I'm a curious woman. People tell me things. You'd be amazed what people tell you when you listen.'

The woman is a pro. 'So, now you're going to tell me that Jim has given you a referral for Nathan.'

'Got it in one.'

'Wow. You're a genius, Shirley.'

There's comfortable silence for a minute. 'Well, I better go off and wrap this up,' she says, getting to her feet. 'Thanks again, Dan – you know, for the referral and all your support. You've been amazing to me.' She pauses.

I move around the desk to shake her hand, but she leans in and puts her arms around me. I inhale a wave of her perfume, and I can feel the pressure of her sharp red fingernails against the back of my shirt.

We stand awkwardly at the door for a moment, a few feet apart. 'I'll get the gang rounded up for Friday drinks to celebrate,' she says. 'Will we say O'Mahony's at six?'

'I'll do my best to be there.'

'You, Dan, had better be there.' She waves a manicured finger from side to side. 'No excuses.' She flashes a smile. 'Not the same without you there, Dan. You're the boss.'

She turns to leave and hesitates for a second, fixing me with her dark eyes. 'We make a good team, don't we, Dan?'

'Absolutely.'

I follow the sway of her hips as she clacks down the corridor in a cloud of scent towards her own office. And I know she knows I'm watching her.

After she's gone, I return to the reports, but my thoughts are like a black hole sucking me in. Like a teenager, I'm thinking about Friday night in O'Mahony's. I won't stay long. It's not fair on Sally. She was right to be angry earlier. I'm just not at the races these days. Andi worries me. And I just don't know how to be a dad to Doll. I mean, Jesus, she hardly knows I'm there. And Sally and me? I don't know. Where did all the romance go? The laughs we used to have, the Sunday mornings in bed eating toast and sipping prosecco . . . That was a long time ago. Anyway, that stuff doesn't last. I need to get a grip. I mightn't even go on Friday. That's it. I'll make an excuse. Joe was right. Steer clear. Too much to lose.

CHAPTER 11

ANDI

The Lainey is almost invisible through the rain as I pedal furiously along the river path. It's nearly half seven, and I'm going to be late for basketball practice. Again.

It's too late when I see the dog leap out in front of me. The bike wobbles for a few seconds, then crashes onto the path, sending me sliding along the gravel. Lucky I haven't ended up in the Lainey. Which is what I shout at the black pair of trainers stopped in front of me.

'Fuck's sake, you should have that dog on a lead. Lucky I didn't end up in the river,' I say to the shoes. I look up. A hoodie, a fringe, a stud earring. Someone my father would call a pup.

'If you were looking where you were going, girl . . .' He points to the bike. 'And anyway, you've no lights.'

He helps me to my feet. 'Your knee is bleeding.' He grins. 'Otherwise, I reckon you'll live.' He picks up my bike. 'You won't be going anywhere with this, though. The wheel's shagged.'

'Oh, brilliant,' I say. 'I'll be sending you the bill for that.'

He bursts out laughing. 'State of you. If you could see yourself. Come on, girl, I'm only living across the road.' He points to a row of redbrick cottages. 'Come up with me, and we'll sort out the wheel. And your knee.' He lifts the bike easily with one arm and leads me across the street.

I limp after him, blood dribbling down my leg. 'You could at least apologise. It was your fault.' The dog trots a sensible distance behind me. We cross the road, and he opens the side gate of number 3 Brandon Terrace. Next door is boarded up; shards of glass lie around the doorway. Farther down the street, kids play around the shell of a car.

'Come on in. She won't bite.' He pushes open the back door. The dog sidles past us. A stack of crockery fills the sink, and there's a strong smell of stew.

'Gran,' he shouts. 'Visitor.' I can see him properly now in the bright light of the kitchen. A dead ringer for Justin Bieber. And when he

36

shakes off his hoodie, I can see a tiger tattoo prowling down his right arm. Trouble, I'd say.

He leads me through to a small sitting room where his gran is sitting by the fire, watching telly. The smoke from her cigarette swirls around her like an aura. The clock on the mantelpiece is stopped at twenty to one.

He jerks his thumb at me. 'She rolled over our Molly, nearly killed her.'

'Oh, Steve!' The woman smiles. 'Don't take a tack of notice of him, pet. Are you all right?'

'I am.' The smoke tickles my throat. 'It's just a cut . . . it's my bike, though . . .'

'Steve'll fix that for you. He's a topper when it comes to bikes.' A yellow smile. 'Get a plaster for her knee, Steve.'

'I'm doing it, Gran.' He disappears into the kitchen and comes back with an old Scottish Shortbread biscuit tin. He plucks out a Band-Aid.

'Sit down there.' He points to a sofa that dips in the middle. 'Give it here.' He kneels down and daubs the wound with a cotton ball and TCP. His fingers are gentle. Thank God I'd shaved my legs. He fixes the plaster across the cut, pressing the edges with his thumbs. His hands are firm and cool, and when he looks up at me, my stomach flips. Blue eyes with flecks of amber. My heart is pounding.

'I won't report you for dangerous driving,' he says. 'I'll leave you off. This time.'

His grandmother laughs. 'Take no notice of him, girl. He's a messer. Aren't you, Steve, you're a messer? Give her a cup of tea. What's your name?'

'Andi.'

'I'm Joanie. Pleased to meet you.' She turns to Steve. 'Give Andi a cup of tea and a biscuit. She looks a bit shook up. Are you a bit shook up, lovey?' She mutes the telly.

I am, but not in the way she's thinking. The dog leaps onto her lap.

She flicks her cigarette into the fire and ruffles Molly's ears. 'You're a bold girl, so you are. Watch where you're going in future.'

A lump of coal falls onto the hearth, and she leans sideways and scoops it up with the tongs. Her hand shakes, and she coughs. 'The fags have me kilt, girl. You don't smoke, do you? I hope not. They're bad news, love.'

Steve reappears with a mug of tea and a Club Milk.

'Sugar?'

'No thanks.'

He hands me the mug. 'You okay now?'

'Sure.' I smile sweetly, thinking, *Why do the good-looking guys always come from the wrong side of town?*

I sip my tea and look at the Sacred Heart picture over the fireplace, the sorrowful figure pointing to his own thorny heart. Joanie follows my gaze. 'I suppose you don't even know who that is, do you, love?'

'Yes, I do, Joanie. My granny used to have him in her kitchen – the Sacred Heart of Jesus.'

'Oh, thank God you have some bit of religion in you, girl. Not like most of them today.'

'Very impressive, Andi, for sure, like,' Steve adds. I give him a sideways look, and he winks.

'Get Andi home safely now,' Joanie says. 'She can't walk with that knee.'

He looks at me. 'I can give you a spin on my crossbar . . .'

I nod and finish my tea as he pulls on his hoodie.

'Come on, let's get you home, girl.'

I say goodbye to Joanie and follow Steve into the yard.

Sitting on the crossbar cycling along in the drizzle, I can feel his heartbeat against my shoulder. I just hope he can't hear mine.

We skid to a halt at 6 Bluebell Grove and exchange numbers. 'I'll buzz you tomorrow,' he tells me, 'and you can collect your bike after school.'

'Thanks. I mean it. And . . . sorry about shouting at you earlier.'

'No worries. See you tomorrow.'

I limp up the driveway, hoping no one has seen me with Steve. I tell Mom what happened, leaving out the bit about Brandon Terrace.

'Sounds like a lovely boy,' she says. She wouldn't say that if she met him, that's for certain.

I check myself in the hall mirror on the way upstairs. I look a right wreck, my eyeliner streaked across my cheek. Mortified. Inside, though, I'm buzzing at the thought of seeing Steve again.

Funny how life can be such a grind and then something happens and you're catapulted from a two to a ten, just like that. Despite my sore knee, I do a little dance around my room as I peel off my clothes. And as the shower water cascades down, I'm even thinking that Mr Crosby could be a sweet guy. It isn't easy being a teacher. I don't know how he does it.

CHAPTER 12

DOLL

'You haven't stopped smiling since you got up, Andi,' Dad says, pouring milk over his Alpen. He adds a few blueberries.

'It's almost Friday. What's not to like?' She grabs a bowl and smiles over at me. 'How are you, Doll?' I'm sitting on the easy chair by the Aga, my pink coat buttoned up, waiting for my school taxi to collect me. I'm thinking about what Granny said last night. I can't think about anything else. I'm to keep on dreaming and hoping . . . and I'll figure out how to escape. Woo-hoo. Grannies don't lie.

Mom's gone to work early, and Dad looks up from his crossword when the doorbell rings.

'That was the postman,' Andi says, carrying in a fat box, wrapped in brown paper done up with twine. 'It's an African postmark, Dad. It must be from Will. Maybe it's a present for your birthday on Saturday, Doll.' She winks over at me. 'Will I open it, Dad?'

He looks up from his paper, glances at me. 'I think that's a yes,' he says, smiling, before he gets back to his crossword.

Andi shoves the milk carton aside and lifts the box onto the worktop. She snips the twine, and the brown wrapper falls away from a slatted crate. I miss Will. He always made a fuss for my birthday. 'What is it this year?' Andi says, pushing her fingers through layers of screwed-up newspaper. She pulls out a bundle wrapped in grey paper.

Dad looks up, curious, but I'm not bothered. Presents? Toys? Who needs them? 'Fair play to him, he's never once forgotten her birthday,' Dad is saying. 'I remember one year—'

'I'm not in the mood, Dad.' Andi doesn't like when Dad goes on and on about Will.

'I'm just saying,' Dad says, 'how he never forgets. Credit where it's due.'

She bites her lip. Her and Dad are always at each other.

Dad's on a roll now. 'I recall one birthday when he saved all his pocket money to buy her a big bunch of balloons. Remember, Doll?' He smiles over at me. 'And the Christmas he bought a huge pink teddy bear with a vest saying *DOLL* in silver letters . . .'

'He's a legend, yeah. Yawn.'

Andi pulls off the wrapping, and underneath is the most peculiar doll I've ever seen. She has a tall Oliver Twist hat with red cloth hair peeping out from under the rim. On top, she's wearing a blue silky blouse with a pink belt studded with tiny seashells.

'Have a look at her, Doll. Isn't she gorgeous?' Andi walks her over to my chair. The doll comes up past her knees. I reach out to touch her orange cotton skirt. It's got tiny flowers stitched on and a border of perfect pink roses. The hem is scalloped with orange lace. I've never seen a doll like this before.

'I think she likes her,' Dad says, smiling. 'Do you like her, Doll? She is very pretty, very lifelike.'

I turn away. I'm nearly eleven, not six. It's a ridiculous present. And I don't like toys. I never did. Especially stupid dolls. A wave of misery washes over me.

Andi is saying, 'I feel like I'm seven again. I want to put her in a buggy and take her out for a walk. Show her off.'

I sneak another look at the figure in her black hat. On her sackcloth feet, she's wearing a pair of red shoes, and around her throat, a string of sea-green stones shimmers in the light. Her eyes seem to catch my gaze, and there's a ghost of a smile around her cotton-pink mouth. How did they make her so . . . real?

'Welcome to Cork,' Andi says, fingering the silver hooped earrings and holding her up for Dad to admire. He reaches into the crate to retrieve a sheet of parchment. 'Hello, what's this?' He pushes his reading glasses down his nose and begins in a very deep voice:

'*This is Nan-Nan, your soul doll, drawing good energies into your life.*' Even though it's an annoying present – no offence, Will – Dad's put-on voice is funny. '*Do not leave your doll unattended for long. Wrap her in a clean cloth when not in use.*'

He smiles, rolls his eyes.

'Wait, there's more: *Nan-Nan's necklet is made from tourmaline. It brings with it the sacred gift of driving away sadness and is most powerful by moonlight.*' He laughs. 'Wait for this, girls. *Whoever carries this soul doll is safe from his enemies, cannot drown in water, nor can any unjust sentence be passed on him, so help me . . .*'

'So help me God, is it, Dad?'

'No, that's it. *So help me.* Well, I have to hand it to them.' He chuckles, dropping the sheet onto the worktop and lifting Nan-Nan onto his lap. 'They really know how to market their merchandise. All this hocus-pocus appeals to people.' He shakes his head. 'Beautifully made, I'll grant you that. But the big question is . . .' He looks over at me. 'Are *you* impressed with Nan-Nan, Doll?'

I'm thinking, *What a load of rubbish.*

Andi shakes her head, frowning. 'Can't you see, Dad? She has no interest.'

Dad says, 'You're right, love. Doll will buckaroo her into a corner. It's a pity. Don't tell Will, though; his heart is in the right place.'

Andi lifts Nan-Nan onto a chair, smoothing her skirt. 'There's something about her that sort of draws you in, though, isn't there, Dad? All that stuff about energies and sacred gifts and things . . . who's to say it's not true? We all want to believe in magic, don't we?'

But Dad's gone back to his crossword.

'Three down, holy envoy, six letters beginning with *n*,' he says.

'Nan-Nan,' Andi says as the doorbell rings.

Dad jumps to his feet and taps his watch. 'It's nearly half eight. That'll be your driver, Doll.'

Andi gets the door, and Dad grabs my bag and walks me out the hall. I can't swear to it – it all happens quickly, so I can't be sure – but as I'm passing Nan-Nan propped on the chair near the kitchen door, may I be struck down, she actually looks at me and smiles. Though I know it must be a trick of the light, I still jump.

Dad looks down at me. 'What's wrong, Doll?' I keep walking, clutching his strong hand in mine, and when I look back, Nan-Nan is staring straight ahead, lifeless.

Dad chats to the driver as he straps me into the back seat of the taxi. 'Thanks, Bill.' As he waves me off, Nan-Nan is forgotten. I sit back against the leather seat. I'm trying hard to think happy Granny thoughts, but instead, dark figures parachute down, grey shape-shifters brushing my face with their feathery feet. I close my eyes and lean in to catch their sly whispers. It's what I do.

CHAPTER 13

SALLY

The secretary looks up and smiles as I rush into the reception room, closing the door carefully behind me. 'Sorry I'm late . . .'

'No problem.' The blonde girl behind the desk taps her keyboard, scans her screen. 'Mrs. Sally Redmond, isn't it?'

I nod.

'Go on ahead.' She points down the corridor. 'Second door on your right. Dr Winters will be with you in a few minutes.'

The room is hushed, with muffled sounds of traffic and a lingering smell of wax polish. Reminds me of the convent where I went to school. Beige blinds are pulled down though it's not yet four o'clock. The carpet is brown, patterned with cream roses. Two leather armchairs are set near a small table where a night-light is flickering in a lantern – the only sign of warmth.

On a desk nearby, there's a jug of water with two tumblers placed upside-down on paper coasters and a box of tissues. Man-size. Tools of the grief trade, I suppose. *You seem upset. Would you like a glass of water?* Or a tissue discreetly placed on your lap.

I sit on the armchair nearest the door. There's a certificate on the wall – *Mary Winters, Member of the Irish Association for Counselling & Psychotherapy* – next to a framed quote: *Life Is Not a Rehearsal.*

Life's a Bitch is what it should say.

I lean back in the chair. The armrests are scuffed and scratched. This chair has probably held hundreds of people before me. People who needed attention, solace, hope. Always hope. People always need hope. Just a glint of it up ahead in the brow of the hill. A glimmer of light to keep them trudging on. A candle in the darkness. Because that light means that somewhere up that lonely hill, there is a house. A chance, maybe, that someone will be there. They might spot you outside in the moonlight as you stumble through the grass and shingle. And they'll come to the door and reach for your hand and draw you in. It might be an old woman with wispy hair, her face dripping with kindness. And she'll gesture for you to sit by the turf fire. 'Sit down,' she'll say. 'You're cold. You don't have to say a word.'

And she'll bring you strong tea from a tea-cosied teapot and a slice of toast slathered in butter that she toasted herself on a long fork over the fire. And if you're shivering, she'll fetch you a rug, an old fleecy one full of softness and compassion. And she'll place it on your knees and tuck it in around you like you're a lost child. Which you are.

And she'll just know, by being near you, what words – if any at all – are needed. She'll sit down opposite you then and stoke the fire. After a while, in the golden quietness, you might just shatter and fall asunder. And she won't say, *Ah, no, girl, don't be crying now. Hush, girl.* She'll leave you off, spilling all the rubbish from the dumper of your life all over her flagstone floor, and she'll dab the tears off your face. *Cry away, girl,* she'll say. *Cry away, cry away. Let it rain.*

And your heart will thaw. And you'll be consoled. And you'll be ready to climb another hill in the darkness. Another day for another dollar.

'Sally? Mrs. Redmond?' I'm startled out of my daydream.

'Oh,' I say. 'I am so sorry; I was miles away.'

'Sometimes,' the woman in the tailored cream shirt says, '*miles away* is a far better place.' She smiles. 'I'm Mary Winters,' she says. 'Nice to meet you, Sally, and welcome.' She lowers herself into the chair opposite.

I wait for her to speak, and after a few moments of awkward silence, we both start to speak together. 'You first,' I say, hoping she will rattle on so I won't have to talk just yet.

'Okay, Sally, you might start by telling me a little about what brings you here today?'

I groan inside. Don't even know why I'm here. What is the point, really? Talking about all your flaws doesn't change anything. Just get on with it. But that's the trouble – I can't do it anymore . . .

'Sally?' Mary Winters is waiting for an answer, one delicate hand cupping the side of her face. She's in listening mode. *Active* listening mode.

'Oh, yes, I'm sorry. What brings me here? Good question, Mary.' I hesitate. 'Well, actually, my doctor thinks it's a good idea . . .'

'And you?'

'Me? Yes, I suppose so . . .'

'You feel you're coming with an open mind?'

43

'Yes, that's it exactly. I have an open mind. Absolutely.'

People will believe anything if you use the right tone.

She waits for me to continue.

But I can't. I can't wrap words around how I feel. How do you talk about shame? How do you say, out loud, that you're not good enough? That you can't function, that you're weak, that you cry for no good reason whatsoever? How can you tell a stranger that you scream in your kitchen? That you know that, shamefully and carelessly, you have lost yourself?

'Sally?'

I look towards the candle for inspiration. My mind is blank. My lips are sewn. I'm programmed to withhold, to not let those words march – left right, left right – up my throat and right out of my mouth. Words are dangerous bastards; you shouldn't trust them. Like a drunk at a party, you never know what they're going to say.

And they drift into my dreams, those words. Wandering like smoke-ghosts. *We're lost*, they say quietly. *Can you show us the way out of here, please? Sorry*, I say, even in my dreams. *Sorry I can't help you. I'm a stranger here myself. I wouldn't know.* They seem okay with that, and off they drift into the shadows.

'Sally? Are you all right? Would you like a glass of water?'

'Yes, please.'

She splashes the liquid into the glass, a few drops spilling onto the coaster.

'Thank you, Mary.' Her nails are painted pale coral; she wears a huge diamond solitaire on her ring finger. My hands are shaking.

'Take your time, Sally.'

She sits back, ready to resume, but I can't do this. I reach sideways to leave my glass on the floor and lift my handbag onto my lap.

'I don't think this is such a good idea really, Mary,' I say, sitting on the edge of the chair. It's nothing she said or did. It's not her; it's me.

I stand up, button up my trench coat. She gets to her feet. A manicured hand hovers over mine. 'Are you sure?' she says. 'Are you sure, Sally?'

'Yes, thank you, Mary. Another day perhaps. My head today . . . I just . . .'

'I understand.' She nods. 'I do understand how you—'

'You don't, actually.' It sounds like a slap.

'Sorry, no, I didn't mean . . . I'm not suggesting . . . it's just that when someone is feeling depressed—'

'I'm not depressed.' I say it loudly, and she steps back, the painted hand falling to her side. She's probably already thinking, *This poor woman is in denial; lots of work to be done there, I'm afraid.* She opens the door and we part cordially, shaking hands.

'You know where I am,' she says. I thank her.

I step out into a chill October afternoon, relieved to be out of that oppressive room, to feel the sharp wind on my face. I feel like an alien, separate from the crowds on Main Street hurrying between the bright shops and cafés. Like there's a thin membrane between me and everyone else in the world.

I take a left towards the car park and change my mind, double back, take another left. I wander down towards the prom. The waves are grey and wild, crashing onto the shore. I sit on the metal bench, feeling the coldness seep through the thin material of my trench coat. It starts to rain. But I want to be wet and cold. It feels right. Like a penance I deserve. Good for the soul.

I watch the swell, the ebb and flow of the tide. I listen to the crash as a wave disintegrates and then the roar as the water gets sucked back over the shingle. Crash, roar, crash, roar. Never ending, never changing, solid and dependable. Not like us humans, scrambling and stammering and longing and lost. Inconsolable in the valley of tears.

I check my watch. It's after five o'clock. My phone's on silent. I have four messages and six missed calls. Andi needs to be collected. Dan will be late. Doll's day-care telling me she's poorly. Ring the office. Please can I make an editorial meeting in the morning? There's a number I don't recognise. I feel like flinging the phone into the sea.

And what if? What if I hurled myself after it? The shock of the icy water, the slap of the waves, your arms flailing, salt water flooding your mouth, and then . . . peace. No more tears. Floating face-down like a star-fish with shoes. Sweet oblivion.

I hurry back to the car through a curtain of rain, thinking I'll get steaks for dinner – that'll be fast – and some coleslaw in Kate's Deli. Don't think; move. That's the job. Best foot forward. And don't forget to smile. Say cheese.

CHAPTER 14

ANDI

I can't get the boy out of my head. Couldn't sleep last night. I want to kiss his mouth. I want to touch his face, trace my finger across his cheek. Get up close to him. If he only knew! He'd have a laugh.

I've had a few boyfriends, but no one ever made me feel like this. Not even close. There was Jamie Corry, so okay, I did fancy him at the start. I thought he was fit – until our second date, when he tried to eat my face off in the back row of the cinema. That was the end of him. I could taste the Taytos off his tongue. Rank. Haven't eaten crisps since.

And JD, 'The Body'. Captain of the under-eighteens football team. Smoking hot – not! And he was a lousy kisser. We might have lasted the whole summer, though, if my mom hadn't spotted me on the back of his motorbike in June, doing 150 on the motorway to Cork. No helmet; that didn't help. 'You're fifteen, for God's sake. So irresponsible. Wait till your father hears about this.'

But she didn't tell him in the end. And when I came back from holidays in Majorca in mid-July, JD had moved on. Not that I cried any tears. He was so up his own arse; I mean, calling himself *The Body*. Hello? Any guy can look cool in a biker jacket.

It's half four. I'm sitting cross-legged on my bed, waiting. Steve said he'd be in touch after school. Will I text him?

No, I'll wait. I change into my new jeans and pink hoodie just in case.

The phone pings as I'm brushing out my hair. Bike sorted. Collect after 5. I high-five the mirror. *Fair play, Steve.* A straightener on my hair, a slick of Mac gloss, and I'm out the door.

When I get to Brandon Terrace, Joanie is sitting in the same chair in a blue fog, Molly asleep on her lap. 'Come in, girl, come in. Sit down. You look gorgeous. Pink's your colour. How's your knee? Did Dr Steve sort you out?'

'He's very good, Joanie. He's just finished fixing my bike.'

She gestures toward the kitchen. 'He's a kind boy, is Steve. Very good to me, lovey. A soft heart, not like his father. Don't get me started on him.'

'Is his mother . . . is she . . . ?' Steve has become a fascinating subject. I want to know all about him.

'Is she dead? No, she's not dead.' She frowns. 'But you could say she's as good as. She up sticks and left for London when that poor boy was only seven. Off with a new man. Said she'd send for him . . .' She shakes her head. 'But she never did. And after a while, he got used to her not being around. That's ten years ago now. Where do the years go?'

'It must have been lonely for him?'

'Well, it broke my heart, lovey, seeing him drawing pictures for his mammy and sitting by the phone waiting for her to call. How any woman can do that to her own child . . . but that's what I reared.' She straightens up in her chair then and flicks on the telly with the remote. 'I'm not saying any more about it. She's my daughter; I'll keep my lips sealed.'

'Andi!'

Her face softens. 'He wants you, lovey. Off you go. Take it easy on that bike now. And don't go breakin' Steve's heart. He's distracted since he met you.' She winks as Steve puts his head around the door.

'See you, Joanie. Mind that cough.' I'm thinking *distracted* sounds promising. That makes two of us.

'Cycle back with her, Steve,' Joanie says, 'just to make sure it's safe.'

I follow him out the garden gate and across the road onto the river path.

We stop when we reach the entrance to Bluebell Grove. 'Good as new,' he says, pointing to my front wheel. We look at each other awkwardly. He nods towards the redbrick Victorian-style houses behind me. 'Which one is yours again?'

I point to number 6. 'The one with the yellow door. You can't miss it.'

He takes in the gravel driveway and the pillars visible through the trees.

'You're all right. I don't think I'll come in for tea, Andi.' He faces his bike toward home. 'I'm sure Daddy wouldn't approve.' He grins, like it doesn't bother him anyway.

He's right. My dad would freak if he thought I'd even spoken to someone from Brandon Terrace. Nothing but trouble, he'd say. Trouble with a capital T.

I give a little laugh, can't think what to say.

And then he's gone. 'G'luck. See ya round, girl.'

I'm stunned. That's it? I shove my bike against the garden shed. I'm gutted. Will I see him again?

I let myself in and go straight to my room. I look in the mirror. Did I misread the signals? Didn't his gran even say he was distracted? I pace the room, plotting all sorts of ways I might get to meet him again. I could tell him the wheel is still not right. Or the brakes are dodgy . . . or I left my bracelet in his house?

When I get out of the shower, there's a message on my phone. U free tmrw nite?

My heart is hammering, and I punch the air. Yes. No point in looking too keen, though. *Andi, play it cool.* I dress and blow-dry my hair. I'm free. Smiley face or not? Nah.

*

We're going to the cinema. After school on Friday, I spend two hours deciding what to wear. I settle on black jeans and my new green Zara top. I can't eat. Butterflies in my tummy have morphed into bats, flying blind at a thousand miles an hour.

I arrive at the Carlton a couple of minutes late. Fashionably late, as my granny would say. Through the huge glass windows I can see him in the foyer. He's wearing a black leather jacket, and his blond hair is gelled back. His eyes catch mine, and he flashes a dazzling smile as I approach.

'I thought you weren't coming,' he says, leaning forward and kissing me on the cheek. I can smell his aftershave. Pour Homme, I think. There's a wild fluttering in my stomach. He is so handsome I can only stare at him.

'Why wouldn't I?' I say, after a beat.

He shrugs.

'Well?' I say. 'Which movie are we going to?'

He pulls a pair of tickets from inside his jacket. 'I had to think about what you'd go for.' He taps his finger against his chin. 'Hmm. What would a beautiful girl like Andi want to see?'

'And you thought . . . ?'

He grins. 'I thought something romantic. Something with an edge to the story.'

'Very good, Detective. I like your style. You're spot-on.'

'*A Star is Born*?'

'That's what I was hoping you'd say. I love Bradley Cooper.'

Half-way through the movie he slips his arm around my shoulder. I don't move, afraid he might hear my heart hammering under my silk top. He strokes my arm very slowly, and I can't concentrate on what's happening on the screen. After a while, he cups my chin and brushes my lips.

Once when our house got flooded, I touched a live wire under a socket in the hall and got an electric shock. Well, that's how it feels now when he kisses me. I'm breathless, and I know he feels it too. He pulls away. Our eyes lock. Everything around me blurs. After a minute, I can't help myself. I lean towards him and kiss him slowly. Above the roar in my chest, I can hear Lady Gaga singing about being off the deep end and far from the shallows. It's how I'm feeling now. And even though it's scary, I'm loving it.

When I feel his tongue slide over mine, I have to pull away. I'm afraid I'm going to faint. I never knew you could faint from pure desire. I take deep, slow breaths. He catches my hand then, rubbing my palm ever so slowly with his thumb, like he's touching some exotic fabric, feeling the satin against his skin.

I'm in a trance. My outer self watches Bradley Cooper and Lady Gaga on the screen.

Yep. I'm in at the deep end. They warned us in school about drugs – ecstasy, weed, cocaine – and how they'd make you feel. Steve is my new drug . . . I can see how you could get hooked.

Afterwards, we walk back to my house, his arm loose around my shoulder. We don't talk much. The rain's gone and the night is clear and cold. For me, it's enough just to walk together under the streetlights. One very slow kiss under the dripping maple tree outside my house and he's gone. Running off, sidestepping the puddles, waving without looking behind him.

I touch my mouth and bolt up the driveway. My dad meets me in the hall. 'Where have you been?'

I slip past him, heading for the stairs.

He smells of beer and perfume.

'I told Mom I was over at Stacey's house tonight. Her dad dropped me home.' I scoot up to my room.

My phone pings in my pocket. Ur beautiful.

I sit on my bed. *He thinks I'm beautiful.* I don't brush my teeth – I want to hold on to the taste of him.

I climb under the duvet, but I can't sleep. Can't concentrate. I tiptoe to the window and stand there, gazing at the night sky like 'tis the first time I've ever seen the stars.

49

CHAPTER 15

DAN

O'Mahony's is humming with the Friday after-work crowd. As I push open the stained-glass doors, I can hear the din of voices and trad music over the clink of glasses. I let Claire, our operations manager, in ahead of me. Down towards the back of the pub through the archway, there's a reserved area for parties and staff do's. All the gang are already gathered there.

'You go on, Claire. I'll get the drinks in. What are you having?'

'Dingle gin and tonic. Fever Tree, if possible.' She winks. 'I'm very particular about my drinks.'

Claire is one of my favourite people. Kind, solid, dependable. She's the go-to whenever there's a crisis.

'Because you're worth it,' I shout after her.

She grins, making her way through to the back. 'I'll keep a seat for you.'

The service in O'Mahony's is fast, and I'm sitting down within five minutes. It's only half six, but the tables are already laden with empty glasses.

'Amazing when there's a tab at the bar, everyone gets into the party mood very fast,' Claire says, smiling, as she squeezes up next to Joe to make room for me.

At the far end corner, I can see Shirley, and she gives a little wave. She's talking to a few of the younger lads. I can feel – *Get a grip, Dan* – a tiny tug of jealousy. Shane Maher is a rugby player for the Blue Tigers, and Kevin Owens in accounts coaches the local senior hurling team. Two charmers, capable lads who know how to look after themselves.

Shirley and the lads are deep in conversation, leaning close together. Every now and then they laugh out loud. For a moment, I feel old. Forty-four isn't old, is it? It is, though, if you're thirty-two.

'Dan, you look like you've lost your wallet,' Claire says. 'Are you okay?'

I smile, take a long drink of my pint.

'I was just saying to Joe,' Claire says, 'it's been a superb month sales-wise. It makes a difference. Everyone's buzzing.'

'It's true, Claire. The figures are looking good. We're on a roll.' I take another long drink, trying not to let my attention wander towards the back of the room. I can feel the alcohol relaxing me already.

She purses her lips. 'I hate to say it, but it's down to Shirley Lovett. Even I can't argue with that.'

'You don't like her, Claire?' Joe says, arching his eyebrows.

'I don't trust her, that's all, Joe. Don't ask me why.' She nudges his arm with her elbow. 'And do not quote me on that, okay?'

More drinks arrive. Joe is talking about Rob Colbert now. 'I met his wife, Joanne, in Centra today,' Claire says, nodding. 'It's so tough on her. She's off work now; she has to rest. And she was the confectioner in the business. It'll be tough financially to replace her. Life is not fair.'

'How is she?' I already knew Rob wasn't coping well.

'Oh, depressed. Stressed out. You can imagine, multiple sclerosis is the unknown. The kids are her main worry.'

'You've been there, Dan,' Joe says. 'You know what it's like when something tragic hits a family.'

'It's not the same, Joe.'

'I know, but still, he's right,' Claire says, 'You do have experience of a child with special needs – a child suffering, in pain. It can't be easy either.'

'How is she anyway, Dan?'

'The same, no change. It's just circles, you know?'

Claire squeezes my arm. 'That's tough. And Sally, how is she?'

'She's good, all things considered. She gets upset, you know, but she doesn't talk about it. It's harder on mothers, I think.'

I'm relieved when Laura from the front office interrupts the conversation. 'Are you guys coming for something to eat after here?' She shifts unsteadily, and her voice is louder than normal. 'Ah come on, Claire, don't be a fuddy-duddy.' She hiccoughs. 'It's Friday. Thank God it's Friday. Woo-hoo.' She doesn't wait for an answer but shimmies to the music as she makes her way to the bar.

Claire smiles at me and rolls her eyes. 'She's had enough, I'd say. Can you imagine what she'll be like in another hour? Someone needs to keep an eye on her.'

An hour later, the music is louder and the younger ones are singing along to 'Galway Girl'. Some of them are up dancing. Kevin is grabbing

Shirley by the hand and shouting, 'Come on, Shirl.' The finger food has been cleared away. The light tapas and canapés have been devoured, and the gang is getting ready to head for pizzas round the corner in Luigiano's. Everyone's in good form. The drink does that. Oils the wheels. Gets people to drop their masks. Loosens us up. We chill. Not a bad thing.

Shirley is dancing with Shane now, and she swivels easily in her high heels. Personally, though, I think there's a limit. She's the financial advisor, a senior executive. She needs to take a step back, not get too familiar with the more junior staff particularly. You have to have some reserve. Am I right or just old-fashioned? I'm about to ask Claire, but she's gone to the loo.

Joe disappears and returns with another round of drinks. People stop by, mingle, come and go.

'Ah come on, come on, the table's booked for nine thirty. Hurry up.' Laura is shushing everyone to their feet. She roots around under her seat. 'Jesus, has anyone seen my handbag? Brown with a silver clasp. Oh, Dee, you're a star. Thanks, hon.'

I take Kevin aside. 'Keep an eye on Laura, Kev. Make sure she gets home safely.'

He gives me a thumbs-up.

Everyone piles out the door, gathering up coats, mobiles, scarves. 'Did anyone leave this pink umbrella? 'Is that yours, Kev?' Guffaws of laughter.

'I'm off home, Dan,' Claire says, buttoning up her jacket.

'So you're skipping Luigiano's? I don't blame you.'

'The girls have ballet in the morning. Better keep a clear head.' She taps her temple. 'And you?'

'I'm just going to finish this and I'll be off home myself. See you Monday, Claire.'

The bar is much quieter now, and the silence is a welcome relief. As I drain my pint, I spot Joe, tucked away in a quiet corner at the bar. He's talking to Shirley and signals me over.

'I thought you two were gone to Luigiano's.'

'No, we're having a nice quiet chat here, aren't we, Shirley? How about you, Dan?' He smiles lazily. He's well on.

'Nah. Not a chance. I'm heading home.'

Shirley has her back to me, and now she turns around and pats the stool next to hers. 'No, you are not. Sit down here, Dan. Sit down. One

drink.' She signals to the barman. 'A pint of Heineken, please, and . . .'
She looks at Joe. 'A pint of Guinness. Go on, Joe, you're having it. And
a vodka and tonic.' She pulls a blue wallet from her handbag. 'No argu-
ments. This is on me.'

A sliver of annoyance crosses Joe's face, but it's gone in a flash.

I take the stool on the other side of Shirley, and she helps me shrug
off my coat. I feel like a teenager, enjoying the thrill of sitting this
close to her. *You're drunk*, I say to myself. *Watch it*. But I'm grateful she's
ditched the lads and decided to stay with us. I know that sounds pathetic. Was she avoiding me all evening? Is it a game? Does she fancy Joe? Is
he interested in her? Or am I reading too much into all this?

I take a sip and place my glass back on the bar counter.

'I want to propose a toast to our financial wizard,' I say. We raise our
glasses and clink them many times. Cheers. Cheers.

She smiles from under her lashes. 'The best of company,' she says,
slurring slightly.

'And what about Kevin?' I mock–look around. 'I thought you two
looked very cosy earlier?'

I regret it the moment the words are said. She puts her hand to her
mouth, smirking. 'Stop it, Dan. You'll start a rumour.' But her eyes are
smiling. 'As a matter of fact' – she wets her lips – 'I like my men a little
more mature. A little more . . .' She flashes a white smile. 'A little more
experienced . . . in life. Emotionally, I mean.'

She pours the rest of the tonic into her glass and takes a long sip.
She turns to Joe. 'And what sort of woman do you go for?' She's teasing
him now. He throws his head back and laughs. 'Any woman who'll have
me, Shirley.'

She looks at me from under her lashes. 'And you, Dan? What draws
you to a woman?'

Joe says, 'He doesn't think about women, Shirley. He's an old married man. Aren't you, Dan?' He winks at me.

I smile and nod and take a long drink of my pint.

Shirley giggles. 'Ah, I wouldn't say that.' She's flirting with us both,
and she's loving it. She's playful. A practiced hand.

'Hmmm. Let me guess.' She strokes her chin with her thumb and
forefinger. 'I'd say, Joe, he likes a bit of mystery and a woman who
knows what she wants, am I right?' She looks at us both. 'Aren't I the
lucky girl to have ended up with not one, but two handsome men?'

She wraps her arms around our shoulders. I place my hand on the
small of her back and leave it rest there. She stiffens for a moment, then

moves a little closer. I can feel the soft wool of her skirt against my palm. Jesus, she's a stunning woman. And she knows it.

Joe drains his pint. 'We thought we might go for a Chinese, Dan. Are you heading home?' He fixes me with a look.

'Yep. I'm going to walk. You two go and enjoy your meal.' I do my best to hide my annoyance as I help Shirley into her leopard-print coat. A cloud of perfume puffs through the air, and the scent of it, of her, unnerves me. I need strong coffee. Too many pints.

Still, a man could do with a bit of silliness, couldn't he? I mean, she is a very attractive woman, and she is right about me. Spot-on. Let's face it; when I think about it – and I don't think about it very often – I do like a bit of mystery, and I do like a woman who knows what she wants. Funny, that. And I never actually realized it till tonight.

Joe offers her his arm. 'Come on, then, we'll try the Gourmet Palace. Best chow mein in town, trust me.'

Outside O'Mahony's, Shirley sways unsteadily.

'It's the air.' She puts the back of her hand to her forehead. 'And the vodka.' She smiles and takes a deep breath. 'Actually, I think I should head home myself. Sorry, Joe, we'll do it again.' She waves her hand about. 'Just a little dizzy right now.'

'No worries. I'll get you a cab,' Joe says, pulling his mobile from his pocket.

She shakes her head. 'No, thanks, Joe, I'll walk. I need the air. I really do.'

She looks at me. I know she lives in the Churchberry Avenue apartments just off the Mill Road.

'I might go with you, if that's okay?'

I take a breath. Jesus. 'Of course. Can you manage in those?'

She looks down at the print heels and takes my arm. 'You can always carry me, Dan.' She giggles. Joe lifts his shoulders and looks at Shirley. 'Looks like a takeaway for *solo mio*,' he says, putting on a sad face.

Shirley leans forward to kiss him on the cheek. 'Goodnight, Joe. Safe home. See you Monday.'

He gives me a look that says *Don't say I didn't warn you* before he weaves towards the Palace takeaway in the Square.

She slips her arm through mine, and we start to walk. It's a small town, people talk, but right now, I don't give a toss who sees us. The streets glisten after an earlier shower, and the night is clear and fresh. We cross the Lainey bridge, the waters below gurgling in full flow, and we take a right down the quay onto Main Street. Our steps are in rhythm, and there's an easy silence between us. The town is quiet now as we cut across the green, through the SuperValu car park, and out onto the Mill Road.

In the cool night air, I feel slightly light-headed, that happy, careless unspooled feeling you get after a few pints too many. Shirley on my arm adds to the buzz. I feel ridiculously happy that she stayed back tonight. I *want* her to want me. I'm flattered she might. It's just a fantasy. Harmless stuff. A bit of fun. It won't go anywhere. It can't. I love Sally. But doesn't everyone need a diversion now and then, some flash of brightness, some quickening of the spirit and the heart?

'Are you okay, Shirley? You're very quiet.'

She gives my arm a little squeeze. 'I don't need to talk when I'm with you.'

We turn left into Churchberry Avenue and stop outside the tall granite block that was built during the Celtic Tiger years. Her ground-floor apartment, number 27, has its own entrance, and she fumbles in her bag for her key.

'Thanks, Dan. Appreciate that. I feel better now, actually.' She turns towards me and draws me close. Her coat has fallen open, and I can feel her softness against my chest. She reaches up and her lips brush my neck, sending a shower of sparks through me. She seems to sense my reaction.

'I don't know what you must be thinking . . . ' She runs her hand through her hair. 'What am I like?'

'You're fine, Shirley; forget about it.' I dig my hands deep in my pocket. Christ, I feel like a schoolboy. I'd want to get a bit of sense. I need to go. Now.

She looks upset. I reach out and take her hand, and she lets it rest in mine. I'd only have to trace a line with my finger along her wrist . . .

She turns her brown eyes towards me for a lingering moment, trying to read the signals in mine. Then she squeezes my hand and moves away. 'Goodnight, Dan.'

'Goodnight, Shirley. See you Monday.' My voice doesn't sound like mine. She twists the key in the door and disappears into the shadows.

When I get back to Bluebell Grove, Sally's watching *The Late Late Show*. She doesn't look up.

'Want a cup of tea?' I ask.

'No thanks.' She turns towards me. 'So much for *I'll be home before eight.*'

'I texted you.'

'You smell like a brewery.'

'When is the last time I've stayed out after work? You know how it is, Sal. It's hard to walk away; I needed to be seen to be there.'

She gives me a look. 'Doll is off form. And her temperature is up.'

'Will she be okay for her birthday party tomorrow?'

She rolls her eyes. 'It's not a party, Dan. It's just a little gathering to celebrate the day.'

The front door opens as I head to the kitchen for a sandwich. It's Andi.

'Where have you been?'

'I told Mom I was over at Stacey's house tonight. Her dad dropped me home.'

She takes the stairs two at a time, humming. Someone's in a good mood.

Later in the shower, I try to scrub Shirley Lovett out of my hair. It's like taking an aspirin for a toothache; it only lasts an hour and the pain is back again.

CHAPTER 16

SALLY

The candles blink and flicker on the pink ice cream cake. There's a picket fence of Cadbury's chocolate Flakes round the edges and Smarties scattered like confetti on top. Ruby sneaks a chocolate button off the side, ice-cream dribbling down her chubby fingers as she pops the sweet into her mouth. She sucks in her lips and looks around to see if she's been spotted.

'Happy birthday to you, happy birthday dear Do-oll . . .' We all stand around and sing it together. Ruby and her friends, the twins Lauren and Louise from number 12, hold hands and smile, eyes on the glowing cake. Dan is holding Doll in his arms, but she's struggling, wants to escape the party, retreat to her couch.

Andi tries to hold her hand, but she pushes away, digging her thumb into her cheek. I can't watch.

'Come on, Doll, blow out your candles. Make a wish.' Audrey, Ruby's mom, my friend and neighbour, forever cheerful. She picks up her iPhone. 'Big smile, girls.'

I lean against the kitchen door and gaze at the little group around the birthday party table. It's late October, a hazy drizzle on the window-panes, and I feel I'm looking at a stage set with actors and props. I see the three little girls, blonde braids, party dresses, chocolate mouths. Happy faces lit up in pink candlelight. I see Dan smiling, jolly, saying, 'The cake's for me! There'll be none left over. It's all mine,' in a scary monster voice, but the smile doesn't stray far from his lips. What's up with Dan lately? Serves him right if he's suffering from a hangover. And there's Doll in his arms, twisting away like a restless horse tethered to a gatepost.

I can't believe it's been eleven years, and I ache for Doll, for the hole that is her childhood.

And Andi, my beautiful Andi, her dark curtain of hair, leaning forward over the table, saying, 'Girls, girls, come on. Audrey's taking a picture. Smile! Say cheese.' So happy lately. Lovely to see that.

Doesn't life keep waltzing by regardless of how much we cry? *One-two-three, one-two-three . . .*

The moment passes. The candles are blown out by Ruby. *Whoosh.* Ruby beams. 'Did you make a wish, Doll?' Doll disentangles from her father's arms, stumbles back to her couch. Ruby follows with a plate of ice-cream, picking out the Smarties. 'I'll make sure there's no Smarties innit, Sally. She won't choke, I'll make sure.'

'Good girl,' I say. 'You're the best girl, Ruby.'

She plucks out a green one, then a yellow. Crunches them and licks her lips. 'Come on, Doll, eat up.' But Doll is already curled up.

'Leave her be,' Audrey says. 'Don't annoy her.' Ruby sets the plate of melting cake on the coffee table, sucking ice-cream from her fingers. Louise and Lauren join her on the couch.

They crowd around Doll. 'Look, Doll, your new friend, Nan-Nan. D'ya want to hold her? Isn't she beautiful?'

Doll looks up, one eye open. Slowly she reaches out for her, rubs her black hat, traces her finger over her arm, peers closer, and without warning, flings her onto the floor. Nan-Nan lands face-up on the polished wood.

Everyone laughs. 'She don't like her, Mom,' says Ruby, picking her up off the floor and sitting her on the chair by the fire.

'*Doesn't*, Ruby, not *don't*. Mind your grammar. Yes, I know, love. Leave her be.'

I pour tea, and we sit around the table, me and Dan and Audrey eating cupcakes and sweets, swiping through the photos. *Get rid of that one; I look awful . . . here's a lovely one.* Andi's opening birthday cards and placing them carefully on the mantelpiece. The three little girls are still sitting in a huddle on the couch, arms folded across their chests, chatting like three old busybodies.

'They're only short a few shopping bags and headscarves,' Audrey says, nodding in their direction.

We all laugh. Laughing is good. The wind is whipping up outside. In here, the room feels comforting and safe, the flames leaping in the hearth.

I stare. My eyes are playing tricks in the dull half-light. On the chair by the fire, Nan-Nan's eyes are closed, her legs crossed at the ankle. She looks like she's dozing off, her head lolling sideways, her arms folded across her chest. *Like a real person.* When I blink and look again, she's back to normal, eyes static like a ragdoll.

58

It's been a long week; I probably need an early night. Hank Williams is singing 'Tennessee Waltz' on the radio.

One-two-three, one-two-three. Life keeps dancing by. Eleven years down. Eleven years done.

Happy birthday, little darling.

CHAPTER 17

DOLL

'Sleep tight, love. Happy birthday.'

The door clicks shut. I'm glad it's over. My party, I mean. I hate all the silly fuss. Pointless, really. It's about making memories, they say, but please don't bother. So annoying. Everyone trying to be jolly. What are they celebrating – am I allowed to ask? Baking cupcakes, flapping out the pink tablecloth – and the flowery paper cups and bendy straws. All for what, Alfie?

I suppose they're trying to make an effort – and it did look nice – the ice-cream cake, made by Andi, my cool sister. The pink balloons and the cards on the mantelpiece with glitter and purple-and-red *11*s on the front. And the presents, too, done up with ribbon and bows and envelopes stuck to them with Sellotape.

Mom says, 'Look at everyone who's remembering your birthday, Doll?'

Big wow.

I usually get lots of clothes – cardigans and packs of T-shirts. Very nice. Lovely. Put them in a drawer, somebody, please. Sometimes a teddy – imagine, a teddy at my age? Hello? Today there are cardboard books – those baby ones for zero to three years. And a DVD of *Frozen*, and Ugg boots – like I'll be going somewhere. The twins brought me a toy dog, a shaggy fella with a cute face and a blue lead. Sure, I'll bring him for a walk around town, will I? Yeah, that's a great present. Not. Amn't I a bit old for a toy dog?

I know what people would say if they heard my thoughts, but I don't care. They can think what they like. That's their own business. I didn't ask for a stupid party and presents and fuss. And I don't like people singing 'Happy Birthday' and making wishes and pretending it's me blowing out the candles when it's actually them.

I wish I could've blown them candles right off the cake . . . and I'd keep blowing till they took off into the air and out the window and across the garden and into the Lainey and then off into the ocean, tossed around like matchsticks, sodden and useless. Useless, *like me!* And what would be left? Well, the cake would still sit on the table, little melted holes where the candles were standing, and the room would be dark and the singing would *stop*. And that'd be the *end* of all the jolliness. And everyone would look at each other, biting their lip.

Anyway, that's not going to happen, 'cos I can't even blow a bubble.

I turn around in my bed and feel Nan-Nan's hat against my back. What did they put her in here for?

I'm so mean, saying all that about my party. After all they did, it's not right. I feel my fists curling up, getting tight and sore, and I need to squeeze some of this guilt and misery out of myself. I reach up with my thumb and dig into my face. If I stay with it, the plaster will move, and if I keep pushing, pushing, then I can dig in properly. I search around with my thumb and feel the dip, the little hollow in my cheek where the wound is. It's sore and tender . . . aah, yes, that feels good. An instant flash of pain and a sharp rush of relief.

'Sweetheart?'

I stop for a second. Silence. Just the faint hum of the TV downstairs.

I go back to my face and concentrate on those delicious pinpricks of pain zapping along under my skin like one-hundred-mile-an-hour dominoes of pure pleasure.

'Sweetheart?' A question, whispered. Is my granny back? But Granny never called me sweetheart.

I stop again, absently rubbing the sticky residue around the open wound where the blood is oozing nicely. I hear a voice. Low and smooth as caramel, a whisper. For definite. I am not dreaming. I turn slowly and remember Nan-Nan is in my bed, and I understand now. A doll with a microchip built in for talking. I turn towards her and see her lashes move ever so faintly. It's the breeze, as Mom often leaves the top window ajar.

This time, there is no mistake.

'Sweetheart, you're sad?'

I grab Nan-Nan and turn her towards me. The moon lights up her face. How do I turn this off? I remember Ruby getting a doll last Christmas from Santa. You pressed a button in her middle, and she spoke. Trouble was, she kept saying the same things over and over until you were driven mad. Things like *How are you today?* or *It's a beautiful day* or *It's very nice to have a friend.* As if she cared. Huh. I wouldn't fall for that rubbish.

I search for a button or a switch or something to press, but I can't find it. Oh no! She could be jabbering here all night. I'd love to buckaroo her out of my bed . . . but then she'll be talking all night on the floor and I won't be able to fling her out of earshot. Looks like I'm stuck with her.

'Yes, it looks that way.'

She's sitting back against the pillow, and I can see her lips move. How many more phrases are on that chip? *Oh, very clever, dolly*, I'm thinking, *and now will you shut up, please!*

'That's a little rude, don't you think?'

She has a gentle voice, soft like the edges of a baby's blanket. I think I must be dreaming.

'You sure do a lot of thinking, Doll.'

I look closely at her in the moonlight, my sore face well forgotten now. Is she actually talking . . . to *me*?

I nearly jump out of my skin when she answers.

'Yes, sweetheart, I am talking to you, and I'm glad I've got your attention.'

Ha-ha, just because I've special knees, she thinks she can fool me, but I'm eleven now and I know about microchips. What'll be next? as my granny would say. What'll be next?

'Well, let me tell you what's next.' Nan-Nan folds her arms across her chest – yes, folds her sackcloth arms across her chest – and asks me this: 'Why are you hurting yourself, sweetheart?'

I've never been called sweetheart before, and it feels nice.

Then she reaches up to my face and touches the sore bit very lightly, like a feather brushing my skin.

I stare at her, blink my eyes, stare again. This dream is so real. I don't want to move in case I wake up. I feel sleepy, so calm. I reach for her other hand and touch it. It feels worn. And warm. Like my granny's. I'm caught in a moment, like in a sparkly net. It's like she hears my thoughts, and that's . . . that's mad.

She smiles. 'You're a good girl, Doll. A special girl.'

I think of my granny saying I was one of a kind.

'Yes.' She holds my gaze. 'That's exactly right, honey, you're one of a kind.' She can hear my thoughts!

Honey. I lean a little closer to the black hat. So close I can feel the butterfly movement of her lashes brushing my cheek. I close my eyes and just for a few silvery moments, I feel – it's hard to explain – I feel like my sour-milk life is ebbing away, getting sucked out into the ocean.

Maybe my granny was right. Nan-Nan is a sign from her. She couldn't come again herself, so she sent a friend. Maybe those new worlds are spinning towards me? Will a magic door open up? When I close my eyes and stay perfectly still, I think I can hear the creak of hinges. And when I concentrate, I can see a golden light slicing through the crack. I know I need to push that door open and step through into the light.

*

The bowl of warm water sits on the kitchen table. Cotton pads, plasters, Dettol, the usual rigmarole. 'Well now,' my mom says, as she turns me away from her and cups my chin. 'Well, if you didn't dig your face every day, Doll, you wouldn't have to endure this.'

Or *you* wouldn't, I think, guiltily. How come she doesn't get mad?

She's still talking. 'And you've only yourself to blame if it hurts, love.' And it does. Hurt. Ouch! I wince and try to escape, but I can't break free. I start to cry; it's just too sore. I try to think of nice things. Like Nan-Nan last night. Remembering her helps to colour the moment, and I brighten up.

'Her temperature is normal again. Thank God for that.' Mom smiles as she turns to my dad. 'One less thing to worry about.' She ruffles my hair. 'You're done, Doll.'

Now I'm on my couch, plastered, drinking my beaker of tea. As in my face has new plasters on, clean as a whistle. Sausages are sizzling under the grill, the kettle is boiling on the Aga, and Mom's singing along to a song on the radio. 'I love Cilla,' she says as she sings her favourite song, 'Something Tells Me.'

She looks happy. Dad's clattering out some cups and plates, and he smiles over at her. *Ping!* The toaster pops. Mom drowns out Cilla. 'Don't give up the day job,' Dad says. She twirls around the kitchen with the coffee-pot.

'You're making up your own words,' he says. She laughs.

I drift off, curling the tartan rug up around me. I think about Nan-Nan. Her folding her arms, smiling, calling me sweetheart and honey. It's delicious even thinking about it. The memory feels like hot chocolate in my heart. Could it be real?

Later, I finish my Weetabix for my mom. Every last spoon, yeuch, but it's done. I feel so bad for having mean thoughts about my party that I really make an effort to eat.

Now Andi is buttoning up my pink duffle coat and putting on my scarf. We're going for a walk in the sunlight.

The leaves are sailing down from the trees, and they're crunchy under my new Ugg boots. I love leaves. And matches and daisies. I bend forward and pick up a green leaf from the pavement. Andi is holding my hand. 'That's a lovely one, Doll. Look, here's an even better one.' She hands me a goldier leaf. I take it.

'Good girl,' she says.

I'd love if I could talk to Andi and ask her things and tell her about Nan-Nan. I wonder what she'd say.

Andi squeezes my hand. She has green nail polish with silver stars. Cool.

I look up at her, but she's gone all dreamy. So pretty, so perfect. Wish my name was Andi. She's got millions of trophies. Player of the Year, top of the heap. Granny used to say she was a topper. *A topper.* I'd love to be a topper. That means you're tops in everything, no one can beat you.

I'd love to swap places with her for a day. Would she swap places with me? *Yes or no, Andi; swap places? Just for a day, even?*

'Stop at your face, Doll. Stop it. Stop digging.' She's cross. I stop and think of Nan-Nan again. *Why are you hurting yourself?* Good question. Can I phone a friend? Sorry, I forgot – I don't have a friend.

We stop under a skeleton tree. The sun is shooting through its bare arms, lighting up the leaves on the pavement: red, gold, brown. Seagulls *kwee-kwee* overhead, swinging through the blue. A church bell is pealing in the distance, clear and pure like the hymns Granny used to sing.

I look up. Just for a moment, there's a hush . . . the world seems to shimmer. The air is bright. I can smell turf. Now the bell is chiming again, and I catch my breath. My heart is light, and a thought drifts into my brain: there's nothing to be sad about. *There's nothing at all to be sad about.* I'm trying to hold on to it but it's darting away. I don't know what sparked it – the thought of Nan-Nan back home? Andi's hand in mine? The sunlight fingers on my face? Something somersaults inside me, like a bird tumbling out of my heart. A glimmer of joy.

Joy, come back, come back! Don't go.

Andi says, 'C'mon, we better get home, Doll. There's a shower coming.' The spell is broken. It's business as usual.

But on the way back I'm singing Cilla's happy song in my head. I can hear the guitars, the trumpets, the drums. And something is telling Cilla that something's going to happen, something magical. And everything is going to turn out right. Woo-hoo. I'm thinking to myself, even though the raining is falling hard and we're getting drenched, I quite like this pink coat; I think it suits me.

CHAPTER 18

ANDI

The Ice-Cream Café is quiet this Sunday evening, just a couple of kids queuing for takeaway slushies in radioactive colours. We've arranged to meet outside the café, and I'm scared he's not going to turn up. But as I turn the corner onto Main Street, he's already there, his hands thrust into his jacket pockets, one foot leaning back against the café wall. My heart swivels inside my red sweater. He smiles as I cross the road, and he leans in to kiss my cheek.

'You smell nice.' He opens the door and gestures me through. We slide into the booth at the back and go through the business of melting the ice all over again.

'How've you been?'

'Good, yeah. You?'

'Good.'

My fingers close over the pastel-pink menu. One Direction is singing 'What Makes You Beautiful' on the radio, and it drowns the awkward silence.

'What's your favourite?' I say, pointing to the menu photos of chocolate strawberries and exotic fruit and swirls of ice-cream in ten flavours.

He turns the page and glances up at me.

'I'm easy. You?'

'The chocolate strawberries with vanilla ice-cream. Definitely my favourite.' Why am I talking about ice-cream? He's not interested. I'm trying hard to think of something cool to say as the girl comes down to take our order. She flicks her eyes over Steve approvingly.

'What can I get you?' She beams at him, barely giving me a glance. He orders for us both and watches her as she totters off behind the counter.

'You're only having a Coke?' Why can't I think of something interesting to say instead of stating the obvious?

'I'm not an ice-cream kind of guy.' He grins.

'I think she fancies you,' I say, nodding to the server, who's smiling over at him now as she scoops up the ice-cream and shovels strawberries into a pink dish. 'You have that effect on girls, you know.'

He grins, twisting a napkin around his finger. 'Really? You think so?'

'Tell me you don't do it purposely.'

'So do I have *that effect* on you?' He places his elbows on the Formica table and leans towards me, tilting his head to one side. When I don't answer, he smiles. 'Well, do I?'

'Yes.'

'I'm glad to hear that, babe.'

'I bet you are,' I say, annoyed. 'Guys like you . . . you're full of yourselves. It's not a very attractive trait, you know.'

'You've got me wrong, Andi girl.' He shakes his head. 'I'm not like that. Just saying I'm glad *you* like me. Because, well, I think you're hot, and I'm glad that, well, that you . . . you know what I'm saying.' He sits back and folds his arms.

'Oh.'

He takes off his jacket and pulls up the sleeves of his khaki sweatshirt. It's tight across the chest, and I can see the band of muscle under the thin material. I think of my dad when I see the tiger tattoo. He'd kill me.

'C'mon, tell me about you, Andi.'

I shrug. 'There's not much to tell. I was born in Dublin – we moved here when I was three or four. And trust me, I can't wait to move out of here the first chance I get.'

'That bad? Go on. I'm listening.' He runs his hand through his hair, and it looks almost white-blond under the strip lighting overhead.

'I hate school – St Mary's is an open prison.' He laughs at this. 'I love basketball. I have one single good friend, one sister, one brother, and a dad who's constantly getting on my case.' I tilt my head. 'Have you heard enough? It's all boring, really.'

The girl comes back with our order, flashing him another smile. 'Enjoy.' I offer to share, but he declines. Why, why did I order chocolate? What if it smears on my face? So embarrassing. *Oh, Andi, you've got some melted chocolate on your nose.* I need to remember to dab my mouth after every bite.

'What about you, Steve? You're very close to Joanie, aren't you?' I take a delicate bite of my strawberry and dab my mouth.

'Yep. Me and my gran are very close. She's fantastic.'

'I can see she's mad about you.'

He shrugs and takes a swig of Coke. 'It works both ways.'

'And your mum?'

He sucks in his cheeks. 'What do you want to know?'

'Joanie told me she . . . she wasn't around . . . do you ever see her?'

I hold my spoon in mid-air. 'Sorry, Steve, you don't have to talk about this. I shouldn't have asked . . .'

He puts his finger to his lips for a moment.

'It's okay, Andi.' He pauses, and I can see a ripple of sadness move across his forehead and travel down across his face. A flicker of something painful. But it disappears quickly, and I wonder if it was my imagination. He looks beyond my shoulder when he answers. 'My mum's a heroin addict. She lives in London. I haven't seen her in two years.' He brings his eyes back to mine again. 'I'm over it now. She made her choices. We all do.' He takes a pink napkin from the cutlery box on the table, double folds it to make a tiny triangle. He straightens the creases to keep it flat.

'I'm sorry, Steve.' I take his hand in mine without thinking, and I can feel a tremble under his skin. I'm not sure if it's because he's thinking of his mother or if he feels the electricity between us. He lets it rest there.

'Are you mad with her?'

He considers the question for at least ten seconds.

'Not anymore. I feel sorry for her, though. We've both missed out. You don't get it back.'

He smiles and gently traces his fingers along the back of my hand. It's hard to concentrate when he does that. My skin is tingling.

'What's your mum like, Andi?'

I take a spoonful of ice-cream – it's cleaner and safer than the melting chocolate.

'She's great; I love my mum. She keeps us all on our toes. And she works so hard. Sometimes – and I know this – I don't make her life easy.'

'You're very lucky.'

'I know.' I dab my mouth again.

I decide not to ask him about his dad.

'And you're lucky you're finished school,' I continue. 'What's it like, working at the garage?'

Steve had told me he's a trainee mechanic at O'Herlihy's Yard. O'Herlihy's Sales & Repairs, to be precise.

His eyes light up. 'Yeah, it doesn't even feel like work, to be honest. And Bertie's sound. He took over from his father last year. He's great plans for the business. It's the bike repair side that buzzes me up.' He grins. 'Motorbikes, that is.'

'Do you see yourself there in ten years' time? Twenty years?'

'Maybe. What is this, an interview?' He retrieves his hand and leans back against the seating, nodding. 'I know what you're thinking.' His smile is hard.

'How do you mean?'

'You're thinking working-class boy, grease monkey. He'll hook up with some young one before he's twenty-one and then it's a council house and a life of ham sandwiches in his lunchbox and a few pints in O'Mahony's on Saturday night. All mapped out. Poor sod.' He avoids my eye as he pulls on his jacket and finishes his drink.

I've obviously hit a nerve. 'You're accusing me of judging you, but it's you who're judging me. That is not fair.' I hear the anger in my own voice.

He stops and looks straight into my eyes. A long pause. 'You're right, Andi. I'm sorry. Forget I said that.' He settles back into his seat.

I dab my mouth again for the tenth time.

'It's okay. You definitely don't have chocolate on your face.' He laughs then, and I laugh, and the moment passes and we're back to that friendly, flirting place again.

When it's time to go, he places a tenner on the table and helps me on with my jacket. I feel like a princess.

Outside, he takes my hand, and we cross onto Church Street and along the quay. When we get to the river path, we dawdle along, holding hands, not wanting the evening to end. It's not quite dark yet. There are still some Sunday evening strollers and cyclists out and about. I'm torn between wanting to linger along the riverbank and not wanting hassle if I get home after nine. They think I'm at Stacey's, and I don't want to push my luck.

'You can leave me at the Avenue,' I say, when we turn off the Mill Road. I can't tell him I don't want my parents to spot him and start asking questions. We sit on the low stone wall under the beech tree skirting the entrance to the Avenue. He traces his finger lightly around the outside of my lips, and my heart skitter-scatters as he leans in to kiss me. It's hard to pull myself away. He squeezes my hand. 'I'll call you tomorrow.'

I float up through the Avenue onto Bluebell Grove, hardly feeling the pavement beneath me. Even the thought of school tomorrow doesn't faze me.

I'm nearly home when I hear footsteps stealing up behind me. Two girls appear on either side of me on the footpath, and I am relieved to see it isn't some weirdo following me. The girls fall into step next to me. The one with long blonde hair and tons of eyeliner says, 'Slow down, girl. We just want a quick chat.'

I turn to look at her friend, who's wearing a dark-blue beanie, and she nods, smiling. 'That's right. It's Andi, isn't it?'

'Do I know you?' I look from one to another, puzzled, and there's a corner of my heart that starts to pump and squeeze alarmingly.

'We just want to warn you,' eyeliner girl says, also smiling.

'Warn me about what?' I'm almost outside my house, so it's safe, but these two have completely caught me on the hop.

Eyeliner girl shoves me hard, and I stumble against her friend.

'Be careful there. Watch where you're going,' hat girl says to me, pretending to steady herself.

'What do you want?' My legs are jelly and my heart is thumping.

'I'm Chelsea,' the blonde girl says. 'This is Tania.' She flicks the front of my denim jacket. 'Pleased to meet you, Andi.'

I nod.

'What do you want?'

Chelsea starts to walk backwards. 'Just a warning, Andi girl.' She points a painted fingernail at me. 'Stay away from Steve Thompson.'

I can only stare after them as they sprint down the Grove onto the Avenue and back out onto the Mill Road. Fucking hell. My hands are shaking as I turn the key in the door.

CHAPTER 19

DOLL

I can't wait to go to bed and see Nan-Nan again. The room is dim, just a thin slice of moonbeam falling across the duvet.

'Night, love. Sleep tight.' The door clicks shut.

Nan-Nan is leaning back against the pillow, arms folded. I reach out to hold her, check for that button. I press as hard as I can – on her back, her tummy. Nothing. It's a glorious mystery. A sixth one, as Granny would say.

'Do you mind?'

She spreads her arms out, like a star-fish.

'Go on, honey, get the search over, and then we'll talk.'

Jeez, I never heard a talking doll say that before.

'You happy now?'

I'm stunned. These questions she's asking me are real. No way are they recorded on a chip.

'There's no chip, sweetheart.'

Oh my God, she can actually hear me thinking. It's not a dream.

She looks at me and smiles. 'Thinking, talking, it's all the same energy.'

I should be whacking her out of the bed at this stage. It is a bit scary; she could kill me. My heart is rattling like a tambourine. Is she a fairy? I wonder.

'No, honey, I'm not a fairy.' Tinkling laugh.

'Wow.' My mouth is dry. I have so many questions, but I'm a bit muddled up and I can't think straight. Who is she? Where's she from? Is she a baddie?

'Ask *me*, Doll. Talk to *me*. Look *at me* . . .'

I turn towards her. She's sitting up against the pillows, her legs crossed at the ankles. She smooths out her orange skirt with the flowers.

'Who are you?'

'Doll, you must listen very carefully.'

'I will. I will.'

'Well,' she says, coughing gently, 'I'll start at the beginning. Settle down please, child.'

I fold my arms just like her, cross my ankles, and move a little closer. I pull my duvet up around her so she won't get cold.

I'm so excited.

'Are you ready, Doll?'

I nod, hoping I'll be able to keep up. 'Nan-Nan, before you start, are you a person or a doll?'

She smiles. 'If you're asking me if I'm real, the answer is yes. Outside, I'm a doll. That's what you see, right?'

'Right.'

'Outside is the shell,' she explains. 'But inside – inside I'm thinking and planning and feeling. And it's what's inside that makes you real.' She taps the side of her forehead with two fingers. 'That's what matters, Doll, what's going on in here.'

'I know.' I get what she means. 'I'm real too. On the inside.'

'Of course you are, sweetheart.' She reaches over and touches my hand. 'You have a heart and a mind and a soul.'

A heart *and* a mind *and* a soul. When she puts it like that, it feels like I'm somebody and not just a goner.

'Are you with me, Doll?' She looks at me sideways, eyebrows arched.

'Oh yes, of course.' I nod my head again, thinking, *Will you come on with the story?*

She leans back against the pillows again.

'Have you ever seen the Mary Poppins movie?'

I'm not expecting that question, but yes, I've seen it. 'She's the one that flies in on a black umbrella to mind the children?'

'Yes, the very one. She flies in when the children need her most. Where does she come from? We don't know – another place, another time, another universe?'

She jumps to her feet, strides across the bed, and edges back the curtain. The moonlight floods in. 'Out there,' she says, pointing at the sky, 'out there you can find many worlds. Right across the universe as far as you can see, Doll, and then a lot farther. And they're all spinning in an ocean of energy, with people living and breathing and dreaming. Maybe that's where Mary Poppins came from?'

'Maybe.'

I follow her gaze across the night sky.

'Do you know my granny?'

She looks puzzled and shakes her head. 'No. Why do you ask me that?'

'She said there were many worlds.'

'There you go! Here I am telling you all this, and you know it already. You understand.' She looks pleased. Like I've made her job easier.

The window is slightly open. A soft breeze lifts the curtains and they billow inwards, drawing in the scent of turf. An owl hoots.

Nan-Nan is talking again, and I try to keep up.

'Now, if you know how to – and I do, Doll,' she whispers, 'you can tunnel from world to world just like . . . like a bus travelling from town to town.'

She must be a spoofer. I can't believe it, but I so want to.

She drops down on her knees next to me. 'Are you with me, Doll?'

'So, you're saying we could take a bus to the stars?'

'No, it's not that simple, honey.' She jerks her thumb towards the window. 'But we can use wormholes to travel across time and space.'

She's off her head. '*Wormholes?*'

She stops. 'Yes, holes in the membrane of space-time.' She jumps to her feet again and steps towards the middle of the bed. 'But I'm telling you all this for a reason.'

I nod like a donkey.

'I can move through space. Here one minute' – she snaps her fingers – 'and gone the next.' Her eyes are glittering in the moonlight. 'I have travelled here from Almazova, a world teetering between ancient magic and new science. A world way beyond that big white moon up there.'

She still has her black hat on, and now she takes it off, using both hands to place it carefully on the bed. She pats it for a moment and begins to smooth her flame-red hair, tucking some stray curls behind her ears. She settles back against the pillows again, clasping her hands behind her head and looking straight at the picture of Goldilocks and the Bears. Silence. She seems to be waiting for me to say something.

I'm bamboozled. Squeezing through holes and crawling through tunnels and sailing – or is it flying – through space and time? It's got my head all muddled. I feel sea-sick. I dig my face. Ouch. It hurts. I'm definitely not dreaming.

'But I thought Will sent you from Africa?'

Nan-Nan looks puzzled again. 'Who is Will, child?' She smiles. 'Sweetheart, I don't expect you to understand. But Doll, I'm for real. And I'm *for* you.' She emphasizes the *for*. Like she's on my side. I do believe her. She's only saying what my granny said.

I'm so excited by this talking doll. She's definitely going to be my best friend. Maybe we can share more stories tomorrow; that'd be cool. And she might teach me how to skip. Or even bring me across the stars and back to Almazova with her. Anything is possible now.

Nan-Nan squeezes my hand again. She smiles. 'Yes, anything is possible.' She places her hat back on her head, then folds her arms and settles back against the pillows.

Then something terrible occurs to me. It's something Will said one night last summer. He was sitting in the kitchen, drinking a beer with his friend Luke, talking about smoking weeds and how they make you feel high and happy. 'You can't stop laughing,' Will said. 'You believe you could do anything, fly even, or conker the world.'

Sounds fun. I'd love to smoke a weed myself.

But Luke said no sooner are you high, up flying around the sky, than you start to come down. You're back to reality and you realise that you can't really fly after all. It's a bummer, they said, and you're forever chasing after a dragon – or a dinosaur, I can't remember which.

I'm thinking that maybe Nan-Nan was smoking weeds and she's as high as a kite, thinking she's a master of the universe, or Nan-Nan Poppins. Soon, she'll be coming down and there'll be no more mad talk about other worlds hiding behind the stars. And that will be the end of all this magic. She will be conked out on my pillow and won't remember a word.

And I believed it all. The twins' mother was on the button when I heard her say I'm not right upstairs.

I reach up and dig my face. Ouch.

Nan-Nan touches my shoulder. 'Child of grace? What's the matter?' She reaches for my hand. 'Don't give up on me yet.' There's a slight sharpness in her voice. 'Please, Doll?'

I turn around to face her. 'I think I'm losing the plot.'

I often heard my granny say she was losing the plot. Forgetting where she left her glasses or getting stuff mixed up. I just don't know what to think.

'Were you smoking weeds in that tunnel?' I ask, brazenly.

Straightaway I regret it. She purses her lips. 'Certainly not,' she says, looking horrified, but I do notice a twinkle in her eye. I believe her; she has that way of getting you to believe everything. Maybe Almazova *is* real. Alma-zova . . . I like the sound of it curling around my mind. Alma-zova.

I close my eyes and feel something wash over me like I'm loosening out, ready to give way, to believe in what comes next. Ready to untie myself from my dark little world and flutter up and away into another life.

CHAPTER 20

SALLY

When I walk into the kitchen, I can sense it. The storm clouds rolling in, something thick and oppressive in the air. These days it's hard to work out if something is real or if it's all just in my head.

The toaster pings comfortingly.

'There's freshly brewed coffee in the pot,' Dan says. 'How's Doll?'

'She looks exhausted,' I say. 'I think we'll leave her home today, Dan. Audrey's free and she'll keep an eye on her.'

Dan pours us both a coffee and nods. 'I can check in on her at lunchtime to see how she's doing.' The unease is definitely in my head. I need to shake it off and get a grip.

'You're okay. I'll do it.'

He butters a slice of toast and stops to wave to Andi as she passes the kitchen window and disappears down the driveway to school. 'Daughter number one hasn't stopped smiling for the last week.' He shakes his head as he opens the marmalade. 'Makes a welcome change.'

I take a triangle of toast. 'I've noticed that,' I say, taking a bite. Which I have – and it does make a nice change – but what was all that about?

I pour myself a coffee. 'It's a bit odd, though, isn't it?' I say. 'I reckon there must be something going on we don't know about.'

I mean, that's all I say. Just that simple observation. Harmless. But he sighs when I say it, an exaggerated sigh, and then he turns to me. I can see his forehead furrowing, a ripple of impatience clouding his face.

'How do you mean? You think it's suspicious? She's happy so there's something wrong, something we're not seeing?' He rolls his eyes.

'Don't be so touchy, Dan. I just think it's odd, that's all I'm saying.'

He topples his coffee into the sink and drops his cup on the worktop with a loud thud.

'Can't you just say, "That's good, that's positive"?' he says, shaking his head. 'Can't you just say, Sally, for once, "Yes, she's happy; that makes life a bit easier for us all"? But no, no, there has to be something suspicious about it. "What's going on? There must be a problem we're not seeing." '

'Is it because it's Monday morning, Dan? What's bugging you?'

And then he says – the cheek of him, when I think about it – 'Why do you always have to look for the misery?'

'I *look* for misery?' I say. 'How dare you. I'm just being realistic. I'm just wondering out loud, if that's all right? I'm just curious as to why she's been in such a good mood over the last week. You're being naïve.'

He turns his palm up. 'What I see,' he says. 'What I see is your misery, Sal—'

'My *misery*? You mean – sorry . . . ?'

'I mean,' he says, 'I mean you need to stop seeing the glass half empty. You need to stop the misery. Like with Doll.' He straightens his tie and runs his fingers through his hair. I can almost hear the clap of thunder.

'You need to get over it. Move on. Accept it. She's sick, she's not happy, it's tough. But there's not much you or I or anyone can do.' His voice is rising like the hiss of heavy rain, and I can hear something in his tone, some undertow of weariness seeping through. It snags me.

His hands drop to his sides. 'Things will change. In time. We will get to the bottom of why Doll is so . . .'

'Get to the bottom of it?' My voice is rising too now. I want to lash back. 'It's not going to happen,' I say. 'It's a bottomless pit. Can't you see that? Face up to reality, Dan; it's a long road ahead. There's no rainbow around the corner. Just more of the same misery for her, for all of us. Why don't you sing it to me: "Don't Worry Be Happy"?'

I need to keep a lid on it. Take a step back. But I can feel the acid of despair churning up inside me like a river on the boil.

He looks at me. Shakes his head. 'Ah, Jesus, there's no talking to you, is there?'

He yanks his keys off the hook inside the kitchen door. I hate that. In the middle of all the fury, he's going to walk off.

'Hey! Don't just walk away.' I scream it.

He waves me away. 'Forget it. I'm late.'

That's when I grab my coffee and fling it at him. He doesn't see it coming. To be truthful, neither do I. I've never thrown a cup at anyone in my life. I regret it instantly. The cup misses him, sails across the room, and smashes against the wall behind him. The coffee inside leaps into the air like a fluid animal. I can actually track it as it shoots across the kitchen, spattering onto his shoulders.

I clamp my hand over my mouth. What was I thinking?

'I'm sorry.'

He rips off his jacket, flings it across the chair. Takes the stairs two at a time. Closet door opening. Banging closed. Silence. Fast footsteps on the stairs. Front door slamming. Silence.

There are coffee drops snaking down the face of the clock. It's eight twenty. I pick up the shards of cup and mop the coffee from the wall, table, and tiles.

My hands are still shaking when Audrey arrives ten minutes later. Makeup has been reapplied. Red eyes turned brown.

'How's Doll, Sally?'

'She's not good, Audrey,' I say, pulling on my coat, avoiding her eye. 'She seems very tired this morning.' I put on my reading glasses, pretend to examine a receipt in my pocket. 'I'll drop in later, and we'll see if she needs to see the doctor.'

In the car, I compose myself. I need to be in control for my nine-thirty editorial meeting. I haven't seen Dan like this before. Those shadows of what . . . discontent, frustration? He's normally so cool and in control. And kind. He used to be kind. What am *I* not seeing? Is it me? My life feels slippery, falling through my fingers. Is Dan slipping away too?

I pull into the office car park and close my eyes for a moment. There's a dark shape pressing down on me, expertly pinning a mask over my face. *It fits beautifully*, the dark shape says. *Like cling film.*

'It's hard to breathe in here,' I whisper in acknowledgement, determined not to cry, not to show any weakness whatsoever. I stay calm. Inhale for four, exhale for four, just like the book says. I rummage through my makeup bag. Another layer of pressed powder, some cherry lipstick. Sliver of eyeliner. I smooth my hair. Good as new. 'Smile,' the masked woman in the rearview mirror says, winking. I do, and the mask moves with me.

I walk through the car park towards the rear entrance. The sun is beaming down, the birds are singing, but there's no fizz inside me. I'm a flat Coke walking.

CHAPTER 21

DAN

I'm sitting at the bar in O'Mahony's. It's Monday so it's quiet. A few locals sip their pints and have the banter. I should've headed straight home. Should've apologised for this morning. Something snapped. I don't know how else to explain it. But right now, I could do with a drink.

There's nothing like slipping in for a pint after a long day. It unjangles you, listening to the banter. Men resting elbows on the counter, embracing their pints and swapping stories on the public dramas of the day. These are bonfires we can all dance around – because they're other people's dramas. Will Trump be back? What's likely to happen in the budget? We knew Brexit was bad news, didn't we, lads? Will Sars win the county? Safe topics. Oiled tongues loosened. Sorting it all out. The pub has to be the perfect networking event. Talking heads, listening, nodding, sharing – 'You're right there, Pat; you're dead on.' A burst of laughter. Unspoken kinship.

When you think about it, everyone is happy in a pub. Headaches are left at the door. The smell of beer and the soft lights act like a crooked finger, drawing you in. It's like a chapel of ease, a respite from the winds. Just what I need right now.

'A pint of Guinness, Dave, please.'

The barman fills the glass with care, lets it settle. Puts his hands on his hips.

'It's cold outside. Still, better than the rain, I suppose.'

I nod.

Just behind me, the speaker is playing Santana's "Black Magic Woman." Dave brings me a perfect creamy pint, and I sink back into the song and close my eyes, remembering.

Music does that to you, doesn't it? Catches you and hurtles you back along the years. It's the summer of '97, and I'm on the Greek island of Mykonos.

Me and the lads had just finished college, spent the summer working in a canning factory in Munich, and Greece was our reward for all the mind-numbing hours of scrubbing vegetables and shelling peas.

The club that night was a heaving outdoor arena. And then in the early hours, the opening bars of Santana's seventies hit cut through the air. A hush fell. No matter how often you hear it, it sounds as magical as the first time.

High on ouzo and cheap beer, we were looking to score. I'd seen 'the one' earlier – green eyes, white lacy top, denim shorts. She was smoking at the bar, and I'd asked her for a light. We'd talked for a minute in the crush, and then she was gone. Now I sloped up, grabbed her hand, and we swayed onto the floor for the opening bars. I remember wrapping my arms around her, whispering the words against her forehead.

The solo guitar and bass slides, the conga and timbales . . . we got lost inside the song. Fell headlong into each other.

It's a visceral memory, loaded with emotion. I can still feel her breath against my shoulder, her hands slipping inside my T-shirt, massaging my spine. The touch of her skin, the coconut scent of her hair – it all melded together, and in that moment everything lit up the shine of pure gold. Our mouths grazed each other's.

The memory crashes forward through the years and tumbles into O'Mahony's Bar.

I take a long drink.

I knew, that night, that I'd marry this girl.

And I did. The following year, me and Sally skipped down the aisle in the San Silvestro Basilica in Rome, still believing the best was yet to come.

How little you know when you're twenty-three. You're a kid. You haven't a bloody clue.

The Six One News is on mute, and there's a game of forty-five starting in the far corner near the turf fire. Candle lamps throw shadows across the flagstones.

I think about the day and how it started. I shouldn't have said what I did. About her being miserable. It isn't true. It's just that lately she seems so fragile and . . . compressed. Not like the real Sally, the old Sally. It's like if you cracked the shell of her, all this melted sadness and pain would spill out. And she doesn't want that. Who would? It's easier to plug the leaks – I think that's the way she's thinking. But I don't understand women. I can't read her mind. She doesn't talk to me about these things.

78

Today I avoided Shirley. I had back-to-back meetings, so it wasn't hard. If I don't see much of her, she's not in my head. That's the plan going forward.

I finish my pint. The phone buzzes. It's Sally. Ring me. I jab her number. No answer.

I fish out my keys and make my way to the car park.

After Doll, we kept the wheel turning. It's what you do – keep the sadness locked up. Keep the lid on it. Keep on keeping on. It's what everyone does in their own quiet way. That's how we survive, isn't it? But does it work? Your mind isn't a mattress; you can't hide all the dark stuff there forever.

I turn the key in the engine and head for home. *Home*; the thought makes me tired.

As I pull into the drive, there's a Saab turning out. Dr O'Brien. I buzz down the window.

'Hi, Dan, just finished up here. I'm afraid Dolly will have to go into hospital again.'

'It's Doll, Frank. Doll, not Dolly.' I never liked that man.

'Sorry, yes, of course. Doll.' He nods. 'She may get dehydrated, so we'll move her first thing in the morning, get some fluids in. And she'll need an x-ray so we can rule out pneumonia.' He checks his watch. 'I'll contact them now and let them know.'

I nod my thanks and kill the engine.

Sally's coming down the stairs. 'Oh. You're home.'

She keeps moving past me into the kitchen. Pushes a bundle of clothes into a travel bag. Drops in a hairbrush, a towel from the rail. Zips up the bag. She looks frazzled.

'I met Frank outside. What time in the morning?'

'Eight, he said. I'm just getting her things ready.'

'I'll take her.'

'No, it's okay. I want to.' She bites her lip. 'She's sleeping so much. I'm worried about her. It's not natural.' She hesitates for a moment. 'I am allowed to say that, aren't I? That I'm worried? Or is that just me inventing a drama?'

I'm not going to react to the sarcasm.

'She'll be in the right place,' I say. 'They'll check everything, and all the staff know her. It's peace of mind.'

We can be so polite. So much left unsaid. She nods. Grabs her jacket off the banister.

'I have to get out for a walk. Get yourself something to eat. Audrey left a casserole in the Aga.'

I check in on Doll. She's sleeping on the couch, wrapped up in a fleecy blanket. I kiss her forehead. Her eyelids flutter for a moment. There's a bluish tinge to her skin. *Where are you, Doll?* I think. *Are you sliding away from us?* That's how it feels to me. A heaviness curls around my heart, like a wet rope.

I sit at the kitchen table. The house is quiet, just the wall clock ticking behind me. Can't shift the feeling that the boat we've built is splintering and the water's pooling under my feet.

I pour myself a glass of wine.

At first, you know, I could understand. Sally was devastated. We both were. Who wouldn't be? The matron in the hospital said, 'Remember, you're grieving for the child you lost.' *The child you lost.* The bundle of sugar and spice, she said, that we'd been expecting. Gone. Now we had to plan for . . . something different. Tougher. More challenging, she said. Rewarding, even.

Such patronising gibberish. I sip the wine, run my finger around the rim of the glass. We were living the dream; we just didn't know it. And then with Doll, we were slapped sideways. Into treacle.

I top up my glass. Put some rice in a saucepan. I think of how we've stopped laughing over the years, me and Sally. There was no talking to her. She was on a mission. But she couldn't fix Doll, couldn't take away the pain.

'Was that my fault, was it?' I ask the question out loud.

There's a key in the front door. Andi's back. I hear a gear bag being flung under the stairs.

'Dinner's ready.'

'Mmm, smells lovely.' She gestures toward the couch. 'Doll's going in tomorrow morning, Mom said?'

'Yep. First thing.'

She makes a face. 'I'll just shower, Dad.'

She sounds chirpy. At least one of us is happy.

I get the plates warmed. My phone rings as I'm setting the table.

It's Shirley. I stare at the screen and let it ring out. There's no message. Part of me wants to ring her back, hear her voice, escape into a bit of fantasy. But there's a warning sound in my head telling me to steer clear.

And I have to admit, if Shirley Lovett made a move, I couldn't trust myself to walk away.

CHAPTER 22

DOLL

The doctor said I have to go to hospital in the morning. Even though I do feel a bit breathless, I can't wait to get back up to my bedroom to tell Nan-Nan. Will she still be there? Will I be back on my own again? Was I dreaming? What if she's disappeared?

No, no, no. Please, no.

I wail so much my dad carries me up to bed early. I'm afraid to look as he turns to close the curtains, but there – oh happy day – there's Nan-Nan propped up against the pillow. Dad slides me into bed, and I close my eyes, holding Nan-Nan's little hand tightly to make sure she won't vamoose on me.

'The doctor said . . . ,' I begin.

'I know, honey.' She rubs my arm.

'You won't leave me?'

She shakes her head. 'Listen, Doll. I'm here to take you back with me. To Almazova. If you'll come. Tonight.'

I stare at her. Waiting for her to smile, to laugh, to say, *I'm joking; you'd believe anything*, but she stares back, waiting for me to answer.

'Tonight? You're taking me across the stars . . . tonight?'

She moves closer and looks into my eyes. 'I'm a scientist, Doll, the Grand Mariner of the Almazova Space Agency. And I'm on a mission. The Council of Grandmothers, rulers of Almazova, has spoken. I am here to bring you back with me. It's your time.'

'The Council of Grandmothers wants me?' She can't be serious.

She sucks in her cheeks. 'It's not my place to question, Doll. The council has requested your presence. I'm just doing my job.' She sits up straight, folding her knees under her.

'Almazova is governed by the Ancients, Doll – five powerful elders. Tough old birds. You wouldn't cross them.' She gives a little smile.

My skin is tingling with excitement but with fear too. Now that things are hotting up, my feet are cooling down. Maybe I'm too young to be speeding off anywhere. I'm only just gone eleven. Maybe next year.

'The council meeting has been set for six bells tomorrow. Your presence is required. The council chamber in the Cathedral of Light is being made ready. That's all I know.'

'And they're expecting me?' She's having me on.

'Our ancient scrolls have spoken of the Child of Summer, an earthly child. A child we need to help us. These sacred Manuscripts predict her coming. And now you have been found. We need to travel before dawn.'

'Me, the Child of Summer? Is it summertime in Almazova?'

'Tomorrow is the first day of summer, child.'

'But Nan-Nan, what will they want me for? What can I do?'

She shakes her head. 'You will learn everything you need to know in good time, Doll. Trust me on this.'

'What's Almazova like?'

'Enchanting. You will love it. Not everyone supports them – but the Grandmothers are visionary leaders.'

'I have a granny too,' I say, but she doesn't seem that interested in talking about her.

I think of these Grandmothers like witches, fearsome, with lips like blades that will slice through you if you say something stupid. When I close my eyes, one of them is crooking her finger at me. *Step up here. You. Yes, you. Step up here NOW.* Inside I'm crumbling like stale bread, my special knees knocking together like castanets.

One of them is glaring at me. *You call yourself the Child of Summer? Well, I never heard anything so ridiculous in all my life. You're nothing but a broken shell of humanity. You're not right upstairs!*

And the others nod crossly, as if I've been wasting everyone's time, and the whisper goes round: *That child is not right upstairs.*

I ask Nan-Nan if I can bring my orange cushion with me. 'No,' she says.

'What about my tartan rug? We could use it as a magic carpet?'

'No.' She shakes her head firmly.

'Andi, maybe?'

'Certainly not,' she says. 'This is a top-secret mission. No passengers allowed.'

I'll miss my mom and dad. And my sister. What'll they say when they find me gone? They'll be searching and searching. Maybe my sour old life here is sweeter that I thought? I have my couch and my family and my school . . . and my bed. And Ruby.

But Ruby thinks I'm a dummy. When her friend came to my house last week, he stared at me and said, 'You're a dummy.'

Ruby put her hand over his mouth like a bandage. 'Don't say that,' she said. 'Don't call Doll a dummy. It's not nice.'

I kinda knew, the way he said it, that a dummy is not a proper person. Like a dummy in a shop window made of plastic and screws. Loose screws.

So am I a dummy if I go? Or a dummy if I stay?

If I wasn't such a dummy, I'd know what to do. I wished upon that star and now here I am, afraid to go. But then, that's me. A mouse. When the magic door swings back, what do I do? I scurry into the shadows.

'I'm afraid, Nan-Nan.'

She squeezes my hand. 'I know, Doll.'

Faintly, through my muddled thoughts, I hear humming. I know the tune. My granny's favourite. They sang it for her Goodbye Party. She never turned up that day. I kept thinking she'd rush in, breathless, at the last minute. But she never made it.

I often think of her, the way she'd sing to me and play the harmonica, a glorious sound that made you think thoughts too deep for tears.

Sometimes when we were alone together, sitting by the fire, she would open her handbag, the one with the gold snake clasp. Then she'd lift out a red box and take her harmonica from its velvet bed. A present from her mother, she said, when she was only eleven years old. Very precious, she said. Priceless.

Then she'd wrap her curly fingers round it and bring it to her lips. Sweet and clear, the notes would rise like smoke and fill the room with a pure-gold feeling. And your mind would wander off to sparkling rivers and wild roses and daisies and bursting trees and pink skies. And then she'd lay the harmonica on her knee and she'd sing about the girl in the song, Lassie – Lassie is a girl, not a dog – and I can still see her, a girl with yellow hair, running across the fields, happy because summer is coming . . .

I can hear my granny singing now, though I can't see her. Nan-Nan's eyes are closed, but the music fills the room

O, the summertime is coming
And the trees are sweetly blooming
And the wild mountain thyme
Grows around the blooming heather
Will you go, Lassie, go?

The harmonica starts, and in my mind, I sing the chorus:

And we'll all go together
To pluck wild mountain thyme
All around the blooming heather
Will you go, Lassie, go?

The notes fall away, and my heart is bursting in my chest. I know my granny is back. I can smell her lavender perfume. And I understand. She's telling me to go. *Will you go, Lassie?* she's saying. *Will you ever just go and stop messing about? Didn't I come and tell you already? Just go, girl.*

I will, Granny, I say to myself. *I will. Thanks, Granny.* And the song says we'll all go together, so maybe, just maybe, Granny will be in Almazova too, with her harmonica. Imagine that!

I open my eyes. Nan-Nan glances at me. She needs to know if I'm staying or going.

'Did you hear the music, Nan-Nan? Did you hear my granny singing?'

'Beautiful,' she says. 'Sweet and clear. She's powerful.'

'I'm coming with you.'

She smiles. 'Are you sure, Doll?'

'Sure. Ready to go, ma'am.'

She closes her eyes and lets out a long, low sigh.

There's no going back now. I'm ready to jump into a new life.

*

I must have drifted off because when I open my eyes, the telly downstairs is off and the house is silent. Nan-Nan is saying, 'It's time to go, Doll. Now, breathe nice and even.' She lowers her voice to a whisper. 'And whatever happens, don't scream.'

I watch her lift her hat carefully off her head and adjust something inside the red lining before jamming it back on. Then she steps across my bed, leans close to the window ledge, and lifts the catch. The window creaks open.

'Close your eyes,' she says, 'and don't open them till I tell you.'

But after a minute I sneak one eye open and see her standing in front of the open window, her face lit up in the moonlight, head high, arms outstretched. The glassy night air drifts in, and I shiver.

Nan-Nan is talking to herself, repeating the same words over and over. Like when my granny used to bring me to Devotions and the priest would list a load of saints' names and everyone would shout,

'Prayfrus, prayfrus, prayfrus.' But instead Nan-Nan is chanting, 'Ago-ye, ago-ye,' over and over.

Then she turns towards me, catches my hand, and loops her shell belt around our wrists. We're tethered together like in the three-legged races at Andi's school sports day.

'Breathe slowly,' she says, 'and close those eyes, honey.'

And then it's like a magnet is sucking us up towards the window. My eyes are shut tight, and I feel my toes trail over the concrete windowsill. There's a sudden heart-stopping drop towards the ground. Jesus! My eyes fly open, and then up, up, up we float, like two helium balloons, over the trees and the red rooftops of Bluebell Grove. I can feel the icy wind in my nostrils nearly taking my breath away.

Nan-Nan and me are rocketing towards the stars. Funny, I'm not scared now. I look down at the earth disappearing into the distance, like when you look in the side mirror of your dad's car and the road behind is racing backwards. I see the yellow street-lights of Glengarvan, and down by the prom, the red Kentucky Fried Chicken sign gets smaller and smaller. Soon all the lights just look like rows of diamonds on a sparkly necklace. Up ahead the Milky Way is like a hundred runways, lit up and beckoning us forward.

The wind snaps at my pink pyjamas, and then . . . everything slows. We're cruising. The wind falls away, and as I close my eyes, I hear the silence. A huge empty emptiness that hovers around me and seeps in through my skin, into my very bones. Such quiet. Such stillness. Like the hush of snow. Not the rustle of a leaf, not the cry of a bird or the flap of a wing; even the very air is asleep. A pure, blue-black nothingness. When I look up ahead, I see a million silver stars, like lanterns lighting our path.

As we float on through the night, the skin of my old world begins to unzip itself, and I can feel it peeling off me, billowing away into the dark. Suspended in the soft silence, I feel rinsed. Clean. Shiny. Brand-new.

In my head, my still-muddled old head, I can see myself lying on my couch, the tartan rug around my shoulders. I can see my mom, brittle and smiling, bringing me a beaker of milky tea. I can hear the spit and crackle of the wood on the fire, and I can feel, I can still feel, the rush of ugly pleasure from digging at my bloody face.

A giant cube of ice, hard as glass, begins to break apart inside me, and slowly I can feel the liquid drip, drip into my chest. Like I'm thawing out. The anger melting away. I feel it all as I sail higher and higher into the velvety night.

In the starlight, I can see Nan-Nan's shell belt wrapped around my wrist; see the pink coral shells, delicate and dainty, stitched onto the yellow fabric. My lifeline.

Don't lose me, Nan-Nan. Don't leave me floating here amongst the cold stars.

We're sailing now, ever upwards on our invisible helium balloons, up beyond the moon where the Grandmothers are already checking their watches and tapping their feet impatiently.

My heart clenches when I think about Mom and Dad. Will I see them again? What have I done? Maybe with me gone, they'll laugh and smile a bit more.

My mind drifts back to last summer at the funfair. My dad, pre-tend-cheerful, hoisting me onto a carousel of horses with gold manes and sparkly straps. There were cars, too, and little red trucks that went up and down and round and round. The man secured a belt around my middle. 'That'll keep you safe, young lady,' he said, and then he looked at my dad as if to say, *Sure, God love her.*

Spare me.

Little kids clung to their reins, giggling and whooping. 'Giddy-up horsey, giddy-up.' Some of them stared. I heard one parent whisper, 'Special knees, darling,' to the little boy pointing at me. And there I sat in my plastic carriage with a pink-and-gold pony up ahead bringing me to the, em . . . ball, I suppose! I was ten, for God's sake. Felt like an idiot.

Andi waved to me as the carousel chugged off. Round and round we went, and my dad would wave and go, 'Woo-hoo, Doll!' Making fac-es, pretending he was excited for me. My mom stared into space. And people stared at me. *Sure, God love us.*

Round and round, going nowhere. My pony – did she think she was in a race? Her head thrust forward, grinning, like she'd her mind made up to win. Poor girl. Didn't she know? There were no winners. Like the rest of us, she was doomed to trot round and round in circles all the days of her life. Always ending up where she started. Same-o. Same-o.

At least *I know.* I understand. All your life's a circle. You end up where you started, whatever way you look at it – you're born, you wade through the mud and then . . . sweet oblivion.

But you know, I can wash all that sadness away now, 'cos I've jumped off the merry-go round. Yes, I am on an actual road now, the

Milky Road, and whether it's good or bad, it's a road, and that's better than a stupid circle any day.

Thoughts drift like clouds in my head as I float on and on.

Now I can see a purple dawn breaking, the glittering stars stepping back like Riverdancers, making way for a coral sky. A hoarse wind rises up, ducking and darting and dragging us down. I feel dizzy. We're somersaulting now, tumbling, then racing backwards like a giant magnet is sucking us off our path. Nan-Nan shouts something, but I can't hear above the thunder of the wind. *Jesus, Mary, and Holy St Joseph.* It's not a swear, it's a prayer; my granny told me that. It's not cursing.

I scream as I feel a sharp tug on my wrist. My arm is yanked sideways. Ahhh! *Christ and his Blessed Mother.* It's a prayer . . .

And then there's a violent thud, and everything turns quiet and black.

CHAPTER 23

SALLY

'I heard her call out.'

Dan stirs next to me and opens his eyes. 'You mean Doll?'

'Yes,' I say. 'I heard her call, "Mom, Mom." I'm sure I did.'

I know that's impossible, but I can still hear the echo inside my head.

Dan whispers, 'It's half two. Go back to sleep. You were dreaming, Sal.'

But I have to check her to be sure.

Even though her window has flown open and there's a chill in the room, her forehead feels hot. When I turn on the lamp next to her bed, she looks lifeless and her breathing is shallow. I stifle a scream. Am I overreacting?

My mind's made up. I'm not waiting till morning.

Dan stirs, blinking as I pull on a tracksuit and grab my mobile from the bedside table. He sits up, fully awake now.

'Dan, I'm taking her to the hospital. She's got a fever. Will you ring the children's ward?'

'Has she got worse?' He leaps out of bed and follows me into Doll's room.

'Will you wrap her in that fleece?' I try to keep the panic out of my voice.

He puts his palm on her forehead. 'I'll go with you, Sal.'

'No, stay with Andi. We both don't need to be there.' I look at him. 'I'm sure she'll be fine, but, you know, I couldn't go back to sleep. I don't want to wait till morning. I can't . . .'

He closes his hand over mine. 'I know. I know. You're right. It's peace of mind.'

He carries her, still sleeping, to the car and plants a kiss on my cheek. 'Buzz me when she's settled in, love. I'll see you in the morning.'

*

In a cubicle in the children's ward, a blue screen glows in the dark, tracking her beats per minute. *Blip, blip, blip.* How fragile a life is. Saline solution dribbles through a tube, and there's a line of antibiotics in her left arm.

She's running a fever, but the nurses tell me they'll soon have it under control. The doctor will do his rounds mid-morning. Blood tests and x-rays say it looks like bacterial pneumonia. In fairness, they moved fast.

I check my phone. Quarter to five. I shift in the armchair, rearrange the pillow, and massage my neck back to life.

Doll's body is barely a ripple under the covers. Two nurses glide like swans along the corridor outside, their soft shoes making a squeaking sound on the tiles.

It's like trying to sleep on a plane. I pull the blanket up around me. The last time she had pneumonia, she came round after two or three days. Turned the corner. All was well in the end. There's nothing to worry about.

This hospital is part of the territory of our lives. The maternity unit, the delivery room upstairs like a graveyard. The birth of dreams. And the death of dreams. *It's unhappy news, I'm afraid.*

The Special Baby Care Unit on the third floor, where Doll spent her first three months. After three months, you slowly come undone. For shame. *Shhh! Don't tell anyone.*

And now here, the children's ward, with its cheerful staff wearing teddy bear tunics and kind smiles.

I close my eyes again.

We've been here so many times. The years melt into each other. When your child is diagnosed with a disability – I hate that word – you enter another world. You stumble through the double doors and there you are, in another country entirely. It starts with a corridor, paint peeling. You look behind you; the doors lock like a prison, and you can't go back.

You press on. What else can you do? There are doors along the left-hand side; on the right are wooden benches with cigarette burns.

You see a signpost: *Corridor of Loss.* You keep walking; you've got no choice. And you start looking for . . . I'm not sure, really. The way out, I suppose. Or a reason.

And yes, you look for the child you lost, the one who disappeared into the mist. You know you'll never kiss her face. You'll never dress her teddies or dance with her or wait outside a club for her at two in the morning on junior cert night. You'll never find her; she's gone forever.

God. Forever is a long, long time.

But you have to keep marching on.

Cardboard files are piled high on shelves, papers crammed inside. They're in alphabetical order: A for Attitude, B for Breaking Point, C for Confusion. When you take a closer look, you don't understand the words, like they're in Arabic.

A girl shuffles past. She stops and grips my elbow. 'I'm lost,' she says. 'Don't know where I'm going. Everything is gone.' She clicks her fingers, but they don't make any sound. 'Just like that,' she says. 'Gone.' Her eyes shimmer, and the tears flow down her face like a waterfall. They pool around her bare feet.

'You poor thing,' I say. 'You poor thing.' I can't think of anything else to tell her.

She leans a heavy forehead against my shoulder, sobbing, stroking my arm. 'The car started spinning like a fireball. My poor boys . . .'

The water is rising around her knees. 'Stop crying,' I say. 'You'll drown. We'll both drown.' But she won't listen, and as I pull away, I can still hear her wailing.

Sorry, I have to get away – misery is contagious.

The corridor yawns on. I sit on a bench to rest. There's a woman nearby in a polka-dot headscarf, leaning forward, legs crossed. She's humming a tune, pointing a shabby toe this way and that to the rhythm of the song in her head. She looks sideways at me. 'You're lost?' she says.

I nod.

She points to a door on the left. Silver lettering on frosted glass. *Lost & Found.*

I thank her. Knock at the door, walk in.

'Lost and Found?'

A spider of a man looks up, jerks his thumb towards the door. 'That's what it says, ma'am.' He grabs a wire notebook and turns the page over, his penholder ready on the countertop. 'How can I help you?'

'I've lost my way,' I say. 'I hope you can direct me.'

'Hold on, ma'am. Start again.' He writes *Urgent* on the top left-hand corner of the page. I like that. He's taking this seriously.

'I didn't want to come this way. It's just those double doors . . . I couldn't go back. There was no way back . . .'

He nods. He understands.

'Yes, there's no way back, ma'am. That's correct.' He sucks on his pen. 'You do know,' he adds, 'you're on the Corridor of Loss?'

'I do indeed. I saw the sign.'

'Well,' he says, 'it's a one-way system, so you'll have to keep moving.' He makes a sweeping motion with his arm. 'You have to keep on keeping on.'

'There must be a way back?'

He rolls his eyes, a ghost of annoyance in his smile. Like he's talking to a child.

'Like I just said, ma'am, there's no way back. Keep on left' – he turns his palm sideways – 'and you'll eventually reach a stairs to the next floor. Climb that stairs, and you're onto another corridor.'

'And then?'

'I'm not sure. You'll have to ask again when you get there.' He shakes his head. 'Sorry I can't be of more assistance.'

I try to keep the panic from my voice. Don't want him to think I'm mental.

'My husband,' I say, twisting my wedding ring round and round my finger. 'I think I've lost him too . . .'

'Go on.'

'At first,' I say, 'I didn't notice. I wasn't paying attention . . .'

'Yes?'

'Then I began to notice it.'

'You noticed what?' He's still not writing anything down.

'That he was missing. He keeps going missing.'

He scratches the back of his neck, nodding. 'Very common, love,' he says, 'especially along here.' He sweeps his hand from right to left.

He leans in like we're conspirators. I can smell mints off his breath. 'It's that kind of place, ma'am. Anything can happen.' He nods again. 'I mean anything. I've seen it all. The stories I could tell you.'

I point to the notebook. 'Will you log it anyway?'

He hesitates.

'Listen,' I say, fumbling for my purse, 'I'll pay a reward.'

The man shakes his head. 'Look, ma'am, he may not want to be found. And if he don't want to be found?' He leaves it hanging. 'Anyway, we have to wait forty-eight hours before we report a missing person. Why don't you come back then?' His eyes are moving to the door. He's already thinking about his next customer.

I grab his wrist. Brazen, I know. A risk. But I have to get his attention.

'And my baby,' I say. 'She's gone too.'

He looks sympathetic this time. 'You've lost her?'

'Yes, I've lost her. I know you must think I'm very careless.' The tears are coming. *Stop it. Compose yourself.*

He hands me a tissue. 'What happened, love?'

'I miss her,' I say. 'She disappeared years ago. I was so looking forward to meeting her, you've no idea.'

'And then?'

'Well, she never came. They said she wasn't coming after all.'

I wail. Tears free-fall onto the countertop.

He hands me another tissue.

'We had to pack away all the dreams.' I bury my face in my hands. 'But it's not easy,' I say. 'It's not easy!' I shout the last bit.

I swallow hard and bring my voice down. 'Sorry for shouting,' I say. 'I'm not blaming you.'

The man comes round from behind the counter and leads me to a chair. He rubs my arm, and I'm grateful. 'Ah, don't talk to me, love,' he says. 'It's all a mystery to me, all the upset and the sorrow. There's no sense to it all.' He pats my shoulder.

Someone puts their head around the door, but he waves them away. 'Give us a minute,' he says.

'I better go,' I say. 'I've taken up enough of your time. Thank you.'

He squeezes my hand. 'Take it easy, ma'am.'

The phone rings on his desk.

The sound startles me, and I jump. There's a nurse shaking my shoulder. The heart monitor's alarm is going off; the screen is blinking. Another nurse bustles past. The alarm stops abruptly.

'Is she okay? What's going on?' My own heart is hammering, and I feel dizzy.

One of the nurses pats my arm. 'Don't worry, Mum, she's fine. Sometimes the cable can work loose.'

I don't believe her.

'Her heart rate is higher,' I say.

'It's not unusual with pneumonia,' she says, 'but we're giving her oxygen now, just to give her a boost.' She picks up my pillow from the floor. 'You get back to sleep. We'll keep a close eye on her.'

She checks the chart at the end of the bed. It's five twenty a.m., and I'm full-on awake. Doll's heart rate is steady again. The nurse called

Rachel is sitting at her bedside. 'She's fine,' she says. 'If you can't sleep, you can make a coffee for yourself.'

I'm glad to get away from the bedside chair, away from unsettling dreams. I tiptoe into the kitchen and put the kettle on. Find a corner to finish a work report. I'm glad to have something concrete to think about, and anyway, pneumonia is very treatable and Doll is a fighter. Didn't she have it three years ago not a bother? It's only old people, really, who have to be careful with pneumonia. Two days and she'll be on the mend again. She'll turn the corner – nothing to worry about.

Still, I'll be glad when this is sorted, glad to be home again.

Outside, the world is beginning to wake up. I stare out the window. A man in an anorak revs up his car and speeds off. Two women hurry along the pavement, scarves wrapped tight. You can see their breath in the glow of the street-light. A taxi driver beeps as a cyclist swerves across the road and breaks the lights. Normal life, chugging along, regardless.

She'll turn the corner in the next day or two. She fought it before; she'll fight it again, I repeat to myself. *There's nothing at all to worry about. It's just that hospitals . . .*

I hate hospitals. Who doesn't? You never know from day to day what might happen. I don't mean with Doll; she'll be fine. It's just the worry and the waiting, that slippery something swimming through your stomach. Not that's there's any need to worry, but you just do. It's ridiculous, really.

CHAPTER 24

DOLL

Yellow sunlight leaks through the lace curtains, making patterns on the dark wood floor. I'm snuggled in a big brass bed between crispy sheets, and there's a pink blanket trailing onto the floor. Am I in a hotel? Or is this Heaven?

A warm breeze lifts the curtain, bringing with it the smell of cut grass. Outside, birds chirp and chatter, and I can hear sounds of crockery and doors closing in the distance.

My shoulder hurts. When I reach up and touch my cheek, I remember who I am and groan inside. Funny, though, I don't feel like digging my face; there's too much else going on in my head right now.

I remember leaving my bedroom, swooping into the night sky, and then floating along and falling. I suppose I must be dead.

I hear footsteps on a stairs. Maybe this is God's house. The door creaks, and my mouth drops open. It's Nan-Nan, but she's not a doll anymore; she's as real as me. Smooth black skin, red curls resting on the collar of her white shirt. Her navy skirt has pleats and gold buttons.

'Good morning, Doll. How are you?' She picks up the pink blanket and tosses it back on the bed. The mattress dips as she sits down next to me. I can see her red shoes.

She smiles as she ruffles my hair. 'I'm sure you've lots of questions, Doll, but first, how's your shoulder?'

'Wow, you're real,' I say. 'You're an actual person.' As I reach out to touch her fingers, I wince – my shoulder does hurt. Ouch.

She unscrews a jar sitting on the bedside table. 'Sit up if you can,' she says. She begins to rub ointment into my shoulder. It smells like Christmas spice.

'It was the gravity zone. You took a tumble when you fell,' she says, 'but it's just bruised.'

'So, am I alive? Or is this Heaven?' And then the thought hits me like a firework. I sit upright in the bed. *I can talk.* Properly. I just heard myself say words, like a real person. 'Nan-Nan, I can talk! I can talk!'

94

She motions for me to sit back against the pillows, quietly. 'You'll hurt your shoulder if you jump about. Be careful, honey.' She smiles. 'You could always talk,' she says, 'just not through your mouth.' She pats my hand. 'You'll find there's a different energy here on Almazova. You will be stronger; your head will be clearer – but you're still Doll. Just a healthier Doll. Our air, water, and food are therapeutic and pure.'

Inside I'm twirling.

'So I'm not dead?'

'No, this is my home, and you're very much alive, Doll. We've crossed space-time.' She screws the jar shut and rubs a last sliver of ointment on my sore cheeks. 'I'm going to run a bath for you, sweetheart.'

She crosses the room to a door near the window, and I hear the gush of water. 'This is your bathroom,' she shouts out, 'so have a soak and get dressed. I'll have breakfast ready, and then we have a busy day ahead of us.'

She comes back to sit on the bed and pats my hand. 'Doll, come on, any questions?'

I feel like I'm floating inside a bubble, so light am I.

'Well, Nan-Nan, can you tell me . . . can you tell me . . .'

I have a thousand questions, and I don't know which one to ask first. I'm too excited. I can actually *talk*. I'm in Almazova, another world up beyond the stars. My granny might even be here somewhere.

And what about home? For a moment, guilt ties a knot across my throat. I don't want to go back. I feel bad for saying it, but that's the truth. And they'll manage just fine without me. Who could blame them for secretly thinking, *It's for the best; she's in a better place*? Well, I actually *am* in a better place, thank you very much.

'Doll, are you listening to me?'

'Yes, yes.' I shout it out. 'Sorry, Nan-Nan. I just love my voice. Yes, I'm listening.'

Nan-Nan gets up and stands at the foot of the bed. Her hand slides across the brass bed frame as if she's trying to rub out a stain.

'You're here for a reason. I told you that already, didn't I?'

I nod.

'Later today, we are going to meet the Council of Grandmothers, Almazova's leaders. I will be with you. Remember, the fact they are meeting you at all means you are a very important visitor.'

'I'm the Child of Summer, you said?'

'Yes. You are here to complete a mission, Doll. According to the Manuscripts, only you can complete it. Whether you succeed or fail has yet to be seen. But for now you are here to work; it is not a holiday.'

She sees that I'm looking alarmed.

'I will help you all I can, Doll, but your mission is set out in the scrolls, and it is not for us to argue or question. We must trust in our ancient history and the wisdom of the Gods. Are you with me?'

I kinda am, but what choice do I have? She's not going to pack me off on a bus home, is she, if I don't cooperate?

'But Nan-Nan,' I say. 'I'm only a dumb kid . . .'

A shadow crosses her face. 'You're not dumb. You're a sensitive, perceptive little girl with lots of courage. That's what I see.'

She's saying I'm brave and other stuff, and it sounds good to me – better than being cracked or a goner. My spirits are rising again. Nan-Nan always makes me feel like I'm somebody.

'Just remember, Doll, the ancient Manuscripts are sacrosanct. The Grandmothers are duty bound to obey their instructions. Their writings are divinely inspired. We trust in them. Implicitly. And you must, too.'

She turns to open a closet behind her and lays out some clothes for me on the wicker chair next to her. White cotton dress, straw hat with a pale-blue ribbon, blue cardi. White trainers. Cool.

'After your bath, you can stand there' – she points to a circle inside the bathroom door – 'and you'll dry off in a few seconds. I will do your hair, as your shoulder will be sore.'

Ha! I've never brushed my hair in my life, or dressed myself, and I can't see how all this is going to work. But I just nod and say, 'Thank you, Nan-Nan.' And I'm thinking, *Thank you, thank you, for rescuing me and picking me to be the Child of Summer.*

When Nan-Nan's gone, I buckaroo the covers back and slide off the bed. So far, so good. As my dad would say, *How do you eat an elephant? One bite at a time.*

There's a glass of water on the bedside table, and I lift it up with both hands. It tastes like an iceberg might – cold and super-clean. I can feel a shock of energy run through me.

I walk to the bathroom easily. Steady as a ship! The sunlight is flooding in through the skylight . . . and through me. I lift one leg and then the other into the sunken tub and melt into the foaming warmth. Jets of water massage my back and shoulders. I squeal with delight.

Getting out of the bath is a bit trickier, and I slip back twice but finally make it. Like Nan-Nan said, a few seconds in the circle and I'm dry. Wow.

Nan-Nan comes back and helps me to do up the blue buttons on the back of my dress. 'You've done well,' she says, as I tighten my Velcro shoe straps.

She reaches for the hairbrush and motions for me to sit, lifting each section of hair and chasing it with the dryer. My hair is shiny and smells of apples. 'You've lovely green eyes, Doll,' she says. I smile, but it still feels alien. She fixes a blue slide in my hair and looks at her handiwork in the mirror. 'Well, what do you think? Are you gorgeous or what, honey?'

'I'm gorgeous,' I say, not forgetting to smile.

I skip down the corridor of Nan-Nan's lovely sun-filled house. It's not easy, but I'm getting the swing of it.

In the kitchen the breeze is bringing in the scent of thyme. Granny's favourite. A small table is set outside with china cups and little bowls of fruit and yoghurt. Nan-Nan pours me a glass of juice and shushes me when I protest that I can't eat hard foods. 'Just try everything,' she says. 'In Almazova, food is medicine.'

I nibble on strawberries, melon cubes, and grapes. *I don't choke.* The yoghurt is like ice-cream. I let it melt under my tongue, creamy and warm. I crush a blueberry between my teeth. Such rainbow tastes.

A butterfly lands on our table. 'That's a red admiral,' Nan-Nan tells me. 'They love people. Put out your hand.'

The butterfly perches on my outstretched finger. I can see little black markings and an orange border on his body. He opens and closes his wings nervously before fluttering away like a tiny fairy.

'Your face is healing up well,' Nan-Nan says, bringing pancakes and maple syrup from the kitchen. She makes up a plate for each of us.

'Andi loves maple syrup,' I say, dipping my pancake in the puddle of syrup. I lick my fingers and scoop the sugar from around my mouth with my tongue. I laugh. 'Nan-Nan, you have a syrup moustache,' I say. 'You look funny.'

'You mind your clothes,' she says, flicking crumbs from the front of my dress with her napkin.

I want to stay here, sitting together and soaking in the sunshine, but Nan-Nan has other ideas.

'When you're done, take a walk around,' she says, 'and then wash your face and brush your teeth. We must be in the Cathedral of Light for six bells, so we need to be on our way by and by.'

Nan-Nan's garden is huge. There's an avenue of trees leading up to a front door with tubs of pink roses on either side.

I go inside, stepping into a room with tall bookcases, a squashy couch, and dark beams across the ceiling. I sit on the couch, listening to Nan-Nan humming in the kitchen. There's a red wool blanket slung across the arm, and for a second I think about pulling it over me and curling up, piercing my face for a minute. What harm would there be?

I push the temptation away, and the moment passes.

On the table just inside the door, I spy a red box. Is it a harmonica? I get up to investigate and prise open the lid. Old photographs. Faces from another era smile back at me.

I flick through them. Soldiers sitting round a campfire, one raising his hand in salute, a cigarette in his mouth. Another has a guitar. There's a photo of a younger Nan-Nan with one of the soldiers. His arm is resting against hers and she's leaning towards him, her palm on his chest.

'Doll!'

I bundle the photographs back and close the lid, making my way upstairs without holding the banister rails. Hurray! When I glance in the bedroom mirror, I see something I've never seen before: shiny eyes and a wide smile. All the misery has bled away.

'Hello!' I say, beaming back.

When my mom and dad flash before me, I can see the girl in the mirror clamp her hand over her mouth. She doesn't want to think about number 6 Bluebell Grove. Not now.

'It's my life, my second chance,' I hiss, and I turn away, skipping down the corridor. *One, two, three O'Leary* . . .

I laugh as I trip and fall over. Serves me right. I pick myself up and continue on down to Nan-Nan, who's tapping her foot at the front door.

'Are you all set, honey?' She takes my hand, and I can feel her warm fingers close around mine. I kiss the back of her hand, and for a moment I feel a pure happiness. 'I'm so excited, Nan-Nan,' I say. 'It's all happening for me now.'

She kisses two fingers and presses them to my head. She looks away then, her face stern. 'Don't get carried away, child,' she says, squeezing my hand tightly. 'You and me both, we don't know what lies ahead.'

CHAPTER 25

ANDI

'Poor Doll. I hope she's going to be okay.'

We're sitting in Stacey's kitchen after school.

'Any update yet?' she says over her shoulder as she fires two tea bags into two white mugs and fills them with steaming water.

'She has pneumonia. It's not her first time. I think she'll be okay. Doll's a real fighter.'

'Thank God for that. She doesn't have it easy.'

She squeezes the tea bags out and hands me a mug. 'Any more on Chelsea?'

I wasn't going to tell Stacey about the incident with the two slappers on Sunday night. She was off school yesterday, and I didn't plan on bringing it up today. I just wanted to forget it happened and move on. Talking about it, I reckoned, would make it more real.

But it sort of tumbled out when I was telling her about Steve earlier.

'Well, what do you think I should do about her, Stace?' I couldn't sleep on Sunday night, but since yesterday I've been realising it was just a silly prank and maybe I should just forget about it.

'I know her, Chelsea Nolan.' She makes a face. 'Long dyed-blonde hair, panda eyes, fake tan.'

I nod. 'You know her? How?'

She pushes a packet of coconut creams towards me. 'Well, I don't *know her* know her, but her brother Lee plays on the same soccer team as our Trev, and I've heard about the Nolans. She's in transition year in Factory Hill and works in Suzanne's Hair & Beauty Salon after school.'

'What's Lee like?'

'Lee Nolan is a dog.' She milks her tea and mine. 'And Chelsea is a right slag, far as I can make out.' She grimaces. 'The Nolans are bad news. They live in St Michael's Villas. Enough said. The older brother is in Cork Prison for dealing drugs.'

She's like a mouse as she nibbles the coconut flakes around her biscuit, exposing the pink marshmallow.

'So is she his ex, Andi?'

'I don't know. I suppose so.'

She opens her eyes wide. 'What? Didn't you ask him? You did tell him what happened?'

'I wasn't planning on telling him.'

She holds her half biscuit six inches from her mouth. 'Why not? You have to, Andi. Maybe she's his girlfriend – and if she is, I wouldn't mess with her.'

'No way. Steve wouldn't do that.' It's hard to explain to Stacey, but I completely trust him.

'Not half. Steve Thompson has to be the best-looking boy in town. And he knows it. He's a player. I'd back off if I were you, Andi.' She finishes her biscuit and reaches for a white one.

I nearly choke on my tea. 'Back off? Are you mad? I'm well into him. No way is that bitch Chelsea Nolan going to break us up.' I sound stroppy, but Stacey knows it's bravado – who'd want to take Chelsea Nolan on?

She gives me a look. 'You barely know him, Andi. And if your folks found out . . .'

'I know. But it feels like I've known him for months. He's so sweet, Stacey. Sounds crazy, but I think I'm in love.'

She sucks in her cheeks. 'Has he tried it on yet?'

I blush. 'Stop it. I'm not even his girlfriend yet; we're just dating. Don't get ahead of yourself.'

'Ring him, Andi. Tell him what happened.'

'It was a prank. She's jealous. That's her problem, not mine.' I bite into a biscuit.

'Tell him, Andi. He's a right to know.'

'Okay, I will, but I'm not letting Chelsea Nolan win.'

On my way home, I admit to myself why I haven't rung Steve before now. I don't want him to think I'm a baby, running to him about such a silly thing. He might laugh. Think it's a bit of craic – girls fighting over him. Or worse, what if he said, *Yeah, she is my girlfriend; sorry, babe?* The idea makes me shudder, I couldn't handle that.

He picks up on the third ring. 'Hi, babe.'

His voice sends my heart into a spin. When I don't answer, he says, 'You around?'

'No, why? Is there something . . . ?'

'No . . . I thought that's why you were calling.'

'Do you know Chelsea Nolan?' I just blurt it out. And hold my breath.

'Why?' Have I caught him on the hop?

'Just asking, Steve. Do you?'

'Yeah, I know her.' His voice is wary.

'Were you . . . I mean . . . are you dating her?' I can't bear to say the *girlfriend* word.

I hear him sucking in his breath. 'Where's this coming from?'

'Answer yes or no.' I sound like Mr Crosby.

'No and no.'

'That's not what she said.' I'm just trying to smoke him out.

'What? You wouldn't want to believe a word out of her mouth.'

'She told me to stay away from you.'

He laughs then. It's all a joke to him. 'She what?'

Tears sting my eyes.

He tunes in to the silence. 'She's not my girlfriend. Never was. Never will be, trust me.'

'So why . . . ?'

'I went out with her once or twice last year. It was nothing. She's not my type.'

'She followed me home on Sunday night. With her friend Tania.' I'm trying to keep my voice cool.

'I'll fuckin' kill her.'

'Leave it, Steve.' This is what I was afraid of: him having a row with her and then the whole thing escalating.

'I'm sorry, Andi.' His voice is soft.

'It's not your fault. I believe you.'

'She's not getting away with this, Andi. I'll have a word.' Then he adds, 'How are you, anyway? I miss you.'

I laugh, secretly thrilled. 'It's only been two days.'

'Too long,' he says. I can feel my heart pirouetting around my chest.

'I've basketball on Thursday. I might see you after practice.'

'Sounds good, babe. I'll call you.'

I dance up the hill towards Bluebell Grove.

*

Mom's home from the hospital. She's sitting at the kitchen table, staring out at the garden.

She looks up when I come in. 'Hi, love. I've just ordered a takeaway for us. Dad's gone to the hospital for an hour or two.'

'How is she, Mom?' I put on the kettle.

'Stable, they say. Sleeping all day. She's a line in for fluids and antibiotics.' She yawns. 'I'll see the consultant in the morning.'

'You're wrecked, Mom.' I lean down to kiss her. 'You're going to bed after dinner. You know she's in safe hands.'

She nods. 'You're okay, Andi? School all going well?'

'Yep. All good, Mom.'

'I'm glad,' she says. 'Sometimes I think . . . maybe you've missed out.' She looks out at the garden again. 'With Doll, you know, you might have felt left behind, over the years . . .' She waves her hand in a circle. 'Don't mind me. I'm not myself lately.'

I hunker down and hold her hands in mine.

The doorbell rings.

'Get that, love,' she says. 'It's probably the takeaway.'

But it's not the takeaway. At the door are Chelsea Nolan, Tania, and two other girls behind them standing on the redbrick flowerbed border so they look six inches taller than they really are.

'Hi, Andi, love.' Chelsea smiles.

'Get away from my door. My mom's inside.'

Tania turns back to the others and says in a squeaky voice, 'Oh, her mummy's inside.' They all laugh.

'I had a call from your loverboy,' Chelsea says. 'You're not getting the fucking message, are you?'

'Are you insane? He's not interested in you.' I know my voice is tinny and small, and I know she can smell my fear. They all can, like wolves in a pack.

My mom shouts out, 'It's paid for, Andi.'

'Second and last warning, love,' Chelsea hisses, her orange face close to mine. As my mom comes out, they all move away, waving goodbyes. 'Thanks, Andi, see you soon.'

'Who was that?' Mom says.

My heart is racing. 'Just a couple of girls from school. Fundraising stuff . . .'

She doesn't believe me.

Before she says anything, I run upstairs to my room.

When I hear the doorbell go again, I jump, but this time it's our food. I'm not hungry. There's a gnawing emptiness inside me, and it's the intolerable thought, like a physical pain, of not seeing Steve again. All because of that jealous bitch Chelsea Nolan.

CHAPTER 26

DOLL

Nan-Nan points to a turnstile up ahead. 'We're taking the MP to the Cathedral of Light,' she says, as we cross the road at the end of the avenue. 'That's a moving platform, like you see at the airport. They overlay our ancient pilgrim paths. The journey will give you a chance to ask more questions.'

There are four platforms trundling off in different directions, and we step on the one with the blue arrow. Nan-Nan takes a seat and motions me to sit down next to her.

'Settle back,' she says, 'and enjoy the afternoon sun. It'll be an hour before we get to the cathedral.'

'Are there any cars in Almazova, Nan-Nan?'

She nods. 'In the cities, yes, there are cars, trains – hovercars too. The city people want speed, technology, progress, a fast-paced life.' She chews her lip. 'Here in the countryside, it's the opposite. People want to hold on to the slow, natural rhythms of life. They want to keep the ancient ways, the old magic of their ancestors, the sacred and the mystical.' She sighs. 'It's not easy for the Grandmothers to straddle the divide. In Almazova, sadly, two worlds collide.'

'Which side are you on, Nan-Nan?'

'I'm a scientist. I embrace progress, of course.' She waves her hand. 'But look around you, Doll. We need to hold on to the old ways too. There is a peace and tranquillity of the soul here that we cannot afford to lose.'

We sit in silence. Nan-Nan takes out her compact and starts to apply red lipstick. She's slung a navy jacket over her shirt. 'You look very smart,' I say. 'Not at all like a doll.'

'We're going to meet some very important people today,' she says, pressing a tissue against her lips. 'Top brass.' She makes a salute, cupping her palm against her forehead.

'Who else will be there?'

Nan-Nan slides her tongue over her teeth. 'Well,' she says, 'the Council of Grandmothers will be presiding. They will tell you why you're here and answer all your questions. And they may have questions for you.'

'What kind of questions?'

'I don't know,' she says, looking into the distance. 'They'll want to know they have the right person for the task, I suppose.'

'Who else?'

'The Ministry will be there, the people who represent the citizens. And of course, Jasper, director of the Space Agency.'

'And?'

'And the Headscarves would always be present at an event like this—'

'Whaaat? Headscarves?' I know what headscarves are – pirates wear them. And when Granny was young, she said everyone wore them to Mass. Even men, I think. If you hadn't a scarf, a hanky would do. I try to picture my dad in a headscarf. 'Are they on people's heads or for sale?'

Nan-Nan laughs. 'Have you ever heard of a Greek chorus, Doll?'

'Greek yoghurt?'

'No. In ancient times on earth, if you went to a play, there'd be a choir in the shadows who'd sing and tell the audience what was going on or warn them of what might unfold.'

'And do the Headscarves sing?' Can you imagine? Singing Head-scarves. What a thing. It makes me laugh.

'The Headscarves are spirits, Doll. They can swoop through the air like a many-headed bird.' Nan-Nan drops her head and brings her thumbs to her chest. 'Those scarves hide ancient faces, ancient souls earning their right to eternity.' She lowers her voice to a whisper, even though there's no one near us on the MP. 'They are spirits locked into haggard bodies, making amends for missteps in their lives. They can forewarn us, guide us, alert us to what's ahead.'

She sees my face fall. 'Don't worry; they stay in the shadows. They won't bother you. But we must respect their presence and wisdom.'

'Sounds spooky,' I say, and I vow to stay well clear of this bunch. 'Why do they wear headscarves?' I wonder.

'I don't know, Doll. To hide their hideous old faces, maybe, or just to stay anonymous.'

Wow. The thought of the Headscarves whirling in the darkness is scary, but I want to see these strange old creatures. Or is it creature? Anyhow, there's no way back now.

We fall into silence as we pass fields laced with buttercups. The late-afternoon sun is warm on my shoulder. Children playing outside wooden cabins shade their eyes and wave as we pass by. I wish I could join them, but I'm on an important mission right now. I wave back.

A bell chimes in the far distance, and I remember my walk with Andi and my new pink coat and the shimmer in the air that afternoon when the church bell rang out. How long ago it feels now. My first life.

'Do you miss home?' Nan-Nan asks.

The bell rope of guilt jangles in my head. 'No,' I say. 'I'm never going back.'

Nan-Nan purses her lips.

'No, I mean it. They can't make me go back.'

'That's no way to talk,' Nan-Nan says crossly. 'Your family loves you.'

We travel along in silence and after a while she says, 'Not long now. Not long at all.'

She buttons up her jacket.

'Get ready to move.' We step off, exit through another turnstile, and cross the road that will take us to the foot of Cathedral Hill.

It's a steep climb up. The cathedral glowers down at us. A giant of a woman is carved into the high stone wall, her arms outstretched. She's gazing upwards with annoyed eyes. 'The original Grandmother, Cornelia,' Nan-Nan says. 'A formidable woman.'

As we reach the top, Nan-Nan hunkers down and holds my shoulders in a tight grip. 'Remember, I'm for you, Doll,' she says. She kisses my cheek and gives me a hug. 'Now, when we get to the cathedral, no holding hands. We walk in side by side, okay?'

Up close, the cathedral casts a dark-winged shadow. Nan-Nan nods to a man with a ponytail and dark glasses, and he smiles and leads us through a door with crusty handles. Inside, it's like a giant cave with a million candles lighting the gloom.

A shaft of sunlight floods through a glass dome above the altar and falls in a circle onto the stone floor. Way up, a giant crystal bowl seems to hover, like a floating chandelier.

'We'll sit here, Doll,' Nan-Nan whispers, pointing to the top row of blue velvet chairs facing the altar.

We're the first to arrive. Behind us, up in the gallery, carved seats shimmer in the candlelight.

I shiver as I hear it – a whispering. Like women chattering in low voices outside Mass on a Sunday, *sss* sounds spilling out like cats hissing.

I turn and see shadows in the gallery swaying like small trees in the wind. Nan-Nan follows my eyes as I grip her skirt. 'That'll be the Head-scarves, Doll,' she says quietly, glancing behind her. 'Don't stare.'

I cling to her jacket, terror suckering my heart like ivy. It's hard to ignore the *whisper, whisper, whispering* behind me. A chorus of old souls in haggard bodies, Nan-Nan said – but who's to say they wouldn't haunt you if they took a dislike to you?

A lion of a man walks towards us.

'Meet Jasper,' Nan-Nan says, 'director of the Space Agency.' He takes off a white cap with gold stars and bows slightly as he shakes my hand.

'Welcome to Almazova. An honour to meet you, Doll. I trust you're being well looked after.' He winks at Nan-Nan and strokes his white bushy beard. I can see my face in the medals pinned to his uniform. Dapper, my granny would call him. He takes a seat next to Nan-Nan.

The chairs are filling up now. People in orange cloaks whisper and nod to each other as they file in. On the altar, five carved chairs are set against a curly-legged table. Five chairs for the five Grandmothers.

Behind the table, a door opens, and a man with white gloves shuf-fles through it, carrying a door-sized book. He places it on the table and lines it up dead centre. He blows on the leather cover, flicking the back of his hand over it before hobbling away. He reappears with a tray of glasses and jugs of water, which he arranges on the table by each chair. Nan-Nan checks her watch as he disappears inside again.

'That's the council chamber,' she whispers, pointing to the door behind the altar. 'Five minutes to go.' She squeezes my hand. I always feel safe with Nan-Nan; she has this way of making you forget about Headscarves and cross Grandmothers.

A man slips in next to Jasper. 'That's Earl, head of state security,' Nan-Nan whispers. 'You'll meet him later.'

I just can't believe that yesterday – was it only yesterday? – I was lying on my couch, desperate and dreaming of escape. Was that really me, or was it another girl? A straw girl stuffed full of anger. And misery. Misery so strong that it could scrape away at you with its claws and drag you under. *Under* is an actual place, like Cork or Dublin. I've been there, did that, wore the teapot. Businesses go under, my dad says, but people do too. My mom is slipping under; I can see it. I'd love to warn her. *Mom, turn back before it's too late!*

The chamber door opens again, and a boy in black appears, a huge drum strapped to his chest. Single notes crash out across the cathedral and drown out the Headscarves. That will put manners on them.

106

He circles the cathedral. *Crash. Boom. Crash. Boom.* I think he's trying to get our attention so the Grandmothers can enter in style.

There's a final *boom-crash* from drummer boy, and the chamber door creaks open. A hush falls across the orange cloaks as five black-clad figures stride out in single file. They take their places behind the five chairs on the altar. Five pairs of pointy shoes stand to attention; five pairs of eyes scan the room, no detail missed. Five parchment faces, chins thrust out.

The small figure in the middle raises her arms and greets us. 'Ago-ye.'

Everyone rises and sits back down. My legs are like spaghetti, and I'm grateful to be seated again.

The figure in the middle stays standing. 'That's Nell,' whispers Nan-Nan. 'She's the leader, a visionary.'

Nell pats her coiled grey hair. As she raises her arms in mid-air, the sleeves of her black dress fall back, and I can see that her left hand is actually a metal claw. I can't take my eyes off it.

'Close your mouth, Doll.' Nan-Nan nudges me.

'Good people all, thank you for coming.' Nell's voice is like a power hose spraying over us. 'Let us begin.'

The man with the white gloves reappears with a silver pot on a chain. He swings it in front of him, and a cloud puffs out like cigarette smoke. I know it's incense, the stuff Father Roche used for the Easter services in St Mary's. He'd swing the silver teapot, and all the grannies in the top pews would mutter, 'Prayfrus, prayfrus.' And the priest would say, 'C'mon now, raise up your voices to Our Blessed Mother.'

Bring flowers of the rarest
Bring blossom the fairest

And he'd bless us then, like he was slicing a cake in four. and all the old folk would shuffle out whispering to each other, 'Isn't the weather grand? Please God now, we'll get a good summer.'

Granny said it was mostly old wans there, praying for a happy death. She was funny like that, was Granny. Or she thought she was, Dad said.

Nell is saying, 'And the response is "Ago-ye," and please stand now for the prayers.'

The Grandmothers sing:

I arise today
Through the strength of the Gods

107

Light of sun (Ago-ye)
Serenity of moon (Ago-ye)
Depth of ocean (Ago-ye)
Faith of our ancestors (Ago-ye)
Mother Cornelia (Ago-ye)
Guide and protect us (Ago-ye)

For a strange moment, the Headscarves break into the opening lines of 'Desperado', my dad's favourite song. No one seems to recognize the Eagles tune.

Nell motions for silence as everyone sits back down.

'Thank you for your attendance.'

She hesitates. You could hear a pen drop.

'For centuries our community has lived in harmony with our environment, the rhythms of life beating like a finely tuned drum all around us.' She pauses, her eyes sweeping the room. 'There is congruity in our world.' She spreads her arms wide. 'Almazova blossoms. We are not perfect, but we know the Gods have bestowed great bounty on us – our teeming rivers, our fertile lands, and our kind climate.' She kisses her palm and rests it on her heart. Everyone holds their heads high. 'The ebb and flow of existence is beautifully undisturbed.'

Her shoulders drop. Everyone waits. You can see it in her eyes, some big, bad wave about to break. Nan-Nan grips my hand.

'Until now!' Nell's voice rises up like an angry lion, and she pauses, crossing her palms over her chest. She takes a long breath.

'Everyone here knows that all that harmony is maintained through the Orb.' She looks up at the crystal bowl suspended far above her. 'The Orb's magnetic heart balances our world. We know it is the source of life.' Her voice cracks, and she stops to steady herself. 'It is the source of all natural intelligence, the powerhouse of our world.' She pauses. 'It is a dark hour. Our sweet life, as we know it, is in peril. The Orb' – she sweeps her arm towards the Circle of Light' – is gone. *It has been stolen.*'

As everyone looks up, there are gasps of disbelief. Even Nan-Nan looks shocked. The murmur of voices grows louder.

Nell pauses for silence. 'And that, I don't have to tell you, is a cosmic catastrophe.'

We all stare at the crystal bowl suspended high up in the Circle of Light.

'It is an act of tyranny. The situation is grave.' She sighs. 'What we may *not* all realise is that without the Orb, we can expect chaos, disorder, destruction. A new dark age.' She steps down off the altar and walks slowly among us. She stops a few steps from me, casting her gaze over the rows of orange cloaks.

No one moves. There is a deathly silence and then a clamour of voices from the Ministry. The Headscarves begin to hiss and whisper in the gallery. They knew, I'd say.

Nell raises her claw-hand to retrieve the silence and moves back to the altar. 'Wait. Please.' She turns towards us. 'Jasper, you may address our assembly.'

Jasper nods and walks tall towards the altar. He takes a remote from his pocket and clicks it. A blue-and-gold ball of light hovers behind him.

His voice is strong and powerful. He is used to being heard, I'd say. 'I have here a hologram of the Orb. All of you are aware, the real Orb has been suspended here in the Circle of Light, powering our world for thousands of years.'

He turns to the hologram and begins to pace. 'We take it for granted, and we can often forget that the Orb controls our entire ecosystem. Without it, we have no future here in Almazova. Our planet dies.'

He clicks to a new image. 'You see here, the outer shell of the Orb is the electromagnetic field.' He clicks again. 'And here is the midsection – the ionic plasma protecting the core. And the core . . .' He taps the side of his head. The core is the central matrix, where consciousness lies – the intelligent heart of the Orb, containing all the data and the Orb's electrical energy.'

He pauses. 'The Orb cannot be replaced, copied, created anew.'

I don't really understand any of this, but I'm getting that the Orb is important and someone has taken it.

Jasper continues. 'The Orb needs sunlight in order to control and calibrate our natural world. To maintain our temperatures, our seasons, even the very length of our day.'

He stops to let the information sink in. There is a stirring in the Ministry, a restlessness. The smell of fear is stronger than the incense. I think I might go home after all.

'I have to say this, finally.' He waits for silence. 'Without light, the Orb can become unstable. Volatile.' He stabs his finger in the air and looks at Nell. 'This is . . . a colossal disaster, make no mistake.'

One of the orange cloaks gets up, moving from one foot to the other. 'What do you mean when you say *unstable*?'

Jasper strokes his beard. 'It is difficult to be precise, Joseph. Limited access to light could mean a lot of unpredictability, fewer daylight hours, cooler temperatures. And that would affect our water supply, our food production. But all this may be gradual.' He folds his arms. 'As I said, it's difficult to be precise.'

A woman at the back stands up. 'What does *gradual* mean?'

Jasper shrugs. 'It depends where the Orb is stored, the quality and quantity of the light—'

The first speaker is on his feet again. 'So whoever has the Orb now controls everything. How could this be allowed to happen? Where was the security?'

There are murmurs of agreement. Angry voices begin to rise, drowning Jasper out. Even Nan-Nan looks stunned, and from what I've seen, it's hard to stun Nan-Nan. She squeezes my hand again.

'I didn't know things were this serious, child,' She shakes her head. 'This is shocking news.' She turns to Earl, her voice like a stone. 'Jasper knew about this. Why wasn't I informed?'

Nell's call for silence slices through the noise. She turns to the figure on her left. 'Kitti, please bring the assembly up to date on developments.'

Kitti steps forward, a long stick dressed in black. Her hooped earrings jingle-jangle as she moves, the sunlight from the dome bouncing off her scalp. She swivels her eyes around the room like a robot, pursing her red lips. Eagle eyes land on me. I think I'm going to faint . . . but her gaze moves on to the gallery. If she was my minder, I'd be under the couch.

'Let me assure everyone, we will resolve this situation.' Her voice is crisp and sweet as an apple. You wouldn't expect that. 'Our lives and the lives of our children depend on it.' She checks a folder in front of her before her eyes sweep across the figures in orange. 'The Orb was stolen one week ago. We are looking into how the security was breached. It should have been impossible.'

'Exactly,' someone says. 'But it wasn't.'

'Indeed. Indeed.' Kitti purses her lips again. 'We have now acquired some intelligence.' She coughs. 'It's a slim lead. The Glenshiquin Mountains in the north are a base for an illegal diamond-mining gang.' I can feel the tension in the room. 'Their associate, an ex–army major, is a volatile character, and we have reason to believe he may be responsible.'

A cry from the back. 'Then what are you waiting for?'

'Listen, please.' Kitti spits the words. 'We intend to find this man, this Major Tom Axel. And we will.' She runs her hand across her scalp. 'But we can't let him know he's in our sights.'

An orange-cloaked figure hobbles up the centre aisle, glancing at me as he passes.

He stabs his finger at the Grandmothers. 'You must have a plan,' he says crossly. 'Spell out your plan. What do the Manuscripts say? I trust you've consulted them?'

A third Grandmother rises. The man runs his tongue along his teeth. 'Well, Valda, you are the expert; don't keep us waiting. What have you found?' He cocks his head sideways, arms folded over his barrel chest.

Valda is whiter than anyone I've ever seen. Her white hair is scraped back from her pale rubber-like face, the skin stretched over dead eyes and pale lips. A seahorse tattoo snakes across her left cheek, its tail flicking the corner of her mouth. I lean closer to Nan-Nan and push my new straw hat down over my eyes. Valda must be a witch.

Her voice is like a river, flowing deep.

'Like all of us here, my heart is sick and sore.' She sighs, a long, sad sound, like the wind. 'Of course we have searched the spiritual writings of the Ancients. These instruments have served us well. We trust them to tell us truths.'

She leans forward and drags the book in the middle of the table towards her. She turns the giant pages like they're made of delicate lace.

'The Manuscripts point us towards a resolution.' She looks up. 'They tell us a perilous journey must be undertaken to retrieve the Orb. Someone from across the universe, someone whose energy the Orb will gravitate towards. Someone without whom the Orb cannot be recalibrated. Someone who has knowledge we do not; someone with courage, power, and fortitude. A glorious contribution will be made, a miraculous deliverance.'

What is she saying? I'm losing the thread. Nan-Nan slips her arm around my shoulder, and I think of my mother so very far away now. I might just change my mind about staying around here. I mean, I'm only gone eleven. I'd say they're probably missing me, in fairness.

'Isn't it good,' I whisper to Nan-Nan, 'they've found someone to get the Orb back?'

Nan-Nan is about to answer when Valda raises her arms.

And then I know. The penny is rolling along and just about to drop. My special knees begin to knock together, and I wonder how jelly can make that knocking sound. *I'm the hero.* The jelly hero.

And Valda is saying, '. . . and our august visitor, our star traveller, is here amongst us. The Child of Summer. Please welcome her.'

I hear applause. Hundreds of eyes follow me as I stand up. I take off my hat and start to walk towards the altar. Everyone rises, and they're all smiling at me. It's a thrilling feeling.

The Headscarves start to hum 'Danny Boy'. The harmonies make me gasp. *What is going on?*

A chair is brought forward. White gloves gesture for me to sit. Valda quietens the Headscarves.

'Your name, dear?' She points a white finger at me. I'm glad I'm sitting down.

'My name is Doll Redmond,' I say, 'and I'm—'

'And you arrived when?'

'This morning.' I turn around to look at Nan-Nan, and she nods.

'Hmm.' She catches her lip between her finger and thumb. 'And you are willing to undertake this mission?' She looks around the room.

'Em . . .'

'I can't hear you, Child of Summer. Speak up.'

'I . . . I . . .' Is she off her head? *Me?* I want to ask. *Why me? What can I do?* Who am I to be chosen and carried – dragged, really – across the universe to fix their problems? I want to shout at the white witch, *Who do you think I am? I'm a nothing-girl.*

Granny used to say I was the berries. She used to say I was perfect, just as I was. Imagine that. That's how much she loved me.

'Well, child. Speak up.'

I feel my granny here now. Like a ghost beside me. *You're one of a kind, Doll.*

My voice is shaking. 'Yes, I am willing.'

Hello, what am I saying? Jesus, the pressure.

'Please step forward and place your right palm here.' She gestures to a small handprint on the top of the page of the open Manuscript. My hand fits over it like a glove.

'Good. Good.' She glances at Nell and nods. 'The co-ordinates are correct. The handprint is a match.'

Nell leans forward. 'The Manuscripts have directed us to you,' she says in a low voice, 'so your presence was sought out. We welcome you, and we are grateful.'

She pauses, pats her coiled hair. 'Presently, you will be fully briefed in the council chamber. There is no time to waste.' She turns to the Ministry and gestures for them to rise.

'The Manuscripts have an ancient wisdom that we mortals cannot fully understand. Can a child complete this perilous mission?' She shrugs her shoulders. 'But, like generations before us, we place our trust in the wisdom of the Gods.'

Nell gestures to the other Grandmothers to follow her. She turns to the Ministry. Her voice is grave. 'Do not speak of what you have heard here today. No word must reach our citizens of this calamity.' She waves her hand in dismissal. 'Ago-ye.'

'Ago-ye.' They all begin to shuffle out, huddling together outside in little groups.

The council chamber door creaks shut behind me and Nan-Nan as we follow behind the Grandmothers, Earl, and Jasper. A voice in my head is saying, *Who are you kidding? Child of Summer? Hello? Sooner or later you're going to be found out, and what then?*

CHAPTER 27

DOLL

In the council chamber, we take our places around a huge table. I'm wedged between Kitti and Valda.

'Let us begin,' Nell says, giving me a brief smile. 'Let us look at our primary lead first. Mauran?' She gestures to another Grandmother. Mauran springs to her feet, a tiny birdlike creature with black-currant eyes and a mouth like a beak.

On a screen behind her, a photograph appears. She nods at the screen. 'This is our man. Thomas Damian Axel. Age forty-six. Born in Teslar, Northern Rassmussen, only child of professional parents, now deceased.' She clicks again to a man in a purple gown, carrying a scroll. 'Tom Axel was a gifted student and studied physics to master's level . . .'

Nan-Nan's hand trembles as she lifts her glass of water. No one else seems to notice. Mauran continues to move from one photo to the next, and I try to keep up.

'He joined the military after university and was decorated for bravery in the Northern Territory war.' More images. 'He earned the nickname The Lion for his fierce combative style.' Mauran's eyes dart around the room. 'He's enjoyed an impressive army career – an expert horseman but ruthless and stubborn, commanding fierce loyalty from his units . . .'

The pictures on the screen change. Major Axel with medals pinned to his chest. Major Axel with two soldiers, head back, laughing. My mouth is dry. There on the screen, that man, the one they're after . . . is the same man I saw in Nan-Nan's photo box.

Valda, the white one, interrupts. Her voice is a sigh. 'You were in the military, Nan-Nan. Did you know him at all?'

'Yes, vaguely.' Nan-Nan reaches for her glass but seems to change her mind. 'We served in the same unit many years ago. I hardly remember him.'

Mauran nods and returns to the screen. 'He disappeared while in post-traumatic stress therapy and was discharged in absentia. Earl, you might pick up here.'

'Of course.' He stays seated. Fixes his glasses carefully on his nose and opens the folder in front of him.

'As you say, a commendable soldier. However . . .' He looks around the room. 'It's not unusual: a soldier often pays a psychological price for sustained combat.' A hospital appears on screen.

'We call it traumatic stress. Overt, close-range hostility can assault the self-image and ultimately the mental health of our soldiers.' His brow furrows. 'The result of a powerful innate resistance to killing one's own.'

Nell looks at me. 'I'm sure you must be alarmed, child.' She gives me a little smile that says, *Don't worry*, and I smile back, frozen with fear. What have I let myself in for? And how can I get out of it?

Earl takes a sip of water, consults his notes.

'Axel was undergoing treatment for emotional distress. I'm afraid there isn't always a successful outcome. All too often, we fail.' He shakes his head and places his palms on the table. 'Over the last seven years, Axel has appeared on our radar a number of times.' He turns a page. 'Most recently, we know he has been involved in criminal activity, developing a diamond-smuggling corridor from North to South.' He consults his notes.

'Axel seems to be pivotal figure in those operations. He's wanted for smuggling, fraud, kidnapping. A dangerous man. But elusive.' He shakes his head. 'However, we certainly didn't see this coming.'

Nan-Nan steeples her hands. 'But you said yourself, Earl. He's a damaged man, a casualty of war. He may not be responsible for . . .'

Nell is drumming her fingers on the table.

'Damaged or not,' she says icily, 'if indeed he is our man, he is an enemy of the people.' She cups her real hand around her chin. The claw-hand remains inert on the table. 'He must be cut down. No mercy.'

Earl rearranges his glasses on his nose.

'Yes, well, we know he operates in the Glenshiquin mountain region. And it isn't just about the sparkly gems. Nanodiamonds have outstanding thermal and electronic properties and are highly prized in space exploration.'

Jasper nods. 'Yes, Earl is right. Diamond nanorods can uniquely withstand cosmic ray bombardment, so you can imagine, it's a very lucrative trade.'

Earl steps up to the screen. 'You can see the terrain is rough up here, only accessible on foot. And he moves about, so he's difficult to track. There are hundreds of caves.'

He uses a pointer. 'Here's the territory under surveillance.' An aerial map appears. He taps a triangle highlighted in red.

'You can see the difficulty: it's rocky and remote. Impossible for any aircraft to land.'

'Even so. Why not send the troops in and surround the area?' Jasper asks.

'Too risky,' Earl says. 'He'd realize we're after him. The only advantage we have is that he's off his guard. He has no idea he's under suspicion.'

'I know informers have led you to believe he is responsible,' Valda says, 'but can we be sure?'

Earl grimaces. 'Our intelligence suggests Axel is our man. Can we be sure? No. But the evidence is solid.' He sighs. 'At any rate, it's our only lead. We must go after him. Stealthily.' He takes his seat again. 'The situation is delicate. The Orb must be located. The alternative is unthinkable.'

Earl looks at Valda and Kitti. 'I know the Manuscripts are ancient and divinely inspired, the voice of the Gods instructing us from afar. You say they're a rich source of wisdom and foreknowledge. I am a man of logic and science myself, but I don't entirely dispute their value. I'm happy to listen to your plan.'

Kitti jingle-jangles to her feet. 'Yes, Earl, you are correct. We are duty bound to consult the Manuscripts. They speak of the advent of the Child of Summer. Our hero must undertake a journey – a journey alone along the pilgrim paths from Killala to the Twin Peaks. This is how the Orb can be retrieved and restored. We are hopeful that rescue will be both swift and successful.'

She nods at me, and her voice is warm. 'The Manuscripts point us in the same direction as your intelligence, Earl. The signs are good. We have set out her journey as instructed, and we trust the Gods will inspire her as she ventures forth. The bravery and resolve that will be needed, well . . .' She smiles at me. 'She will have to supply that herself.'

'Alone? Nan-Nan is to accompany her, surely?' Earl asks.

He's right. They can hardly expect me to go alone. I mean, I'm only a child, and let's face it, I haven't a clue how to read a map or climb a mountain. The whole plan is full of holes. Maybe there was something stronger than incense in the pot earlier.

'I'm afraid,' Nell says gently, 'that will not be possible.' She turns to me. 'Dear child, you must venture forth, alone. The Manuscripts are very clear. You must set out from the Cathedral of Light as a sole traveller. The mission is yours and yours alone.'

Earl is about to say something when a chair crashes backwards and the fifth Grandmother begins to pace the room, her black cloak trailing along the flagstones. She tosses a mane of grey hair off her shoulder.

'So help me Gods! Before we start making plans, may I ask a question? And I want answers!' She spits the words out, spraying the air with a light mist.

Nell straightens herself and says quietly, 'Yes, Ki, please do ask.'

'Can someone please tell me *how* this happened? The Orb is triple protected. Only we have access to the cathedral. There was no sign of a break-in. There are layers of security.' She leans forward. 'Well?'

Before Earl can answer, she's off again, slamming the table with her fist.

'We all know that the Orb's security has to be first-class.' She purses her lips. 'I'm bewildered. I'm worried. I'm suspicious.' She flings the words across the room like stones. 'Which one of us here is the traitor?'

She sits back down, folding her arms across her chest. Earl gets to his feet, his eyes flashing.

'With respect, Ki, we've been through this already.' He looks at the other Grandmothers. 'Yes, there has been a serious breach of security. We know that the laser protection was disabled for a very short period. How, we have yet to determine.'

'It's not good enough!'

Valda gets up, the tail of her seahorse tattoo flicking angrily against her white lips. 'What are you suggesting, Ki? That it's one of us? We are the guardians of the Orb. We are the protectors . . .'

Nell stays perfectly still.

'. . . and of course you too, Ki, have access and opportunity. We are all under suspicion.'

Nell thumps her claw-hand on the table. Her face is a stone. 'We are not best served by these exchanges. Ki, you pose a valid point and one, I can assure you, we are pursuing vigorously.' Earl nods in assent.

Ki tosses her hair back. 'Thank you, Nell. It is a serious concern. We must discover how this crime was committed.' She takes a drink. 'In any event, Tom Axel must be pursued. As Earl pointed out, the situation is grave. The Manuscripts are our best hope.'

There is a tense silence.

Nell turns to me. 'Would you like to say something, Doll?'

'I would, Your Majesty.'

She smiles. 'Then speak now, girl.'

This is it. I have to go for it. It's mad, it's scary, it's dangerous, but it's better than lying on a couch feeling hopeless. I dreamt it, I prayed for it, I believed it, and now here I am. There's no going back. *Go, Lassie, go*, Granny said, and she wouldn't see me wrong.

They all glance at each other, but their faces are unreadable.

'Back home, I was scared about coming. But I did.' My mouth is dry. 'And now, some magic is happening. I'm not sure what it is, but it's powerful all the same. My granny said the priest was always talking about the next life, to be ready for it, to be prepared to leave the valley of tears, and here I am. In my next life.'

The Grandmothers nod. They seem happy to hear about another grandmother. There's a lump in my throat.

'Before, I didn't know what to do with myself. I was sliding under. Down and dark. Cutting my face was the only thing that made me happy. I wanted to be Goldilocks, to run away.'

Puzzled faces all round.

'So what I'm saying is . . . I'm ready. I'm not afraid of Major Tom Axel, 'cos I sort of know what's wrong with him. God love us. He's not right upstairs, but I don't think he's a bad man. And if there was a bunch of Gods way, way back who said I was to be the Child of Summer, the one who brings the Orb home, then who am I to say it can't be true?' I'm on a roll.

Heads are nodding around the table. The light is dimming outside; pale-orange fingers reach through the narrow slits in the stone walls. The room is bathed in a golden glow and the light falls across Nell's face, like she's lit from inside. The woman believes in me. My heart starts to swell. Nell *actually believes in me.*

'So yes, I will go and bring back the precious Orb.' I look right into Nell's pale-blue eyes. 'I'll do you proud. I won't let you down.'

When I sit back down, my hands are trembling, but there's a fire glowing inside me.

Nell speaks. Her voice is quiet. 'Thank you, Doll. You are indeed a powerful girl, a girl of fortitude. We put our trust in you as you do in us. Yes, you will meet treachery and danger, but as you do, the power inside you will grow. In the shadow of doubt, you will find courage.' She smiles. 'The ancient paths you travel will protect you; the wind will whisper its secrets to you. The candle in your heart is lit. The sacred earth will hold you in its arms. Along the way, you will meet kindness and love. They will enrich you.' She pauses.

'What I want to say to you is beyond speech, beyond song, beyond longing.' She sighs. 'I'm afraid our world is unravelling. I feel the chaos crackling in my bones. There is unsettlement in the air.' She looks around the room. 'Today I saw an eagle fly backwards into the sun; this morning the blossom in the wood turned grey as I passed by. The waves idle on the shore, reluctant to sweep the shingle in their path. The birds sing a melancholy song; their voices tremble. When I see these things, I am washed in sadness and fear.'

She rests her eyes on me. 'But we must have faith. Fondly do we hope and reverently do we pray that you will return, Doll, with your mission successfully completed. We depend upon you.'

There is applause. Everyone comes to shake my hand, kiss my cheek, smile encouragement. Valda and Mauran hand me a rucksack and a map, telling me where I must go, writing instructions.

So much to take in. My resolve is faltering again, swinging towards hopeless as they guide me out of the council chamber and say their goodbyes.

In the Cathedral of Light, the caretaker is snuffing out the last flickering candles. Nan-Nan is standing in the doorway.

'Thanks for waiting for me, Nan-Nan.'

'Are you ready for your journey, honey?'

'The Headscarves, Nan-Nan. What if they follow me?'

She touches my cheek. 'They are your allies, Doll, there to protect and guide you.'

Stars are arriving in twos and threes across the sky. Soon it will be dark. I shiver, and Nan-Nan helps me put on the purple velvet coat the Grandmothers gave me. She slips a bag of sweets into my pocket. 'That's from me,' she whispers. 'To cheer you up.' Nell has slipped me a gift too.

'How's your shoulder? Don't lose the ointment I gave you.' Nan-Nan fusses over me, and I can see she's upset.

Valda steps out of the shadows, her white face luminous in the gloom. 'Come on, Nan-Nan, it's time Doll was off. We've packed her bag. She has everything she needs.'

Nan-Nan hugs me tightly. She slips off her green necklace and fastens it around my throat. The stones glint and catch the starlight. 'It'll keep you safe on your travels. Be careful, sweetheart.'

I head back down the hill to take the MP going north. I turn around to wave Nan-Nan a final goodbye and blow a kiss. When I look again, she's gone.

My heart is heavy as a gun. What in God's name have I done?

CHAPTER 28

DAN

Sitting here in Doll's drowsy little hospital room, I feel unplugged from life, hovering between reality and some half-otherworld. I loosen my tie and sit on the edge of her bed. Her eyelids are bluish-white, and her breathing is shallow. I take her hand in mind, pressing the fingers gently. Her skin is soft as Play-Doh.

A nurse bustles in, pink and plump.

'You're the dad?' she says, plucking the chart from the end of the bed. 'No, stay where you are. I can manage.' She squeezes past me and adjusts the fluid line.

'She's sleeping a lot, Nurse. Is that normal?'

She takes Doll's temperature. 'Pneumonia can take its toll.' She shakes her head. 'Her little body's bound to get tired fighting infection.'

She writes up the chart and pauses in the doorway. 'I'll get you a cup of tea if you like?'

'No, thanks. You're very kind, but I'll be going soon.'

She nods and disappears down the corridor.

I sit on the leather armchair. My mobile glows silently. It's Rob Colbert again. I hear my breath exhaling like a slow puncture. Back in the day, a bank manager could make all kinds of concessions for a client in trouble. Use their own educated judgement. But now every bloody decision has to be passed up to our Regional Office. Reams of paperwork, online meetings, faceless forms and electronic questionnaires. I wait a minute and jab the recall button. He answers on the second ring.

'Thanks, Dan. I know it's late . . .'

'How's Joanne?'

'She's on new meds since Friday. We're hopeful if things go well, she might be back to work part-time in six to eight weeks.'

'That's positive, Rob.'

He laughs nervously. 'It's a chink of light, Dan. She's a great confectioner. I'll have to get a replacement, but just a temp, hopefully. And I wanted to ask you . . . if maybe you thought about . . .'

'The interest-only repayments? I'll do it, Rob. Under the radar. It's a couple of months; I'm going to say yes, Rob. A one-off . . .'

I can hear the long, low sigh of relief. 'Thanks, man. It'll cover my costs. One less thing to worry about.'

We chit-chat about the business. He clicks off. It's a small concession. I hope I haven't done something I'll regret.

I stare at the waves on the heart monitor screen and drift off to its soothing *blip-blip* sound.

*

When I wake up, my neck is stiff. It's almost nine o'clock. I tiptoe over to kiss Doll goodnight and head for the car park. At the hospital exit lights, I see a familiar figure on the path ahead of me. I buzz down the passenger window.

She leans down. 'Well, hello!'

'Are you . . . ?'

She points to the bus stop up ahead. 'Getting the nine-twenty Glengarvan bus.'

'Hop in, Shirley. I can drop you home.'

She opens the door and slides in next to me.

'Car's in for a service,' she says, pointing to the sign for Gallagher Brothers Garage across the road. 'I get brother-in-law rates, so it's worth the trip.' She smiles, dropping her handbag by her feet and buckling up. 'He'll drop my car back tomorrow.'

She gestures to the hospital building disappearing behind us in the wing mirror. 'My sister's in for minor surgery, so two birds, one stone.'

'You've had a long day so.'

She stretches back against the leather seat and crosses her legs. 'You bet.' She turns to look at me in the gloom. 'How's your daughter, Dan? I heard she went in early this morning.'

'So-so. It's pneumonia. We'll get an update from the consultant in the morning.'

'Must be hard,' she says. 'For all of you.'

'The Long and Winding Road' is playing on the radio. 'I love that song, Dan,' she says, and I turn up the volume. The melody fills the car, and she sings along quietly. She knows all the words.

'You've another daughter at home, I gather?' she says, after a while.

'Yes,' I say. 'Andi's fifteen going on twenty-one.'

I indicate onto the slip road, and the car roars towards the motorway.

She laughs. 'Sounds like me back in the day. Must be lovely, though, all the same . . . having a family, I mean.'

'How about you?'

She sighs. 'I'd like to. Someday. Hope I haven't left it too late.'

'You just haven't met the right man yet, Shirley,' I say lightly, knowing I'm out of my depth in these conversations.

'I thought I had.' She fixes her hair behind her ear. 'I was engaged, you know.'

'It didn't work out?' I flick on the wipers as light rain drizzles along the windscreen.

There's a long silence. Paul McCartney sings the last notes of the song.

She sighs. 'No. It didn't work out. I was a fool. I should have seen it coming. But I didn't.'

'I'm sorry.'

'And you, Dan? How long are you hitched?'

'Twenty-one years.'

'Wow. Sally must've been a child-bride.'

'We were very young,'

'Any regrets?'

'We've survived.'

'Is survival the end game?'

She looks at me when I don't answer. After a minute she says, 'I wish I could say no regrets.'

'You probably dodged a bullet with that guy, Shirley. There's someone else, someone better, out there for you.' I can see her grimace, but she keeps staring ahead.

'Thanks, Dan. I need to hear that, you know. It gets lonely on your own.'

We chat about work, safe small talk that fills the journey home. Off the motorway, I turn right onto the Mill Road and continue down onto Churchberry Avenue. The car growls to a stop outside number 27.

'You're a star. Thank you, Dan.'

She unfastens her safety belt, and her hand presses on my thigh as she leans over to kiss my cheek. She inhales slowly and slips her bag over her shoulder. The rain has eased.

She opens the door a fraction and hesitates. 'Do you want to come in for a coffee?' She smiles. 'I even have a Guinness in the fridge. If you want to. Up to you.' She reaches over and pats my knee. 'You look all in, Dan.'

It would be so easy to say, *Yeah, why not?* Kid myself that I just want a coffee or a chat. That she just wants a coffee or a chat. But the

123

chemistry is there, crackling between us. There's a long silence as we both sit there – she turning back towards me, one foot on the pavement.

'Up to you,' she says again, compressing her lips.

Game, set, and match to guilt.

'Not tonight, Shirley. I better get home. Thanks, though.'

She shrugs. 'Sure. It's been a long day.' She flashes me a smile, but the dashboard lights catch a glimmer of disappointment in her eyes as she looks across at me. 'Okay, see you tomorrow.'

'I can pick you up in the morning, if you like. I mean, I'll be passing . . .'

She brightens. 'Great. See you in the morning, then.'

I drive home with the windows down. I need to get rid of Shirley's scent, and I need the wind and the rain blowing in to bring me back to my senses once and for all.

CHAPTER 29

DOLL

I can feel tears pricking my eyelids, and I have to blink as the road ahead gets blurry. There's a bonfire in my head, and my stomach is ducking and diving. I don't know which end of me is up. At least there's no sign of the Headscarves.

Such strange creatures, the Grandmothers, not a bit like my granny.

They said I had everything I needed in my bag. *Everything except courage*, I tell myself.

Whatever I had of it inside the council chamber, it's gone now. How am I going to do what I promised? What was I thinking? I'm not right in the head. A prize eejit.

A flash of panic shoots up my throat and eases out in a long wail. What am I thinking? Who am I kidding? I feel my legs buckle and falter as they strain to follow my footsteps. My special knees ache, and I realise how un-special they really are. How un-special I am. Just a dummy with dreams. Is the new me fading away already?

My face shames me. When I think of it – me standing in front of everyone, pretending to be great. With my ugly scars and crusty wounds. How they must have smirked behind the smiles. Nan-Nan says my face is healing, but I can feel the skin, thin, puckered, and pinched. A hole in my face. Disgraceable.

Left, right, left, right. I trudge along.

I look at my hands. Hands that can barely lift a cup and not drop it. I struggle to fasten a button, to swallow, to walk. Special knees is right! They just made that up so I'd feel . . . special. When there's nothing special about you, they make something up so you won't feel so bad. And you believe it. When you're a kid, you believe anything, really.

My scrawny body shames me. I want so much to curl up on my couch and dig the hole in my face, go deeper so I can tumble into it, head over heels, and disappear inside myself. A safe house. I want to wallop my stupid fingers hard against a hard wall. Feel the lovely pain.

125

And wail and wail. Or jump off a cliff into the sea, shattering my match-stick legs against the rocks. And then people would know; they would understand. They would say, *If only we listened better. We could've rescued her.* But I'd have been carried off into the ocean by then, lost.

My soul is cold, no rainbow inside my head now. Only rain. It's lashing in my head. Even the bonfire is ashes.

There is no one about as I climb the steps to the platform and step onto the MP. I fling the bag on the seat opposite and sit back.

I pass by moonlit fields. An owl *too-whoo*s in the distance. Trees glide past, shaking their heads as I trundle by, as if to say, *Doll, you are an idiot with your notions of saving us all.* The breeze titters in response.

I feel another long wail climbing up out of my lungs, and as there's no one to hear, I let it escape. I cover my face with my hands and cry out all my years of misery. A drop of blood dribbles down and zigzags pinkly across my knee. I don't want to ruin my white dress, and I rub it away with my thumb.

I wish I was powerful and strong like Nell thinks I am. Powerful and strong and filled with courage. Like someone who can march into life with a shield and a sword, cutting and chopping, never giving up. Or like the boxer Ali Baba, never afraid and winning and winning. Saying, *I am the greatest.* A ten. Not a two like me.

I find the sweets Nan-Nan gave me and unwrap a red one. Straw-berry . . . mmm. I look at the map from Mauran. I need to get off at the last MP station. I must take the windy road up to Hanora's cottage, where I will spend the night. After that, I must make my way to Glen-shiquin Mountain, one of the Twin Peaks. But how?

I just realise I can read as well as talk. *I can read as well as talk.* The map slides off my knee as I clap my hands. Maybe writing will be next. Imagine that! I swirl the sweet around with my tongue, sucking the fruity favour.

I hug the bag to my chest. I feel better inside. I think the sweets are cheering me up. Maybe they're magic. The rain in my head has stopped, and the sun is out. This is an adventure, I tell myself. This is what I dreamed about. This is my second life. Not everyone gets a second chance. There's nothing to be afraid of, nothing at all.

I can see the lights of Killala Station in the distance. The last stop on the Northline. I sling my bag over my shoulder and step off as the walkway slows to a halt. All is quiet. The platform is well lit, but my heart skips a beep.

A humming. I hear it rising in the distance, between the trees. It's those Headscarves again. I know the Beatles' sad tune, and as they sing, I whisper the words of 'The Long and Winding Road'.

There's no way I'm heading out there on my own. I walk toward a counter with a sign saying *Information*. When I ring the bell, a mop of white curls appears from behind a door marked *Private*. The man comes around to my side of the counter and leans towards me. I can smell coffee off his breath.

'Well, missy.' He smiles. 'What can I do for you?' He hunkers down. 'Are you lost, child?' He pushes the red pencil in his hand behind his ear. It disappears into the curls.

'I'm looking for Hanora's cottage. Can you point the way? Is it far? Could I miss the turn?'

I'm playing for time, hoping to give those Headscarves the slip. He disappears behind the counter and returns with a torch.

'C'mon, lassie, it's not far. I'll lead the way. It's late for a young lady like yourself to be out and about.' He shakes my hand. 'I'm Bert.'

Can't believe he's calling me Lassie; he must know my granny's song. I gladly follow his corduroy jacket as he heads along a narrow path. The Headscarves are still singing.

I hurry to keep up with Bert. 'Do you hear that?' I ask him. 'Do you hear those Headscarves singing?'

'I do,' he says, 'but take no notice. They're harmless. I've often heard them over the years, but I never recognise their songs. Nice tunes, though, I'll grant you that. You're not afraid, child, are you?' He pats my head. 'Poor old souls. They're just searching for their road to eternity.'

I relax a bit. I like Bert.

'Are they expecting you at the cottage, child?'

'Oh yes. Hanora is a friend of my granny.' I lie so easily, but it's a white one, so it should be okay with the Man above.

The smell of lavender is thick in the air. 'Do you smell that?' Bert says. He sniffs. ''Twould nearly choke you. It's the strangest thing.' He lifts his eyes to the sky. 'Something's not right.' He laughs. 'Like Mother Nature's overdoing it. What do you think, girl?'

I see a light up ahead. Bert flashes the torch beam up and down the gable wall of the cottage. 'There you go, child. She's a great cook, so no doubt you'll get a good meal and a warm bed tonight.'

He shakes my hand as I squeak the gate open.

'Thanks, Bert.'

'My pleasure.'

I tiptoe up the path and knock at the door. I hear a latch lifting, and a pink face smiles down at me.

'Come in, come in, child. We've been expecting you. You must be cold. Are you cold? At least you have a coat. It's unseasonably cold . . .' She puts her arm around my shoulders and hugs me to her. She smells of apples and baking, and her body feels soft as a pillow. 'Come in, come in . . .'

I follow her into a room lit by a pair of red fireside lamps. She throws a log onto the glowing coals and takes my coat to hang it on a nail behind the door. 'Sit down, sit down, child. Warm yourself. It's Doll, isn't it? Doll, a lovely name.'

I perch on an armchair by the fire.

'You must be hungry,' she says. She wipes her hands on her apron. 'I'll get you a warm drink first. Kurt won't be long.' She turns towards the end of the room and calls out, 'Kurt! Will you come in, man, and meet Doll?' She rolls her eyes. 'Men and their sheds.'

She bustles off and returns with a mug of warm pineapple juice. It tastes delicious, and I can feel energy flashing through my blood. I feel stronger. Hopeful.

'Tastes good?'

I nod, sinking into the chair. 'Thank you, Hanora.'

'Call me Hanni,' she says, tossing a blanket over my knees. 'You'll warm up soon.'

I haven't the heart to tell her I'm not that cold. I think she likes fussing over me.

'How is Nell?' she asks.

'Very good,' I say, like I've known her all my life. Better not mention her claw-hand.

'Yes, Nell is a wonderful person, strong and wise.'

'What happened to her hand?' Jesus. I didn't intend to blurt it out. 'Sorry, I don't mean to be rude . . .'

'Ah, don't worry yourself. It's no secret, lovey. It was a nasty accident. Happened on a climbing trip in the Bullara Mountains, must be about ten years ago now.'

I can't believe a granny would be climbing mountains.

'Was she climbing at her age?'

'She was. No better woman for a challenge, and fit and strong she is. Not like myself.' She pats her middle. 'It was minus twenty at least – don't ask me how she did it. She slipped on ice and fell into a ravine.

128

Luckily, her fall was broken, but her arm got wedged between two boulders and they had to cut through it.'

'The boulder?'

'No, her arm! Just above the wrist. Right there and then. She's some woman. They had to, or she would have died. Frostbite can be vicious. Valda said she was lucky to be alive—'

Kurt appears in the doorway. He's a burly man, filling his wheelchair with no room to spare. He extends his arm towards me. 'Welcome, Doll, welcome. I see you've settled in already. We're glad to see you. I hear great things about you.' He sniffs the air. 'You'll enjoy the lamb stew,' he says, looking at Hanni. 'She's a fine cook. And by the look of you, you need a bit of fattening up.'

Three places are set at the table, and Hanni fills our plates with hunks of lamb and vegetables. There's plenty of bread to mop up the juices. I lick my lips but can only eat half of what's on my plate. Kurt shovels the food onto his big spoon and hoists it to his mouth. His jaws move in semi-circles as he savours the flavours.

'We heard about you,' he says, dabbing his napkin against his furry chin. 'You're the Child of Summer, am I right?'

I nod my head. 'Well, that's what everyone is saying, but I'm not sure myself, to be honest.'

'The Grandmothers are never wrong,' Hanni says. 'You must trust them, Doll.'

Kurt furrows his brows, scoops a spoonful of stew. 'It's a serious business, so it is, a serious business. You know about Major Tom, don't you, and the importance of the Orb? They filled you in?'

'I know a bit. I know the major's not right upstairs.'

Kurt looks at the ceiling, puzzled. 'Upstairs?'

'No, I mean his head isn't . . . I mean, he's a right demon. A lunatic.'

'A lunatic?'

'What she means,' Hanni says, 'is that he's dangerous, don't you, Doll?'

'Yes, that's exactly it,' I say gratefully. 'He's gone around the bend.' I struggle to explain. 'And now he can't stop . . . he's lost the plot.' I've heard my granny speak about this, so I kinda know what I'm talking about.

Kurt is staring at me.

'Or maybe it's just power,' Hanni says. 'The Orb gives him ultimate control of our entire world. He is brazen enough to think he can win, isn't he, Kurt?'

'Do you know him? Have you met him?' I ask Kurt.

'Oh, I know him all right, Doll.' He takes a swig of ale and leans forward, elbows spread on either side of his plate. 'But it's been a while now.' He rubs his chin. 'Your quest won't be easy, Doll, but the Manuscripts are sacred. When they've spoken before, they've never been wrong. The Gods are on your side.'

He takes a hunk of bread, sweeps it across his plate and into his mouth. He kisses his thumb and forefinger, nodding at Hanni. 'The best,' he says. Hanni takes a bow, smiling.

'Tell her about Tom,' she says. 'She needs all the help she can get.'

Kurt leans back, folds his arms. I can see another beard peeking over the top of his checked shirt.

'Our Major Tom is a strange fellow. Ruthless. But courageous too. He's earned medals for bravery, more than any other soldier I've known. But don't underestimate him. He's capable of killing you, and he is also a charmer.'

'Like a snake charmer,' I say. 'I've seen them on telly.'

'Yes, that's right,' Hanni says. 'He could get a snake to slither into its own grave.'

Kurt looks at Hanni. 'Remember, missus,' he says, placing his palm over her hand on the table. 'The major saved my life. You can't forget that.' He leans towards me, his chin resting on his fist.

'He was a lot younger than me, Doll. But we fought side by side in the Northern Territory war close on sixteen years ago. Brothers in arms, we were.' He points to the wheelchair. 'That's when this happened.'

Hanni clears away the plates, and Kurt gives her a thumbs-up sign. I do the same.

'Tell me what happened,' I say, leaning closer.

Kurt spreads his shovel hands on the table.

'Our unit was hiding out in the pine forests off the Northern Rocks. Getting a few hours' sleep before attacking a rebel commander's hideout.' He sits up straight in his chair. 'Our unit was an elite division – trained to kill, Doll. But we woke to find ourselves surrounded, our sentries' throats cut. They surprised *us*. There were mortars and grenades crashing all round us. The heat was overpowering.'

I can see little drops of sweat on Kurt's forehead. I give him my napkin to dry his face.

'You never forget it,' he says, wiping his brow. 'War turns men into animals.'

He takes a long drink of ale and wipes his mouth. He leans closer. 'Next thing I knew, I had been hit. Shrapnel had shattered my spine, but I didn't know that straightaway. I couldn't feel my legs. I heard screaming and realised it was me; that was frightening. I was sure I was going to die.'

He chews on his thumbnail.

'Our unit was wiped out – nine dead, including our commanding officer. Tom and a young sergeant called Albert were wounded.'

'What happened then?' I ask, knowing at least that Kurt survived.

'We were two thousand metres up, girl. We had to make our own way down or die on that mountainside.'

'But you couldn't walk, you said?'

'No, girl, that I could not. I told the others to go. But no way was Tom Axel leaving me behind. We were all going back together, he said. All or none.'

Hanni puts an apple cake in the middle of the table, steam still rising. 'I'll get some cream,' she says, and bustles off.

'Go on, Kurt. What happened next?'

'Well, Doll, I'm in and out of consciousness. Tom gets branches and bits of rope we'd used to haul supplies. He gathers tins, containers, whatever he can find. He tells Albert to help him pare the wood and lash it together and uses the tin containers for buoyancy. "We're goin' for a swim, brother," he says to me. He always called me brother, even though I was old enough to be his father.' Kurt strokes his chin, thumb and forefinger meeting and retreating. He's back there. And I'm there too.

Hanni cuts three slices of apple cake, and the mixture tumbles onto the plates, the apple holding firm. I can smell cinnamon. She pours the cream over and passes the pudding around. 'Eat up, Doll,' she says, smiling. 'Don't let Kurt and his grizzly tales put you off your food.' She rolls her eyes again and looks at her husband. 'Are you finished yet? You will have the child petrified with your stories!'

She holds her spoon of apple cake in mid-air. 'And don't be romanticising him, man,' she says. 'He is a criminal.' But her eyes are soft when she says it.

She looks at me. 'I suppose when someone saves your life and risks their own for you, you don't forget that, do you?'

'You don't,' I say. 'How could you?'

'Still,' she says, licking cream from her lips, 'what he's involved in now, what's he's done – it's treason. And all our lives are in danger.'

'Go on, Kurt,' I say. 'What happened in the finish?'

'The lads got the makeshift raft to the river. It took an hour to drag the damn thing there.' He scoops a mouthful of apple cake into his mouth. Licks his lips.

'Tom came back and carried me to the river. He was bleeding from a head wound. Running on adrenaline. Albert was shivering, shock setting in. They tied me to the raft somehow, and we were off. The three of us.' He slaps his thigh. 'When I think of it, Doll. Hurtling downriver in the dark, over rapids, through whirlpools, paddling with branches or just free-falling, hanging on in the frigid water.' He shivers.

'I don't remember much of it, to be honest. I was losing consciousness. I know we were tipped into the water again and again. That river was swollen from the rains. 'Twas a miracle we made it.'

'What happened then, Kurt?'

'I ended up in a military hospital for six weeks before being moved to rehab. I wanted to die. That was a dark time.' Hanni squeezes his hand.

'And the major?'

'Tom had a concussion, a few cuts and broken bones. He mended fast.' He pauses. 'Well, physically anyway. Psychologically?' He taps his head. 'I'm not so sure. No one escapes intact. Do they, Hanni?'

Hanni shakes her head. 'Very few,' she says. 'And some don't make it at all. Like all your comrades that night. Nine fine men' – she clicks her fingers – 'gone, just like that.'

'Tom was awarded the Silver Star for bravery that night,' Kurt says. 'I loved that man. For what he did, for who he was. A hero.'

'Did you stay in touch?'

'He often visited me in rehab, sneaked me in a flask of brandy.' He chuckled. 'We stayed in touch for a bit, but he wasn't a sentimental man. He moved on. He left the military eventually, drifted off. Haven't seen him for ten years or more.'

Kurt shakes himself into the present. 'Well,' he says to me, leaning forward and loading some cake into his mouth, 'are you up for it, Child of Summer?'

'I dunno,' I say, 'and that's the truth.' I feel I can be honest with these nice people.

'I'm not sure if I can do it,' I say. 'What if they've got the wrong person? What if they made a mistake? They thought they had a ten, but I'm only a two . . . and soon they will find out . . .'

Hopeless is stretching her familiar arms around me, and I'm leaning in.

There's a candle on the table, and Kurt pushes it away from us. He looks from Hanni to me. 'Is there a breeze in this room?'

We both shake our heads.

'Is there a draft coming in that door or through that window behind me?' He jerks his thumb over his shoulder.

'No, Kurt,' Hanni says. 'What are you saying, man?'

He points a stubby finger towards the candle. 'The flame is leaning towards Doll,' he says. 'Look.'

He's right. The flame slants in my direction, like it's straining to reach me.

'I don't understand,' I say.

'Now swap places at the table,' he says to Hanni and me, and we do as we're told.

'Just to humour him,' Hanni says.

The candle flame flickers and starts to lean in my direction again.

'Y'see,' he says. 'Nature tells us the truth. Even the candle flame, in its physical wisdom, in its consciousness, knows where the Child of Summer is.'

Just to convince ourselves, Hanni and me swap places again, moving our chairs a little to the right. There is no mistake. The flame strains towards me, like a dog on a leash that has spotted a rabbit.

They both stare at me. The only sound is the log spitting on the fire.

Maybe, just maybe, I am the Child of Summer. Somebody special. Not just my knees, but all of me. Doll Redmond, Child of Summer. Chimes like a bell.

'The Gods know,' Hanni says. 'There are matters mightier than mere mortals.' She squeezes my hand. 'We're all made of stardust. But Doll, maybe your particular stardust needs the light of Almazova to make it sparkle and shine.'

Kurt nods and heaps the last of his apple cake onto his fork. Scoops up some cream. 'Smells divine.'

The spell is broken. 'Bed for you, Doll,' Hanni says, and she leads me towards my little bedroom. There's a small wooden cot with a yellow quilt. I slip out of my dress and under the covers. 'Sleep tight,' Hanni whispers.

I think of my mother. *Sleep tight.* A stab of guilt, a cut to my heart. I ran away. Disappeared on them. No good can come of it.

CHAPTER 30

SALLY

They bustle in, all business. The matron first, the consultant on her heels. She holds the door open for him, almost curtsies. Two med students squeeze in behind.

'Good morning, Mum.' The matron is all smiles. 'This is Mr Davis.'

I nod. Even though his hair is greying at the temples, he has the look of a little boy making his communion. A studious child. Grey suit, blue tie, shiny shoes.

She checks her chart. 'This is Doll Redmond, Doctor, eleven years old. Special needs. Non-verbal. Third admission for pneumonia. And this is Mum . . .'

She consults the chart again. 'We've started her on antibiotics and fluids.'

Mr Davis says, 'Good morning, Mrs Redmond.' His voice is clipped. He takes the chart from the matron. 'How is she responding?'

'She's stable, but her temperature was elevated during the night.'

'And her heart rate,' I say, 'is that normal?'

He looks at the file, frowning.

My heart hammers.

But he nods, stroking his chin. 'Pneumonia can have a destabilising effect on the heart. Her body is fighting the infection.' He looks to the two silent students at his side. 'Her lungs may be weakened by previous bouts.'

He peers at the matron's notes again. 'These antibiotics are powerful, but they can only do so much.'

'So much? How do you mean?'

He peers at me over silver-rimmed glasses. 'Pneumonia is a serious illness, Mrs Redmond.' He looks at the matron. 'We'll keep a close eye on her response.'

The matron takes a little bow, looks at me. 'Any questions, Mum?'

I hate when they call you Mum. She knows my name. *Mum*. It's so lazy.

I look at the consultant. 'It's just a matter of time, I suppose? She will recover? I mean, there's no real danger . . . is there? It's not *that* serious, is it? She has recovered before, no problem . . .' I trail off, waiting for him to tell me it's a manageable illness; everything's under control; she's in the right place.

But he doesn't. Why doesn't he? He doesn't even smile. I focus on his blue tie.

'I think we should . . .' He stops, looks at Doll, starts again. 'I think we should wait and see. For now, she is stable. Let's take it one day at a time, shall we?'

He turns to leave. The two students – are they props? – haven't said a word. They exit first. Mr Davis nods towards the bed. Doll hasn't moved. Her eyes are closed, her body like a pencil under the pink counterpane. 'We have to factor in her condition,' he says.

Now I want to pull at the sleeve of his jacket. I want to shout at him, *Hey, you, stop right there! What do you mean, 'factor in her condition'?* I want to say, *What exactly do you mean by 'one day at a time'? What's that code for? You stupid little man.*

No, I don't like the sound of that. Like there are battles to be fought; like he's not sure we'll win or lose. I want to yank him back into the room. Say, *Is there something you're not telling me? Are you holding something back? I'd prefer to know.*

Or would I? A few years back when they told us – at this very hospital – that Doll might not be able to fight a bronchial infection *with her condition*, I fainted. The last thing I heard was *with her condition*. My legs began to wobble, a singing blackness closed in, and I ended up on the tiles. I remember they smelt of Dettol. Someone propped me on a chair, and a voice said, 'Keep your head down, that's right. Nice, even breaths. Take a sip of water.'

I remember the plastic cup vibrating as I took it, water spilling over my fingers. 'Sorry. Thank you.'

'It happens,' the voice said to Dan. 'Medical anxiety; not unusual. She'll be fine. Won't you, Sally? You'll be fine in a minute or two.'

So maybe there's a chart somewhere saying, *Mrs Redmond – medical anxiety – keep it vague.*

I text Dan. Doll stable. Dr says take one day at time…what does that mean??? See you for lunch at one.

I stroke Doll's forehead. It feels clammy. Her face is beginning to heal, new pink skin stretching across her cheeks. I dab some Sudocreme around the wounds. She stirs, a brief half smile. I can see her pupils moving under her long lashes. Dream sleep. 'Happy dreams, Doll,' I say out loud, rubbing the back of her tiny hand.

I sit back on the hard leather chair, close my eyes. I hear quiet shoes, quiet voices. A gurney rumbles by. A child wails in the distance. Cups clink on a trolley. A phone rings. I can smell gravy. Nurses gather at reception and laugh at a shared joke. Hospital life marches on. Out there, it's just another day at the office.

Dan and Andi arrive at lunchtime. 'Don't say anything,' he says. 'She wanted to come – it's double PE; she's not missing school. As such.'

Andi holds Doll's hand. 'You go off with Dad and get a sandwich,' she says. 'I'll stay here.'

In the hospital canteen, the ham salad roll tastes better than expected, and the coffee is strong and hot. There's been an awkwardness between us since our row on Monday morning, and I'm not in the mood for another argument.

'I'm sorry for flinging the coffee at you,' I say. 'I was so angry.'

He smiles. 'Yeah, you could've killed me, you know.' He squeezes my hand. 'It was me, Sally. I shouldn't have started on you.' His finger circles the top of his cup. 'Let's forget about it. I know it's tough for you . . .' He trails off. 'For all of us. Anyway, what else did the consultant have to say?'

I tell him. 'Will you call him? I'm probably worrying about nothing. It's just that . . . well, maybe I need to worry. I hadn't the guts to ask. Will you ask? Will you get the facts, what can we expect, that sort of thing?'

He puts his hand over mine. I'm grateful for the gesture, feel the tears brim.

'I'll call him later, I promise.' He looks at me. 'You switch off. You know what they're like. Covering their arses. Won't commit to anything and we've been here before, more than once.'

He's right. I feel better. Of course. I'm running away with things, as usual. Everything will be fine. It's just pneumonia. It's manageable. People don't die of pneumonia. I think they used to, years ago, when we didn't have the range of antibiotics we do today. Not like now. And didn't Doll recover twice already?

I think it's actually lack of sleep that does it. Makes you anxious. Silly, really. *Don't trouble trouble, till trouble troubles you.* That's what my mother used to say. Good advice. *Get a grip, Sally.* Everything's going to be all right. It's only day two. And her face is healing; isn't that great? Every cloud has a silver lining.

I'm back in the leather chair. Reading the same page of my book over and over. A scorpion of a thought is lurking in the shadows, his little pincers clawing at me, scuttling through my neurons so fast I can barely feel the flick of his tail. I can smell the venom, though, and it's making me sick. I want to vomit. Or scream.

I can't scream; I'm in a hospital. People would hear me and think I'm mad. Maybe I am going mad?

My heart is racing, but I won't panic. There's nothing to be afraid of. Only the fear itself. That's what they say: face the fear, confront the rat in your head. He's not real.

I turn down the page of my book, place it on the locker. Walk around the bed. Why is she sleeping so much? She hasn't moved in hours.

The monitor tracks her heartbeat. A steady ninety-nine. My hands are sweaty.

What if, though? What if . . . ?

I sit on the edge of the chair, drop my head between my knees. *Breathe. Nice, easy breaths now. In . . . out . . . in . . . out.*

A voice. Sensible legs in tights, white shoes. 'Are you okay there, Mrs Redmond?'

A tap swishes on. I sit up slowly and take the glass from the out-stretched hand. 'Thanks, Nurse.' I squint at her name badge. Bernie. 'Thanks, Bernie. Just a little dizzy. I'm fine now. Thank you.'

'It's very stuffy in here,' she says. 'You take a little walk, Mum, get some fresh air. It'll do you good. I'll keep an eye on her.'

She's right. I need to get away, out into the cold sunshine. Where life is normal. The glorious, wonderful ordinary.

CHAPTER 31

DOLL

In my dream, my dad is crying and turning the house upside-down. 'Doll. Doll. Where are you?' He stumbles into the garden, pushes a rosebush aside. He swears as a thorn pierces his finger.

'Doll! Doll! Come on, game over.' He drags his palms along his face.

The sound of his voice rocks me awake, and I sit up, trying to push the tangled dream away. I feel the soft quilt under my fingers and remember I'm in Hanni and Kurt's cottage. *Dad, I'm not coming back.*

Morning sun streams in, and from my bed, I can see a buttercup meadow.

My mind is so crowded with people, they can barely fit. Nan-Nan and Jasper. The Grandmothers and Earl. And I feel I've known Kurt and Hanni for years.

I lace my hands behind my head. It's like being inside a story, not knowing the ending. It sure beats lying on a couch in Misery Street.

Dad, please don't come to me in my dreams. I don't want you to be sad. If Dad knew where I was . . .

Dad, if you knew where I was, you would be singing.

I know he would. My dad loves me. He'd want me to be happy. He'd say, *Doll, go for it!* He was always saying that to Andi. 'Go for it, Andi.' If she was playing a match, if she was in some tournament, he'd tell her to go for it.

He never told me to go for it. He gave up on me. The memory scrapes me like a claw. I mean, there was nothing to go for – well, that's how I saw it, anyway.

Looking back, I actually think I broke my dad. At least he has Andi and Will to un-break him. When he realises I'm gone, they'll stitch his heart back together again – a perfect red velvet one.

I can hear Hanni moving about in the kitchen, and I ease myself out of bed. I'm excited about the day ahead, wherever it might take me.

I push my dad out of my head, and I get dressed in the clothes Hanni has left out for me.

'Good morning, child.' Hanni sets a bowl of porridge on the table, and I think of Goldilocks. 'I've never liked food,' I say, 'until now.'

She smiles and passes me a plate of pancakes with raspberries. 'Food is medicine,' she says. 'Eat well, feel well, Doll.'

She pats me on the head. 'You'll need your strength, so clean your plate. I'll pack some food and clothes for your journey.'

'Where's Kurt?'

Hanni jerks her thumb towards the back door. 'Outside,' she says, 'getting your travelling companion ready.'

'Oh, a friend. Wow.' I finish my food and rush outside.

'Come and meet Poppy,' Kurt says. 'Isn't she a beauty?'

Poppy turns brown eyes towards me. I'm stunned. I can't ride a horse; I can't even get up on one. As if Poppy heard me, she leans forward and nuzzles me.

Kurt calls to a boy filling a bucket from a tap. 'Jacko, meet our special visitor, Doll.' Jacko comes over and shakes my hand. His dark hair is tied back, like a girl's. 'Let's go,' he says, leaping onto Poppy's back in one easy movement. He reaches down to help me mount as Kurt helps put my foot in the stirrup.

'Oh, Diamond Jesus, I can't do this. Help! I'll fall.'

'C'mon, Doll. Feet in the stirrups . . . there you go.' Jacko helps me into a sitting position in front of him. He slips his arms around me and holds the reins.

Kurt laughs. 'Ah, you're a natural, Doll. And you're in safe hands. Jacko's a boy wonder with horses. He can nearly make them talk – can't you, Jacko?'

Jacko grins. 'Giddy-up, Poppy.' I close my eyes and pray for a happy death.

'You're nervous,' he says. 'Don't be. Relax your bones. Horses pick up on your emotions.' He lets me hold the reins with him. 'And remember, Doll, when you're on a horse, you feel on top of the world. You're a queen looking down on everybody, and they're looking up to you.'

He's right. I've spent all my life looking up at people, and now I'm ten feet tall. We begin to gather pace, cantering through fields and forest paths. Poppy clip-clops along, and I start to breathe again. Jacko shows me how to get her to slow down and change direction and how to keep her in check. Heels down, shoulders back.

139

I begin to relax, loving the wind breathing into my face and the rhythm of the hooves pounding beneath us. After a while, Jacko says, 'Doll, here, take the reins for a while and let her know who's boss.'

I can feel Jacko's breath in my hair. He is telling me a funny story about his sister, how a bucket got jammed on her head the day before, and I begin to laugh. I can't stop. Jacko is laughing too. The tears pour down my cheeks, and we are both hysterical. I've never laughed like this before.

Well, hello, I've never laughed in my life. I've seen Ruby and the twins laughing, and Andi and Mom often share a joke, but I never got it. I never understood how it felt.

It feels like you're weightless.

We stop to let Poppy have a drink from the river, and Jacko and me share some chocolate, dangling our feet in the cool water.

Jacko says, 'Is it true you're the Child of Summer?'

'Yep,' I say, tossing my hair back like Andi. 'That's what I'm told, anyway.'

'Cool,' he says. 'Can you talk about it?'

'Not a chance,' I say. 'If I did, I'd have to kill you.'

Jacko's face freezes.

'Only joking,' I say, and the two of us laugh again, splashing each other.

If only he knew what a fraud I am. But he thinks I'm cool, and that's a first.

We're back in the saddle. I'm getting the hang of it and have a sneaky feeling that Poppy is really the one in charge. I think she'll be leading me up that mountain rather than the other way round.

I can't believe I'm riding a horse and pinch myself on the way back to see if I'm dreaming.

It's time to begin my journey. Time to find Major Tom Axel and the Orb. I say my goodbyes to Jacko and collect my bag from Hanni. Now it's just me and Poppy and a map, a sleeping bag, and some food. Off into the wild.

Hanni secures my stuff on the side bags and turns to hug me tightly. Kurt spreads out the map again and traces the route I must follow, though Poppy knows it well. 'She could follow that path blindfolded,' he says.

'I hope I see you again,' I say, 'But if I don't . . . I want to thank you both.'

Hanni smiles and pats my head. 'Hear this,' she says, quite sternly, hunkering down unsteadily so she's face-to-face with me. 'Remember, Doll: you have the Gods beside you and behind you. They are your shield and your sword. They will guide you and protect you. The Manuscripts have spoken their truth. You are the Child of Summer. Have faith. You are our rescuer, our brave hero.' She clasps my hands in hers. 'We will meet again, Doll.' She plants a kiss on my forehead.

Kurt shakes my hand, and his gnarly grasp catches my heart. It's hard to stop the tears.

I trot out the gate, and Poppy leads us onto the river path. I turn to wave to my two new friends. Hanni has a hand on Kurt's shoulder as she waves me goodbye. They're both smiling. I want to hold that picture and freeze it, so I can take it out to warm me on sad days.

I'm not far along my path when I hear the Headscarves. Their song echoes against the sheer cliffs on the far side of the river. 'We Are the Champions'.

Everyone loved Freddie Mercury in our house. I know the chorus and sing along loudly.

My voice echoes around the valley, and it's the strangest sound, me singing on a horse. The Headscarves swoop and dive above the cliffs, like a giant multicoloured kite, their scarves flapping in the wind. It's a mighty sight. And I realise I'm not afraid of them anymore. Poor souls on their road to eternal happiness. And their music is a message: I've got to win. I mustn't be a loser, only a winner. I have to be a Champion.

I say to Poppy, 'Do ya hear that, Poppy? I must be a Champion.'

She turns to look at me as if to say, *I've no problem with that. Just go for it.*

'GO FOR IT, DOLL.' I shout out the words, and they echo back from the hills. *GO FOR IT, DOLL ... FOR IT, DOLL ... DOLL ...*

I *am* a queen, half-way between earth and sky, ten feet tall and full of power. Horse power! I laugh at my own joke. Poppy shakes her mane in agreement. She turns and shows her teeth, like she's laughing too.

'You and me, girl,' I say aloud. 'We're a team.'

I feel I'm born again, this time into a golden life. A life with songs and adventure and no digging into your face. Where you can chew and talk and jump on a horse and eat apple cake. And you won't be getting sick after a beaker of tea and you have nice fat legs, not sticks. In this golden life, nobody says, *Sure, God love her.* Only *she's a topper, no mistake. An absolute topper.*

My skin tingles; my heart glitters. I open and close my fingers around the reins. Painless. The sunlight shimmers through the trees, dappling the surface of the water. Insects hum. Crickets sing. A brown fish catapults through the water and plops back into the depths.

I signal Poppy to stop so she can drink from the riverbank while I eat lunch and pick wild-flowers to decorate my straw hat. The sun makes me drowsy, and I lie on the bank and close my eyes, drinking in the warm quietness.

I sit upright when I hear it. A rustling in the trees behind us. I listen, frozen. My heart is hammering. The corner of my eye catches a movement. Something dark, a liquid cloak. I freeze.

But there's nothing. A trick of the light.

We continue our journey, but I can't shake off the feeling we're being watched. Unseen eyes tracking us.

The sun is low in the sky now, and I check the map for the cabin where I'll spend the night. Kurt said it will be easy to find by following the pilgrim path upstream.

He's right. I can see the small wood cabin up ahead at a bend in the river. Poppy slows down. She knows we're here. I'm happy to get back on the ground again, and I do very fast, as my foot gets stuck in the stirrup and I tumble and hit the path with a thud. I roll over and get up unsteadily. Nothing broken.

I lift the latch. The cabin has a wooden cot, two stools, a stove, and a table set against the wall. There's a shelf with some mugs, bowls, and two blackened pots. I drop my sleeping bag on the cot, then head for the river to clean off the heat and dust of the day.

It's icy cold. I duck my head underwater and feel my body tingling with life. I touch my face, feel the dip where the skin is pinched and scarred. What was all that about? I can hardly remember. Was it only yesterday that I hurt my shoulder falling into Almazova? Now there is no pain.

My fingers move freely through the water. I twist my body to get warm, waving my hands in the air. Woo-hoo! Everything's turning to gold.

I heat up the red bean stew that Hanni packed for me and eat outside. Poppy is munching her food, and in the distance the Headscarves are at it again, singing a song about a tiger.

I tell myself to stay calm. I know there are no tigers here on the mountain. Kurt was very clear about that. River eels, yes; deer, wild boar; but no lions or bears or tigers.

Still, I tether Poppy, fix her blanket around her, and slip inside the cabin. I draw the bolt across. Can tigers open bolts?

I cuddle down in my fleecy sleeping bag, and just as I'm starting to melt into dreams, something pulls me awake. A sound outside the cabin door. My body fear-freezes. A tiger?

Fingers of panic grab my throat, and I can't breathe.

I hear it again. A footstep. I lie in the darkness, listening. My blood has turned to water.

An owl hoots. A breeze rustles through leaves. A crack, like a twig snapping.

And then I hear it. A tap at the door. *Tap, tap.* Again. *Tap, tap.* I slither under the cover. Poppy whinnies. I hold my breath. *Jesus, Mary and Holy St Joseph, take me back to my couch. Take me home. Pray for us. Pray for us.* Another tap, and the wooden latch moves.

And then way above, I can hear a choir pouring out a beautiful melody, the notes falling like confetti down around the cabin. The music catches the strings of my soul like a harp.

Outside the door, footsteps quietly retreat.

Have the Headscarves scared someone off? Are they protecting me? The melody fades fast.

After an age, I sneak a sweet from my bag. Tastes like a peach. My heart slows. I relax. But I know one thing: someone or something is following me, and I can't help thinking that they'll get me sooner or later.

So what am I doing, out all alone on a dark and lonely mountain? Have I lost the plot?

CHAPTER 32

DOLL

The sun is filtering in through cobwebbed windows. I sit up, remembering the tapping last night. Did I imagine it? Outside, now, the only sounds are the birds chattering and the gurgle of the river. I swing my legs onto the floor. Not a twinge.

I hug myself inside as I open the door and lean against the frame. Poppy is grazing, and there's a mist burning off the river. I can smell the green. I tip some oats from Hanni's bag of supplies into a tin bowl. I sit outside to eat, checking my route on the map. Still a way to go, but I can see Glenshiquin in the distance, a purple-brown giant of a mountain scraping the sky.

Poppy comes closer and peers over my shoulder. I can feel her breath on my hair. It's like she's telling me she knows the path and it's okay. *No panic, Doll.*

I smile up at her. 'Thanks, Poppy,' I say. 'You're a good buddy.'

A good buddy.

I never had one. It's a sweet feeling. Having a buddy gives you wings.

From the corner of my eye, I sense movement. A shadow behind the trees. I hold the spoon midway to my mouth. I shrivel inside. Something dark, retreating.

Will you stop it, Doll? I say to myself. *There's nothing there.*

One last dip in the river before I move on. I wade in, letting the cold water close over my head. I push my dripping hair off my face. My whole body is sparking. It's like being in a sweetshop with chocolates waiting to melt in your mouth. The sour smell of my couch is just a grey memory. Was it even me on that couch? Am I reborn – a brand-new, golden Doll?

I saw him on the telly, Freddie Mercury, sitting at his piano, eyes closed. I didn't then – but I know now – that he felt golden too, and it soared up his throat and burst from his mouth when he sang Don't Stop Me Now.

I push my palm along the surface, spraying a rainbow of water crystals into the air.

I'm singing and waiting for the Headscarves to join in, but there's not a sound. Maybe they just don't know it.

I stop and listen. The birds are silent. I stand quite still, up to my special knees in water. Black clouds are belching in, and there's a distant growl. Where has the sun gone? A wind curls along my shoulders, and fat raindrops start to fall.

No hum. No chirp. Such quietness. I hurry towards the bank, shivering. Freddie Mercury is forgotten. Goosebumps on my arms are whispering, *Beware*.

It's not just the cold; I feel a slithering deep in my gut. As I wade towards the cabin, the water swirls higher and higher, circling my middle, insisting I stay. *Please, you must stay*. Watery hands pull me back. *Come out here. Stay*. I stumble and cry out as I feel the stones slip beneath my toes, like I'm being hoovered into the deep. The waters roar; the wind howls like a dog. I scream, but there's no one to hear.

I'm circling like a chorus girl from *Riverdance*, caught up in a mad whirly-jig. But I don't want to dance; I don't know the steps. I'm sliding under. *Come on, dance*. My arms thrash about; there's nothing underfoot, and the river slides through my fists.

Water fizzes up my nose and I break the surface, moving my jaws upwards and outwards, snatching precious air. I claw at nothing, disappearing under. The river has swollen to twice its size, like a witch has cast a spell over it.

The curtains are closing – the play is over. It's not fair. Just when I was going places. Anger makes me scream. I don't want to be a Headscarf singing my way to heaven. I grab a branch, feel its slippery bark, and hang on with numb fingers.

Seconds flash past like Olympic sprinters. *Sorry, Dad. I tried to go for it, but* . . .

I shouldn't have stayed on that couch for all those years. I gave up so soon. Threw in the tea towel. And now my life is fading like a dot on a screen.

I hear ghostly clapping. I'm skipping. Fast. *One, two, three O'Leary*. Everyone is looking at me. *Four, five, six O'Leary*.

Well done, Doll . . . you're a topper. All my family are smiling at me. *You done us proud, Doll*. I smile, take a bow.

I feel the green velvet bed lean up to cradle my spine. It's over. I'm tired. *Granny, what a pity. Granny . . .*

CHAPTER 33

ANDI

I'm worried, so I ask Dad again over breakfast, 'Will Doll be okay? How come only family are allowed to visit? Why is she sleeping all the time? Is she in a coma?'

But he says, 'Will you just leave it? The doctors are saying she's stable. It's early days, but she'll pull through.' He's so snappy.

'Mom's worried, isn't she? Are you guys okay?'

He glances at his watch. 'Jesus, look at the time.' He grabs his keys from the hook behind the kitchen door. 'Come on, I'll drop you.'

Conversation closed.

'Put on your belt,' he says when we get in. He's in bad form. I know him so well. He turns up the volume on the radio. Swears under his breath as he listens to one miserable news story after another. A young mother was killed by a drunk driver; a bomb exploded in Syria; one of the lads on the Irish rugby team was seriously injured in last night's friendly . . .

'Christ, what's the world coming to.'

He slams on the horn as a motor-bike overtakes us. 'Stupid bastard.' He looks in the mirror, signals, and pulls in by the kerb.

'See you, Dad.'

He doesn't even answer. I slam the door and spend the next twenty metres coming up with an excuse for being late before I decide to take a right to the bus depot. I'm going to the hospital.

*

Half an hour later, I'm walking through the reception and up into Doll's room. To be honest, let's face it, she's not looking good. I hate saying that – thinking it, even. I don't care what they say; it's pretty obvious to me. It's like she's giving in, floating off, hardly a breath in her body.

I touch her face. It's cold, but the scars are healing. That's something. I kiss her forehead.

A nurse puts her head around the door. 'Hello?'

I jump back. 'Jesus, you gave me a fright.'

'Are you a relation?'

'Yes, I'm her sister.'

She nods. 'That's fine, then. Family only.'

'How is she?' I say.

'Holding her own, considering.'

'Considering what?'

She takes a step into the room. 'Well, considering her condition. You know it isn't easy for her body, fighting this, but . . . well, she's a little soldier. I'd say she's the pet at home, is she? She really is like a little doll. Poor mite.'

'What does that mean, holding her own?'

She looks a bit taken aback. 'It means, well, that she's stable, but with pneumonia, you know, it can be a tough one to shift.' She smiles. 'Aren't you very good to pop in during school time. Giving your mother a break, yeah? Anyway,' she says, checking her watch, 'I'll leave you to it. Give me a shout if you need anything.' She gives a little wink and disappears, her shoes squeaking on the polished floor.

I sit back on the leather chair. I'm no wiser. I don't think nurses are allowed to tell you much anyway. I suppose it'd cause confusion if they started blathering to everyone who came to visit. But am I getting the truth?

It's hard to concentrate on anything while Doll's sick. Poor Doll. She has a crap life. I wouldn't swap with her for anything.

Truth is, I don't think Doll even *wants* to live. Imagine saying that to my parents. We've never had that conversation: the elephant in the room, Doll's unhappiness. It's off-limits, unacknowledged and unspoken. *Don't mention the war.* And now, are they keeping something from me? I'm her bloody sister, so I have a right to know. Mom says, 'She's doing fine.' Dad says, 'Sure, isn't she getting the best of care?'

Yeah, right. What does that mean?

Doll stirs. I lean over and touch her shoulder. She gives a faint smile, her eyes flickering under half-closed lids.

'Doll, can you hear me?'

When I sit back down, I can hear humming – some familiar melody I can't place. Goosebumps erupt on my arms.

My mobile buzzes. It's Steve. Can I meet him later? A pizza or a walk on the beach?

My heart floats to the surface again. I've told him about Doll. But not Chelsea's visit to my house on Tuesday. And I'm not going to. If she

147

comes after me again, I'm going to sort her out myself. She does not get to fuck up my life.

I take the bus back to Glengarvan and head into school for afternoon classes. As I walk along, it comes to me. The melody in Doll's room: *One, two, three* . . . The ball game rhyme. It's stuck in my brain now like an earworm.

After school, I head for the prom. Steve is leaning against the seawall, scrolling through his phone. The ocean is wild today, and the wind is whipping up the sand along the seafront. I love days like this.

'How's your sister?' Steve asks as he laces his hand in mine. He hasn't met her. Not yet, anyway.

'She doesn't look too good, Steve.'

He pushes my hair off my face, and we lean in against the wind and start to walk along the shore.

'What are the doctors saying?'

'Oh, you know, she's stable, the usual stuff.'

'From what you told me, Andi, she sounds like a fighter.'

'She doesn't want to live.' I just blurt it out.

He stops and looks at me, his eyes widening. "How do you make that out?'

'I just know. Why can't anyone else see it? It's not rocket science.'

'She can't talk, so in fairness, Andi, you're just assuming.'

Does he think I'm making it up?

Everyone seems to be an expert on Doll. It's doing my head in.

'What would you know?' I say. 'You haven't a clue.'

'About what?'

'About what it's like to have a sister who hates her life. I *know*. I'm her sister.' There's a lump in my throat, like a stone.

'Andi, don't get upset.' He pulls me closer and kisses my cheek.

'Forget it.' Actually, I *am* getting upset, and I know I'm seconds away from bawling my eyes out. I don't want to cry, because I know if do, I won't stop.

'It's just tough,' I say, pressing my fingers to my eyelids.

'On her, like?'

'Yes, of course. And . . .' I stop for a second. 'And hard for me. No one gets that.'

He squeezes my hand. 'Tell me, Andi.'

'Are you a psychologist now?' I smile so I don't cry.

'Tell me, babe. What's tough?' His voice cradles me, his silence making space for what I need to say.

This far up the beach, the huge granite rocks provide shelter from the wind. We stop and lean against one. I don't know what to say. I kick some wet sand into a rock pool, watching the waters muddy. A baby crab swims to the surface. The waves curl and crash onto the shore.

He's doing it again. Waiting.

The crab scuttles off and disappears behind a rock. I'm not sure what to say. I've never said it to anyone before.

'I know it's hard on Doll. She's only a little one, but she . . . she . . . Steve, she fills the house. It's suffocating.' The stone in my throat's turned to salt.

'How do you mean, Andi?'

'I was just five,' I say, remembering the first day she came home from hospital, mothered in pink blankets, wailing quietly. 'And after that, she took over.'

'She got all the attention?'

I nod. 'In those pre-Doll photos, I'm always there in my pigtails, squeezed between Mom and Dad. Happy and adored.'

'And then . . . ?'

'And then Doll came along and took my space. I became the shadow.' I start to cry. 'Makes me feel so guilty, even saying this. It was like Doll sucked up all their love and I was left on the sidelines. A sub.'

'I can see how it could happen,' Steve says, brushing tears off my cheeks. 'I suppose it wasn't just another baby sister. This one needed more time and love.'

'That's exactly it, Steve.' I sniffle, trying to compose myself. 'Doll's sick, she won't eat, she won't sleep, she needs physio, she's injuring herself . . . it just went on and on.'

He pulls me close, and I can feel his breath on my cheek.

'I know I shouldn't be saying all this stuff.'

He shushes me. 'No, Andi. It's good to talk about it. I'm listening. Every kid needs attention, don't I know it! It hurt so much when my ma disappeared out of my life.'

'It does . . . hurt. You know what it's like, Steve. Even now, if anything is wrong in my life, they say, "You're the lucky one, Andi," or, "Be grateful, Andi. Look at poor Doll." It makes me so mad.' The words tumble out like gravel.

'Once, when I was eleven, I won a silver pen for best student. I ran all the way home, couldn't wait to tell them. But do you know what they said?'

Steve rubs my arm.

'They said, "Well done, Andi, that's great." I was so excited. I tried to show them how to change the colours, but they were already saying, "Look! Doll is holding the spoon herself. Isn't that progress, Andi?" The prize meant nothing.'

I pull out a tissue. 'You know what I did, Steve? I threw the pen in the bin later that evening – and they never even noticed.'

I look at him. 'Do you think I'm a bad sister? Do you? 'Cos I feel mean. And now I'm talking about her when I know she's so ill.'

He cups his hands around my face. 'No way, babe. Are you mad? I totally get you. And you won't lose her.' He wipes a tear from my cheek. 'But you should talk to your parents, Andi. I bet they don't have a clue. Seriously, like.'

I half smile. 'Maybe now isn't a good time.'

'State of you,' he said, taking the tissue and dabbing my eyes. 'You're a sight for sore eyes, Andi Redmond.' He kisses my eyelids. With Steve, I feel it's safe to be the real me.

He leans in and kisses me, putting his arms inside my parka. I can feel his cold hands through my school shirt, but his lips are warm, and I lean into his kiss. For a few minutes I forget everything. I forget Chelsea. I forget school. I forget Doll. My brain shuts down; I'm feeling, not thinking. And inside, I feel a lightness I've never felt before.

*

My dad is at the front door when I get home. He points to Steve's receding figure. 'Who's that? I don't like the look of him.'

'You don't have to.'

'Where were you? It's almost six o'clock.' He puts his palm up. 'No, don't tell me. I'll guess. You had detention because you bunked off school this morning?' He rolls his eyes. 'You take the biscuit.'

'I went to the hospital.'

'I know, and you had no permission to do that.'

'You're welcome,' I say. 'Only doing my bit for the family!' I shout the last bit as I march past him up the stairs.

My mobile pings a message. It's not a number I recognise. I recoil when I open it. Hasn't he told you about us? And there's a picture of Steve and Chelsea. She's planting a kiss on his cheek as he gazes at her, smiling.

I press my face hard against the duvet, hoping the soft material will stifle the sound of my sobs.

CHAPTER 34

DOLL

I'm lying on my side. The sun is hot, and there's a breeze rippling over my face. Like the gentlest hand.

I can smell puke. I start to retch, and it takes me back to all the times I've been sick. The familiar churning inside, the acid burning my throat, and then having to spit out the foul-tasting liquid. The sickening smell as it sprayed onto my top or pretty new dress. The aftertaste like rotting lemons. The panic around me. 'Quick, quick, Doll's sick again!' My cardigan pulled off, baby wipes retrieved to clean my face. 'Quick, grab some TCP. A cloth.' My vest and top carefully peeled over my head, fresh ones bundled on. Vomit, still unseen, dribbling down my nose, making me gag. 'Oh no, there's more . . . quick, another cloth.'

After a few minutes it would all be over. Washed face. A spoon bull-dozed into my mouth. Some cooling medicine poured down my throat, pink and minty. Hair combed. Bib replaced, like I was a baby. The stink of disinfectant. Calm. Inside, some lingering gurgling, an occasional drop of acidy liquid tiptoeing up my throat. On fire.

That's why I started to dig my face – to distract me from the filthy taste and the pain and the drama. And the smell. Who could blame me? But they did. Blame me. 'Stop digging your face, Doll. Do not dig your face.'

Well, they would dig too, if they were me.

How can you fight that fight? Every day? *Come on!*

'She's digging her face again. She won't leave her face alone. Hasn't been sick for a week, Doctor, but she won't stop. Doll's face is destroyed. *What will we do about Doll?*

I hated food. You can see why. Food meant getting sick. I'd often resist. Close my mouth. Hold my lips firm. But they'd win in the end, and all my tears and howls made no difference. I had to eat. So I'd give in after a while. And everyone would be relieved. *Good girl. Good girl.* All the sad faces, exhausted. My mother crying. Tears dropping down on me like shells as she kissed my head. The family worn down . . . by me. In Misery Street.

The blades of grass vibrate in front of me. The vomit is mine. I can feel it in my throat, dribbling down. No smell of TCP though, just the lovely breeze running its fingers over my eyelashes, across my cheek.

I'm starting to remember now. The river. Yes, but am I dead? I can't sit up; there are invisible threads holding me down. Like Gulliver. I close my eyes and open them again. I'm so, so tired.

There's a pair of scuffed boots nearby. One leans against the other, like it's too feeble to stand on its own. *I know how you feel, boot.* The laces are frayed, tips missing. There's a cake of muck around the heels. They look forlorn. As if their owner, in a sudden moment, pulled them off in disgust and just walked away barefoot.

A pair of feet comes into view. Blue-painted toenails. The feet stop in front of me. Just above me, tanned hands rest on tanned knees. A breathless voice says, 'You all right, girl?' The knees hunker down. Slow rivulets of water drip down the skin, shin to ankle bone. I move my gaze upwards. A pair of blue-green eyes, lips pursed, sleek black hair; ironed wet. A small puddle forms around her feet. 'You all right?' she repeats. Ragged breathing.

I close my eyes and lean forward as pink liquid sputters from my mouth. The girl steps aside, reaches behind me, slaps my back, helps me into a sitting position. I wipe my mouth with the back of my hand as she hands me a mug of water. I drink it shakily and spit out pink foam.

'That pink stuff is your lungs coming up,' she says.

I feel dizzy.

'You gave me a fright. Didn't know if you were dead or alive.'

She kneels down closer. I can feel her breath on my face. Black pants reaching just above her knees. Black T-shirt with *Rebel* across the front in white. Drenched. She's about twelve, pretty, with teeth from a toothpaste ad.

'Hello. Do you talk?'

I smile. So grateful. My throat hurts. 'Yes,' I whisper. 'Yes, thank you . . .'

'Tiger. My name's Tiger. Don't even ask.' She rolls her eyes. 'What's yours?'

'Doll.'

'Well' – she licks her lips – 'you do look a bit like a doll, that's for sure. No offence.'

I take another sip of water. 'Thought I was a goner.'

'Well, you came close, for sure. You're lucky I came along. Weirdest thing I've ever seen. One minute the river was calm. The next, it's chaos.'

We both look at the river now, tumbling along like something from a fairytale.

'I know.'

'You okay now? You're looking a bit better.' Tiger leaps to her feet like a panther. 'I think you need to get some warm things on.' She points to her dripping clothes. 'I'm getting out of these too, and then, I think, a nice warm drink. After that, me and Mitch will help you get home.'

'Mitch?'

She moves towards the cabin, and I can see another horse next to Poppy. Tiger pulls something from her saddlebag and disappears inside. I can hear the kettle singing, and she reappears a few minutes later with two mugs. 'Come on, some hot mint tea and chocolate biscuits. Good for shock – and we've both had a shock.'

I change into dry clothes. Comb my hair. Rinse out my mouth. I still feel a bit shaky, but the warm tea and the taste of melting chocolate is rebooting me.

'What happened, Tiger?' Funny name for a girl, but she did say don't ask, so I won't.

She runs her palm over her wet hair. 'You don't remember anything?'

'No. Just that I was sinking, and then I woke on the grass there getting sick.'

'Poor girl, you.' She reaches over, taps my shoulder. Fixes her hair behind her ear. 'Well,' she says, taking a bite from her biscuit, 'I jumped in when I saw you – I have a gold for life-saving or I wouldn't have bothered, to be honest – and I grabbed you by the hair and dragged you to the surface. Like this.' She makes a dragging motion on her own hair.

'The river was actually receding at that stage, so I was able to get you back onto the bank.' She shakes her head. 'Another minute and you would have been dead, for sure. Your face was turning blue. Not a good look.'

She frowns. 'I put you on your side so you wouldn't swallow your tongue. It's a different story when you're doing it for an exam and for real.'

She wrinkles her nose.

'I gave you mouth-to-mouth, kept your airways clear. That got you going.' She reaches for a biscuit. 'Then you started coughing and puking . . . but hey, you were alive, so mission accomplished.' She mock salutes, cupping her hand to her forehead. 'Yes siree, two present and correct, sir.'

We both laugh.

'You're a hero. You are, Tiger. You saved my life. You don't forget that, someone who saves your life.'

She shrugs. 'Like I said, I have a gold in life-saving. Anyway, you don't stop to think, really; you just go for it, don't you?'

'I suppose. Thank you anyway.'

'What's your horse's name?' She looks over her shoulder and jumps to her feet. I follow her over, still a bit wobbly.

'It's Poppy.'

Tiger rubs her mane. 'They love affection, don't they? And they're so clever.' She laughs. 'I'd say Mitch is getting jealous. They can pick up on emotions, you know. Look at Poppy – her ears are forward; that means she's happy. Aw. She's so friendly.'

I rub Mitch, and he nuzzles closer.

'He likes you.' She smiles and reaches into her saddlebag. 'Here, give him this.' Tiger produces some carrot pieces. 'Keep your palm flat or he'll eat your fingers.'

Mitch chomps noisily. Poppy nudges Tiger, and we both laugh.

'See what I mean? Clever girl, Poppy,' she says, as she feeds her some carrot.

The sun is high in the sky as we stretch out on the grass. Everything looks the same as before. The river continues about its business. Birds sing, insects hum, and the sun spreads her warm fingers over us all. A purple butterfly flitters past my nose and settles on Tiger's knee. I can see her velvet wings edged with white lace. A bee nuzzles a nearby cornflower. All is right with this beautiful world. And hey, I'm so alive.

But the flooded river? That was no natural storm. The Orb has been disturbed. Major Tom is letting us know how easily he can unleash the chaos. It's his message to the Grandmothers, scrawled across the sky. I shiver in the heat.

Tiger's eyes are closed, her long lashes casting a shadow over her cheeks. What am I going to tell her? I've only been talking a few days, and already I'm spinning lies.

As if she can read my thoughts, she opens her eyes and leans up on her elbow.

'Better get you home, Doll,' she says. 'What time are you expected back?'

Here goes. I swallow.

'Actually, I'm on my way to my uncle's house.' I say it casually. 'He's lives way up Glenshiquin, and . . . and . . . he's expecting me. My parents are . . . away.'

She looks surprised. 'You're travelling all that way . . . alone?'

I start to pack my stuff. I jam on my straw hat, brushing off the wilted flower-chain I made yesterday.

'Aren't you afraid, on your own?'

'No. Aren't you?'

'Of course not. But I'm not heading up there. It's at least two days' ride and another one on foot . . . and it's not safe, Doll.'

'I have a map,' I say.

She whistles when I show her the route. 'No way. You can't do that journey on your own.' She puts her hands on her hips. 'There are people, dangerous people. It's not safe.'

Do I tell her? The Grandmothers warned me to tell no one.

'Listen. I am heading off now. You go home, Tiger. The Gods will guide me and lead me.'

Where did that come from? I half believe it. Well, I am the Child of Summer, aren't I?

Who nearly drowned, a voice in my head says.

Tiger starts to pack up her things. Wet clothes laid out on the grass have dried, and she rolls them up. 'I'm coming with you.'

My heart jumps. Having her as my friend is the stuff of dreams.

'No, your parents will be looking for you. And you just said it, it's dangerous.'

'No, they won't. My mum is away. My granddad – he lives with us – and he thinks I'm in my friend Sylvie's house.' She points her finger to the side of her forehead. 'He's with the birds . . . so I can go off on my own whenever my mum's away. He doesn't ask questions. Lives for his pigeons – he really is with the birds.' She laughs, and even though I don't really get it, I laugh too.

'And your dad?'

She hesitates. 'He died when I was five.'

'I'm sorry.'

She shrugs.

I so want her with me, but how will I shake her off when I get close to Major Tom's hideout? I can't tell her my secret.

'Okay. You can come with me, but you must promise to turn around tomorrow and go back. I will manage the last bit on my own.'

She's lacing up her boots and stops to look up at me. 'Listen, girl. I'm doin' *you* a favour, not the other way round. So don't spell out the rules for me, okay?'

'I'm just saying . . .' I trail off. I don't want to fight with Tiger; she's my new buddy.

She smiles. 'Let's get tacked up and move on.'

We tidy up the cabin and close the door firmly. The sun is slanting behind the cliff face now, turning the rock from grey to orange. We continue along the forest path, skirting the river.

'I love to disappear into the mountains at weekends and during holidays,' Tiger is saying. 'I like to think I'm an explorer, and when I grow up, that's what I'm going to do. For real. Trek through deserts, fly over the universe, travel back and forward in time.'

'Wow. What a plan.'

'There's so much happening in science,' she says. 'I can't wait to get out and explore the universe.'

'Sounds like you have it all worked out.'

'What about you, Doll?'

How can I tell her that up to a few days ago, I just wanted out? A goner on a couch. Can't tell her that.

'Me? Oh, I always wanted to escape, to find adventure and feel alive.'

'Yes, yes, that's me too, Doll. Escaping into adventure. You and me both.'

In Almazova, there's no one saying *God love us*. Tiger, my dream friend, is actually talking to me like I'm a normal person. A real person. I'm somebody now. I'm really somebody.

So why do I feel so uneasy? Why is my gut telling me to watch out? Tiger is my friend, isn't she? It's going to be more fun with a friend. So why do I feel like something's not right?

Tiger's blue-green eyes are staring at me. 'What's up, Doll? You are okay, aren't you?' She's leaning back in her saddle, the reins looped around her fingers. Back straight, head tall. Like she was born to it. A ten. A topper.

'You'd tell me, wouldn't you, if you didn't feel right? There is such a thing as dry drowning, you know; you survive for a bit, and then' – she clicks her fingers – 'it's lights out.' She chews the inside of her mouth.

'I'm fine.' I change the subject. 'Do you ever get lonely, Tiger? When you come out here on your own with no one to talk to?'

She shakes her head. 'I have Mitch,' she says, leaning forward and patting his mane. 'And nature.' She looks at me. 'And now I have you for a while. That's enough. And who knows what adventures we'll have? Come on, boy.' She raps Mitch's flank and tears off, lowering her head as she weaves through the trees. 'Come on, Doll. Race you . . .'

I ease Poppy into a gentle trot and follow Tiger upriver, trying to push the anxiety out of my mind.

Tiger's waiting for me under the shade of some pine trees.

My back is sore, and I'm thirsty. The sun is slipping behind the cliff face on the far side of the river. I stop alongside her, take a drink, and pass her the bottle.

'I don't think I'll last much longer in this saddle.' I pull out the map and trace my finger along the route, and I can see it's a steep climb for most of tomorrow.

'That's Inchiquin, next to Glenshiquin,' she says, pointing to twin peaks high above us.

She shades her eyes, scanning the horizon, and rests her gaze on the narrow gap between the mountains. 'That's where we're going, Doll. It's a tough climb.'

I nod. I'd say Tiger knows everything.

'Here's a good spot to camp,' Tiger says. 'We can have a swim then and cool down.' She pats Mitch's mane. 'You must be tired, boy.' Mitch snorts softly and dips his head to graze.

'Count me out for the swim,' I say.

She leaps off the saddle in one easy movement – so annoying. Tiger peels off her T-shirt and races in, like Superman, diving under. She somersaults and doubles back towards me. 'Blow me down, it's cold.' She leaps up, sprays water in a circle, and rubs her face.

'Join me, Doll.' She splashes me. 'Come on, pussycat, you'll be safe; I'm here to save you.' She laughs again and backstrokes downriver. I'd say she's good at everything.

I dangle my feet in the water. When I lean forward, I see my reflection. I can't really believe it's me. I look happy, my scars barely there. I touch my cheek. The holes are closed over and smooth. Just a tiny dip in the skin. Those wounds are like an alien thing now, junk from an old life.

As I gaze into the water, another face reflects back from behind me. I spin around, my heart thudding like a drum, but there's nothing there. Just a grassy bank scattered with daisies.

Tiger is still swimming, graceful as a ballet dancer, and as I watch, the poem comes to me in a flash and catapults me into another world. Andi's voice, high and clear. She's about twelve, practising her poem for her electrocution exam. Drove us all mad reciting it again and again for weeks beforehand. 'The Tyger', by William Blake.

> *'Tyger, Tyger, burning bright*
> *In the forest of the night . . .'*

'With feeling,' Mom would say. 'Say it with feeling, Andi. Mind your diction too, love.'

'What does it mean, anyway?' my granny asked one night. We were all sitting round the fire, the telly on mute. Me on my couch. I could nearly sing the damn poem at this stage.

'It's celebrating the beauty of a tiger,' my dad said.

'Doesn't sound like that to me,' Granny said, catching my eye and winking. 'Sounds like a holy terror.'

Andi shushed us. 'Just listen, please. The exam's tomorrow. It's not a joke, guys . . .

> *'When the stars threw down their spears*
> *And watered heaven with their tears . . .'*

The image fades.

Tiger is dressed now and shouting instructions over her shoulder. 'C'mon, we need to get a fire started.' I jump to my feet, glad of the distraction. We gather a mound of sticks, and Tiger, with a lighter and some puffing and blowing, gets a flame going. 'See, easy-peasy when you know how,' she smiles. Tiger smiles a lot.

'You're good at everything,' I say as I hunker down next to her. 'Saving people, riding a horse, lighting fires, swimming.'

She straightens up, wags her finger like a teacher. 'And,' she says, 'I've even got dinner sorted. Ta-da.' She takes a bow, waves her hands towards her saddlebag, and pulls out a parcel. She sweeps me a sort of curtsey. 'Madame, would you care for some trout?' She opens up the paper wrapping, and two brown-speckled fish drop onto the grass. 'Pan-fried, perhaps?'

She puts her finger to her lips. 'Don't tell anyone. I didn't catch them with my fishing rod.'

She picks up the fish with both hands and places them on a flat rock nearby.

'After that flash flood today, some fish were washed up on the bank, and some of them' – she points down – 'didn't make it back.'

'Add *finding dinner* to the list,' I say, clapping my hands. 'You're a topper, Tiger.'

She pulls a small penknife from her pocket, hacks off the heads, cuts a line down the middle of each fish, and scrapes out the slippery insides. Yeuch. She rinses them off in the river. Job done. There's cooked rice too, dried fruit, two oranges. Yum. We have lots to share.

The last of the sun's rays cast a golden light as we sit cross-legged around the fire. The fish is sizzling in the pan, and my mouth is watering. Food actually *is* glorious, like the song says. Tiger tosses the trout onto our plates, and we tuck in.

'It's delicious,' I say.

'And nutritious,' Tiger says, professor-like, waving her fork in the air, pushing pretend glasses off her nose. She is so funny. We both laugh.

'Tell me about your mom,' I say.

'What do you want to know?' she asks. 'She's a single mom. I love her to bits. Works in our local bakery.'

'What else about her? Is she kind?'

'Very kind. Makes up for not having a dad.'

'I couldn't imagine not having a dad. Do you miss him?'

'Hard to miss someone you hardly met.' She sighs. 'My mom doesn't talk about him. She won't go there. So I don't know anything about him, really. Just that he died in a riding accident on a ranch.'

'Do you remember him at all?'

She pauses, her fork in mid-air. Looks straight ahead. 'I do remember when I was about four. We were at the ranch. I remember men moving about with lassoes, training and feeding the animals. My dad lifting me onto a horse. The smell of tobacco off him. I remember him wrapping his arms around me, holding the reins.'

She stops. Her eyes gaze along the darkening river.

'Go on.'

She looks at me again. 'I remember hollering as the horse took off, the sound of the hooves and the thrill, the wind in my face. I was petrified at first, but I knew my dad had me safe. He kissed the top of my head. Told me how proud of me he was. When we returned, he shouted to the men, and they came over in their big hats, smiling. "Well done, girlie." '

She closes her eyes for a second. ' "My girl," he says, "One to watch. She's one to watch. A cracker." '

There's a catch in her voice, and she rubs her eye. 'That's the only memory I have,' she says. 'I'm sure I've filled in some gaps, but I can still feel – when I go back there in my head – how I felt then. It's very real.'

'How did you feel?'

'Safe,' she says. 'Like a princess.'

She throws some more wood on the fire, and it crackles, the flames leaping up and warming our faces.

The river, silver in the moonlight, tiptoes downstream. An owl hoots in the distance. I think of my own dad, and I feel like crying.

'I've checked,' she says. 'I've searched our house for a photograph, a letter, some memory of my dad . . . nothing. Every bit of evidence removed, like a crime scene.'

'You found nothing?'

'Just a birthday card. I came across it in an old cookery book. Slipped out when I was looking for a recipe for a school assignment. The card was for Mum.'

'What did it say?'

'There was a rose on the front, and inside he wrote, *With ever fondest and truest love.*'

'Sounds romantic,' I say. 'Your mom must've been broken-hearted when he died. She can't even talk about him.'

She places her palm across her heart. 'When I grow up, I'm going to find out all about him. I never said that aloud before. But I am.'

She jumps to her feet. 'We better get some sleep. You're a good listener, Doll. I'm glad we met.'

I take my purple coat from my bag and button it up before I slip into my sleeping bag. Tiger puts on a khaki jacket. We both yawn at exactly the same time and laugh again. She slips me a piece of chocolate, and we let it melt, sweet drips of Heaven in our mouths.

The stars are blazing above us as we snuggle down into the fleecy warmth. The water laps gently against the bank. Two swans fly overhead like slow-motion arrows.

'That's where I'm going someday,' Tiger says, pointing up to the night sky. 'Travelling on secret missions beyond our universe.'

I think of Nan-Nan and close my eyes. 'Sleep tight,' I say.

Tiredness pulls me down, and I'm sailing across the borders of sleep. There's a sign at the entrance saying *Here Be Monsters*, but I keep paddling through . . .

I wake with a jolt and scream when I see them. Staring down at us are a circle of hideous painted faces.

CHAPTER 35

DAN

'Come on, Sal. You don't need to be at her bedside day and night. It's Friday. I'm just locking up. Why not leave now, and I'll organise dinner?' I'm doing my best to stay calm. 'I mean, there's nothing you can do while she's like this.'

'That's not the point.'

'What *is* the bloody point?'

'She's been restless. I want to be here if she wakes up.'

'But the doctor said he didn't expect any change till after the weekend.'

'I don't care what he said, Dan. I'm her mother.'

'Her martyr, you mean.' I shouldn't have said it.

There's a thick silence, then an exaggerated sigh. 'Well, someone's got to do it.' As she hangs up, I can almost hear her teeth clenching.

I shut down my PC and pocket my car keys. There's no talking to that woman.

Joe puts his head around the door. 'O'Mahony's for a pint?'

I shake my head. 'No, I'm not in the mood.' He waits for more, but I wave him on. 'Go on, enjoy. See you Monday.'

I hear Shirley's heels on the corridor.

'All set to lock up?' She stands in the doorway, her coat over her arm. 'You going to O'Mahony's, Dan?'

'No, you?'

'No. I'll take a lift, though, if you're heading home.'

'Sure. I might stop for a bottle of red on the way.'

She nudges me as we head into the car park. 'Romantic evening lined up?'

I give her a scowl. 'No chance. I'm dining alone. Sally's at the hospital again, and Andi's out.'

We stop off in Main Street, and I'm in and out of the Wine Vault in less than five minutes. Shirley is picking up bread and olives in Colbert's.

'Nice guy, Rob Colbert,' she says, getting back in the car and buckling her seat belt. 'He's having a hard time, apparently.'

I pull out into the Friday traffic. 'Yeah, Joanne has MS. They're a good team, and I'm doing what I can to cut them a bit of slack.'

'Fair play, Dan.'

'It's not much, just giving him a break on the interest under the radar . . . but for Rob, it's a lifeline.'

In less than ten minutes, I'm pulling up outside Shirley's apartment. She fishes out her keys.

'Come on, you're coming in,' she says, gesturing for me to turn off the ignition. 'For one.'

I hesitate for a beat, then kill the engine. 'Just the one. My treat.' I retrieve the wine from the back seat.

'Deal,' she says, flashing me a smile. 'And there's a chicken-and-ham pie I can heat up if you're hungry.'

'You've swung me,' I say, locking the car and following her into the flat. I wasn't looking forward to going home to an empty house.

Inside, Shirley is switching on two table lamps, and a gas fire remote sends yellow flames licking up the chimney. She draws the curtains and gestures to a metal wine rack. 'Choose one there, Dan, if you like. The opener is on the bookshelf behind you.' She disappears into the small kitchen and returns with two glasses. 'Won't be a sec. Sit down.' She motions to an oversize cream sofa facing the fire.

I open the Rioja from the Wine Vault and pour.

'Nice place you have here,' I say, as she sets a bowl of olives and crackers on the coffee table.

'Help yourself.' She takes my jacket, and when she reappears after a few minutes, she's changed into a grey wool dress.

'Pie's warming in the oven. It won't be long.' She takes the glass I offer her. 'Rioja. Perfect.'

She folds herself into the armchair by the fire and takes a long drink. 'How are you, Dan? You look tired.'

I loosen my tie and stretch out. 'I am. It's been a long week, but' – I wave my glass in a circle – 'good wine, good company, and dinner warming. Just what I needed.' There's a delicious aroma of baking wafting in from the kitchen. 'Do you like cooking?'

'For friends, yes. I like the company.' She refills my glass, and I can feel the warm glow of the wine relaxing me. 'How is your daughter? Doll, isn't it?'

'Stable, you know . . . that's all they'll say. I don't know . . .'

'What don't you know, Dan?' She leans forward, swirling the liquid in her glass.

'I don't know . . . anything, Shirley. Life is a tangled mess, isn't it, sometimes?'

Today, I had a mad impulse. How could I tell her this? A sudden urge to run away from my respectable-bank-manager-golf-playing--father-of-three life, a life I'd carefully crafted for myself. A life that has felt increasingly hollow. It looked real – but when you get closer, you realise your hand can slice clean through it, like a hologram. And earlier – and I'm not going to say this to Shirley – earlier, talking to Sally, I felt an indifference descend on me, an absence of feeling. And that scared me, that disconnect. It was something new to me, an extension of how I've been feeling for months.

The wine helps, though. And Shirley's voice soothes me.

She gets up to take an olive from the bowl and comes to sit next to me. 'Whatever it is, Dan, don't think about it tonight.' She takes my glass and places it on the coffee table. 'Life *is* messy,' she says, rubbing my arm gently. 'But we must get out of our heads and into our hearts.' She places her hand on her chest. 'It's all about the heart.'

'Spoken like a true sales-woman,' I say, trying to lighten the conversation. I can smell her perfume again, and it's making my pulse quicken, like one of Pavlov's dogs.

She leans closer and turns her brown eyes towards me. 'You don't have to be perfect, you know. I think you're too hard on yourself.'

I hold her gaze, caught by the gentleness of her voice. I don't know what makes me say it. 'You're a beautiful woman, Shirley.'

She rests her glass on the coffee table and turns back towards me, holding my eyes. And then, as if in slow motion, she places her hand on my tie and gently pulls me to her. Gently enough for me to gather my thoughts and resist if I want, slowly enough for me to know what's coming next. And I still don't resist when she cups my chin with her soft fingers and grazes her mouth across the side of my mine. And I don't resist – I don't want to resist – as she moves her lips along mine and kisses me. I can feel the wool of her dress pressing against my shirt and the warmth of her underneath the thin material, and I can hear her heartbeat, like a time bomb.

Her tongue explores my mouth, tentatively, as if it isn't sure what it's looking for, and the sensation is thrilling. It's an ache. I can taste the wine on her breath, and I wrap my arm around her shoulder, cushioning her head against my chest. Her hair tickles my skin.

I trace my fingers along her throat and reach for her mouth. Sensual kissing is a language. A way to slowly say things and express emotions wordlessly, and I know this beautiful conversation is only beginning.

'Oh God.' I push her away. Run my palms down my face. What the fuck am I thinking?

She pulls back, looking hurt. 'You want this as much as I do.'

'I know. I'm sorry. It's my fault.'

'Don't say that, Dan.' She takes my hand in hers and traces circles on my palm. 'Don't complicate things. God, I want you; you feel the same. Enjoy it.'

I straighten up, folding her hand away from me. 'You know it's not that simple, Shirley. I wish to Christ it was.'

She puts some little distance between us. 'You're married. I'm okay with that.' She reaches for her glass.

'But I'm not.'

'Didn't look like that to me.' She bites her lip.

'I . . . I'm sorry. Jesus, Shirley, I do find you attractive, but I'm married. And I can't do this to Sally.' I straighten my tie and get to my feet. 'I need to go, Shirley.'

She sucks in her lips, and her eyes are cold now. 'Sure, if that's what you want. I'll get your jacket.'

We stand there in the doorway, a few feet apart, the air still crackling between us. 'I don't want any awkwardness. I hope . . . I mean, you know, working together. Can we forget this ever happened?'

She hands me my jacket. 'Nothing happened, Dan. Get over yourself.'

She folds her arms, leaning against the door-jamb. 'Why did you come here this evening? I'm just curious.'

'Company, a drink with you? I wasn't analysing it, Shirley. It was a snap decision.'

She rolls her eyes. 'Yeah, right.' And when I don't move, she says, 'Go, Dan. Will you just go.'

*

I'm relieved there's no one home. The house is dark and silent. I pull on my running gear and head out into the rain for a long trek. I need to clear my head. And as I sprint off down the Monastery Road, I can't help but think there's a shitload of trouble coming my way.

CHAPTER 36

DOLL

My heart drops like a shot bird. One of the faces crouches over me. I'm sitting up, shivering in my purple coat. It's daybreak.

Tiger says, 'Do whatever they say, Doll.'

I stare at their sandaled feet. Skin like tree bark. They have machetes tucked into leather belts. Knuckles to split a face in two. Diamond Jesus, I think I'm going to pass out.

I can hear the horses whinnying. They sense danger. *A bit late, lads. Why didn't you warn us earlier!*

One of the men shouts something at me. The painted face scoops me over his shoulder like I'm a bag of sugar. He strides towards two canoes near the bank. From my upside-down angle, I can see five pairs of feet following us, and I can hear Tiger screaming as we're both lowered into a canoe.

'Can you understand?' she's saying. 'Please. We're just kids. We can't leave our horses here. Please . . .'

But they don't listen. It's like we're toys instead of people. The canoe nearly tips over as the men jump aboard. The last thing I see before they put a sack over my head is the fear in Tiger's eyes, and I know this is not a Girl Guide's adventure in the wild. The canoe glides out into the river and we veer right, paddling upstream.

I hear the *slosh-slosh*ing of the paddles slapping and pushing through the water. As we gather speed, a drum-beat starts up behind me.

Rat a boom, rat a boom, rat a boom, boom, boom.
Rat a boom, rat a boom, rat a boom, boom, boom.

It's a chilling sound. The rhythm is driving us faster and faster, till it feels we're skimming over the water like seabirds. There's no talk, just the smell of sweat and the spray of water on my skin. And the sound of Tiger sobbing.

My purple coat is too warm, but I'm afraid to take it off. I sink further into the floor. What use am I? When will I learn you can't turn a sow's ear into a pink purse? Granny used to say some people had notions. Notions like the Kerry goat, she said. Well, I had notions. Notions of being a big hero and saving the world. Nell said I was powerful. Hello? I don't think so. I mean, she didn't know me five minutes. They invent all that stuff to fool you into taking chances. Taking chances to suit *them*.

Rat a boom, rat a boom, rat a boom, boom, boom.
Rat a boom, rat a boom, rat a boom, boom, boom.

Is the drum some sort of message – *We've found food?*

When I really think about this Orb, what's in it for me? They'll just buckaroo me home when my work is done. *Thanks, Doll, you're a star. Now off with you; we're done.*

I'm such an idiot. My head hurts, and my heart slides south. I hunch sideways, try to sleep. Maybe I should say some Hey Marys – a whole rosemary might help. Hail Mary full of grace, blessed is the foot of Diamond Jesus. But I can't concentrate on my prayers with the bloody drum behind me.

Rat a boom, rat a boom, rat a boom, boom, boom.
Rat a boom, rat a boom, rat a boom, boom, boom.

Well, at least I'm living, though. I'm actually living and not just a shadow on a couch. For such a long time I was like a human collection box, people dropping in their coin of sympathy. Keep it! Shove it!

I took a chance, though; isn't that something? I went for it. I sailed off my windowsill; not everyone would've. I could've fallen and cracked my skull.

By the time the boat slows and the drumming stops, I feel a little bit better. I'm not giving up just yet. I won't be a pussycat. No matter what they do.

My mouth is sand. I resist the urge to dig my face. That's abnormal, and I'm not that kid anymore. I'm the new golden Doll, the Child of Summer. I need to remember that now more than ever. *Even if they're going to eat us.*

There are voices, greetings; the canoe is dragged to the bank. I'm hoisted up again. Firefighter's lift. The air feels thick with the hum of insects. It's hot inside the coat, and my legs feel like jelly.

More voices. The sound of horses. We move into shade. A merciful cool. Footsteps. A girl's voice. I'm dropped onto what feels like a rug. The footsteps retreat. The voices fade. Silence. I ease the sack off my head and see Tiger right next to me. I reach out and hug her tight. We stay like that, locked together, for a while.

We're in a hut. It smells like a spicebox. There's a low table with a bowl of water and two mugs. We scoop up the water and drink, letting the icy liquid leak down our necks. Happiness is a drink of cold water. We splash our faces.

A girl comes with some oranges. She's pretty as an elf. Her face is painted yellow and purple, and she's wearing a long red dress. She leaves without saying a word.

We sit and peel the oranges and sink our teeth into the juicy flesh. The floor is bare earth, scattered with rugs and pine needles. Sheepskins and quilts are piled against one wall, and there is a carved dresser in a corner with cups and plates sitting on top. Dried flowers are pinned to the walls, and there's a wood-stove in the corner with logs stacked on either side. A cosy home.

Tiger is sitting cross-legged, popping the last pieces of orange into her mouth.

'This is my fault,' I say. 'You did warn me. I should've listened.'

Tiger finishes chewing. 'You're right. I did warn you.' She takes a drink. 'But it was my idea to come with you. So don't go blaming yourself. You're only a kid.'

'What now?' I say. 'Will they eat us?'

She smiles at that. 'No, Doll. These are remote tribes who live like they've done for centuries . . . but cannibals? I don't think so. They often have disputes with neighbouring tribes, but it's all contained. They sort things out their own way.'

'Would they harm us?'

Tiger streaks her fingers through her hair. 'I don't know that. Some of the tribes have links to criminals. To them, everyone is an outsider. Expendable.'

I'm not sure what that means, but I can guess. She looks worried and smooths her hair back again. 'Let's hope . . . or else . . .' She makes a slicing motion across her throat. 'Or else, you and me? We're history, kid.'

Will I tell her? I was warned by the Grandmothers to say nothing about my mission or my identity, but I want to make her feel better, safer. But even more, I want to impress her.

'It's okay,' I say. 'Listen, I've got something to tell you.'

She looks at me, waiting, but the girl in the red dress is back, motioning us to follow her.

Outside, there is busyness. Men cutting wood; women in coloured robes taking washing to the river nearby. I can smell spicy cooking and wood smoke. Children play under the shade of tall trees, swinging from ropes. They stare at us as we pass and fall silent.

We stop at a large hut, and the girl pushes back the door and leads us through. The room is dim, and as my eyes adjust, I notice a wiry man, not much taller than Tiger, smoking in the gloom. His skin is covered in tattoos, red and black whorls and curves that coil and snake up and down his body. He is sitting on a carved chair and gets up as we approach. Yellow smile. Gold earring.

He gives a small bow. 'Good afternoon, young ladies.'

His voice is deep and rich. He crushes his cigarette under a sandaled foot.

'Welcome to my home.'

I look at Tiger. We weren't expecting this. Our mouths are open. Is he taking the mickey?

I find my voice. The voice of the Child of Summer. 'Well,' I say, 'we didn't have much of a choice, did we? We're not exactly guests, are we? We didn't choose to be here. We were dragged here.' My own words give me energy. Tiger is looking at me as if to say, *Don't blow it. Be nice to him.*

'Tell us, mister,' I say. 'Why are we here?'

He extends his arm. 'Pleased to meet you. My name is Archon.' He says it like *Awrchon.* 'And you?'

We shake his hand.

'I'm Doll.'

'I'm Tiger.'

He looks at us, smiling. 'I hope you've recovered from your journey.'

I look at him crossly. 'From our ordeal, you mean. You've kidnapped us.'

I know it's a crime.

When someone is taking a nap and they're a kid and then someone takes them away, that's kidnapping. Kinda like what Nan-Nan did to me. I'm just thinking that now.

'That's a serious allegation you're making there.' He motions us to sit at a nearby table. He pulls up a chair for himself and leans towards us. The candle on the table throws his face into shadow. The tattoos darken and the whorls on his face move as he talks.

'What were you two doing in the valley?'

He doesn't wait for an answer.

'There are ley lines you do not cross. Am I to believe that you are unaccompanied?' His voice is sharp. He folds muscly arms, waiting.

Tiger is straight in.

'Look, we're sorry. It's true, there are lines we should not cross.' She bites her lip. 'Truth is, sir,' she says, 'we were planning to climb up to the pass between Glenshiquin and Inchiquin.'

He grimaces. 'That's dangerous territory. Cutthroats and criminals.'

'Doll's uncle lives there, and he's expecting her.'

Archon's eyes widen. Doesn't believe a word of it, and Tiger is beginning to see how unlikely my story is. Unless my uncle is a criminal – that would explain a lot.

He leans towards me. 'Your uncle?'

'Yes, sir.' I must think fast. More lies. Practice makes a perfect liar. 'Yes. No. I mean . . . Sam, Uncle Sam – he has traumatic stress. He needed to recover, to be alone.' I try to measure their faces. 'I have a message for him. From my parents?'

He doesn't believe me. He calls out over his shoulder, and the elf-like girl appears like magic. He says something we don't understand.

Tiger looks puzzled. Archon gets up, paces around the table. An eagle tattoo stretches across his spine, the beak nipping the base of his scalp.

'Maybe this will explain why I "kidnapped" you, as you so ungraciously put it. What you will see in a moment will shock you . . . and remember, this could be your fate.'

We wait, staring at the entrance as five children enter the room. My special knees are knocking together again, and when Tiger clutches my arm, I can feel her trembling. I think I'm going to faint. Tiger's olive skin has turned white, and her eyes are shut tight. Her mouth is forming the words *no, no, no* and she's shaking her head. *No, no, no.*

'Come closer, children.' Archon crooks his finger, and they shuffle shyly towards him.

Five children – two boys and three girls – stand before us. Puppy eyes, thin faces, sparkling teeth. The girls wear orange cotton skirts with matching tops. Fat ribbons in their hair. The boys' little chests glisten from the heat.

I stare back. *They have no hands.* Each child obediently holds out their arms, each one cut off at the wrist. Stumps puckered and scarred.

I start to cry. Tiger puts her arms around me. The children file out.

'And that,' Archon says, 'is what we rescued you from. Do you understand? *We rescued you.*'

He sits back down at the table and pours us a mug of orange juice. His voice softens. 'You were alone in wild territory. It's not safe. Your parents must be idiots.'

I wince at that. Tiger bites her lip.

'Why didn't your men take us down the river, closer to home?' I ask.

'There are unspoken boundaries, lines of demarcation. We do not roam beyond these high valleys. This is our home; we protect our own borders, our own people.'

'Who did that to the children?' Tiger asks.

Archon lights a cigarette, inhales deeply.

'Ramish is the leader of a neighbouring tribe.' He pronounces it *Rameeeesh*, spitting it out like a swear.

He leans towards us; I can smell the smoke from his breath.

'He's taken over as chief from his father last year. He is responsible for this . . . this savagery. He has a thirst to kill, to torture, to dominate.' Archon taps the ash from his cigarette. 'He has no honour, shows no mercy. You had a lucky escape this morning. Torturing children is his speciality.'

He takes another drag, exhales through his nose.

'He is a sadist. Even his own warriors fear him.'

'Are you afraid of him, Mr Archon?' I say.

'Cos it sounds like he is. And he's the boss here. If the boss is afraid, you have no hope. Even I know that. Fear is a cursed thing. Being afraid makes you shrink, and when you're afraid, everything, even gold, turns to dust.

He hesitates, cigarette in mid-air, surprised by the question.

'Am I afraid? Am I afraid? No, I am not afraid of Ramish. He is a poison on the landscape. Rotting inside. But I'm afraid for my people and for the children.'

He crushes his cigarette on the floor.

'Let me tell you this. He sells children to criminal gangs. It's cheap labour for them.'

'In the diamond mines?'

'Yes. And anyone who resists Ramish gets their hands severed. And you know what happens then?'

We both shake our heads.

'All those hands are collected in a bucket.' He stops to take a breath, eyes ablaze. 'Then they get strung together like bunting from the boats that travel up and down the river. We see them pass by, drums beating, and the strings of perfect hands, cold as marble, arranged across the black sails, waving like mechanical dolls. Grotesque.'

'His trophies,' I say, shivering. 'May he die roaring.'

Archon looks at me.

'It's an old Irish blessing,' I say. I often heard my granny say it.

'I like it,' he says, nodding and lighting up another cigarette.

Tiger hasn't said much for a while. 'Why don't you stop him, Archon?'

'I have something else to show you,' he says. 'But first, you'll have to excuse me. The shaman will be here soon, and I must prepare a welcome.'

He gets up to leave. 'You are hungry. I will have some food brought to you, and then you will see what Ramish has done to my son. And then' – he points his finger at my face – 'I will want to know who you are.'

'Me?'

He opens the door, looks back. 'Yes, you, Doll. I will want to know who you are.'

When he's gone, I turn to Tiger. 'We need to leave.'

'You're joking. We're good here,' she says. 'Archon is a friend; he will see us safely home.'

'I can't go home. I must press on. I have to get to my uncle's house, and—'

'Stop talking rubbish, Doll. There is no uncle. Archon knows that. So, what's going on?'

'Let's eat first.' Two bowls of soup arrive with banana bread. I gulp down the coconut broth, scraping the bowl with the bread to mop up the last drops.

Tiger eats silently, waiting for me to tell the truth, and I think it's about time I did.

CHAPTER 37

DOLL

Before I can begin my story, Archon is back, and he beckons us to follow. Outside, the men are stacking wood and there's a skewered pig over lit coals. He's dead, though, thanks bit of God. There will be a feast tonight, Archon tells us, in honour of the shaman's visit.

We stop when we reach another hut. There's a woman in a pink dress sitting outside, and she gets up to greet Archon.

Inside, candles flicker on either side of a low carved bed. Dried flowers and herbs bunched together hang from the bedposts, and I can smell incense. Rugs are scattered on an earthen floor. There's a deep stillness in the room.

Lying on the bed, covered in a cloth of gold, is a boy a bit younger than my brother, Will. His eyes are closed, and he is perfectly still. The cloth is edged in black silk, lovingly set in a straight line across his chest. It's a cloth of grief, I think to myself. Is he dead?

Tiger and me step closer, linking arms.

I can see a wolf tattoo on the boy's right shoulder – green eyes, red jaw. A jagged cut runs from the animal's mouth to the boy's wrist, the skin spliced open, pinkly healing. Another cut runs like a swollen purple river down his left arm. I stop myself from reaching out and touching the hand lying outside the cover.

Tiger walks around to the other side of the bed. I keep my head down as a sadness seeps through me and a tear drips onto the boy's palm. His eyes flicker for a moment.

Deep down inside me, I can feel the suffering in this room. It's like a bird beating its feathers around the bed. The boy's hand reminds me of my brother.

Don't you always remember a kind hand that touches you? I remember when Will would come in from school and throw himself next to me on the couch. So annoying. I'd nearly bounce in the air. 'How's it goin' Doll?' He'd switch on the telly, settle for the wrestling, and then, absorbed in the fight, slip his arm around me.

I'd feel his hand resting on my shoulder. A hand that smelled of Taytos and chocolate. A hand that was good at catching a ball, drawing a picture, gripping a hurley. Or giving someone a dig if they were asking for it. A hand that threw itself around me every day.

Will loved me. I don't know how, because I always pushed him away. He kept coming back, hoping maybe that one day I would lean into him. But I never did.

I step back, rub my eyes. Tiger tiptoes towards me. 'Did you see that?'

On a chair in the far corner, a hawk is perched on a bundle of rags. As Archon moves towards it, the bird rises up, and the rags begin to rustle and sway. We both grab each other, frozen to the spot.

'Welcome, Spirit,' Archon whispers as he embraces the bird.

'It's a shaman,' whispers Tiger. 'Like a witch doctor. He's here to help heal the boy. Look' – she points to the figure – 'the bird is just a headdress.'

I can make out a face under the bird hat, the skin carved from clay with raisin eyes that dart about the room. The shaman's cloak is a patchwork of ribbons and rags and feathers and fur, with chains jangling over curly hands. He kisses Archon, embracing him like a brother.

'He must be roasting,' I whisper.

The hawk's dead eyes swivel towards me, and Archon calls us over. 'Come and meet Spirit,' he says, 'our trusted and powerful shaman.'

Spirit lays a crocodile finger on my chin and gives me a gummy smile. Then he cups his bony hands over mine, closing his eyes and singing a tuneless air.

'You are a stranger?'

I nod.

'You're on a soul journey, little one.'

It isn't a question; he just says it like he knows something. He touches the scar on my cheek with a skinny finger.

'Be very careful. Don't trust too easily.'

I can count three teeth.

He nods at Tiger, touches her shoulder. He turns to leave. 'Archon, I will be back very soon.'

He shuffles out, and Archon leads us back to the sleeping boy. He strokes the pale forehead gently.

'My beautiful son, Casimir. Just sixteen. Holding on, just holding on . . .'

'What happened to him?' Tiger whispers, though we can both guess the answer. *Ramish*.

It's like he hasn't heard her. He looks down at the sleeping body. 'I'm proud to call him my son. His mother died as he was born, you know. He's my only boy, tough as a tree.' He traces a crabbed hand down his son's arm, strokes his fingers. 'Brightens my heart,' he says, almost to himself. 'My boy.'

What colour is love? It seeps from Archon, coming off him in waves and washing us all in sorrow. Our heads are bent like mourners at a Goodbye Party.

I don't know why I say it.

'He will survive, Archon. You said it; he's tough as a tree.'

His eyes are cloudy. 'Whether he lives or dies, I will avenge this.'

'How did it happen?' Tiger asks again.

'There were four boys went out that morning to fish. Two came home.' He puts his finger to his lips, motions us outside.

We sit in the shade as Archon tells us the story.

'They had sailed up to Kinoka Creek at sunrise, sitting on the bank, getting their bait ready. It was trout season, and they were going to catch enough to feed the whole village.' He shakes his head slowly. 'Ramish surprised them from behind. Casimir's closest friend, Jason, was be-headed first. No prayers, no mercy. The others were ordered to play football with his severed head.' Archon winces and closes his eyes.

'They refused. It was a bloody battleground.' He clenches his fists. 'I don't want you to hear all the detail,' he says. 'It would haunt your dreams forever. You are only children.' He swallows. 'Lani, another boy, was stabbed through the heart. Casimir and Arron plunged into the river. Arron got to tell us what happened.'

'Did he survive?' I ask.

'Yes, he was wounded, but he's recovered well. We searched the river for Casimir and found him, collapsed on the bank, just before nightfall. Butchered. Bleeding to death.' He rubs his palms over his face.

'His wounds are slow to heal, but . . .' Archon taps his forehead. 'His mind is scarred. He has had a – how do I put it – a traumatic event.' He pauses. 'His soul is dead. But I thank the stars that the sacred river brought him back to us. His heart still beats.'

'But there's a thorn in it,' I say.

He nods. 'Yes, yes, a thorn, like a skewer through his heart. He's abandoned his life. Psychic hurting, too much to bear for now? I don't know. He has been like this for weeks.'

I know what he means. *He's abandoned his life* – isn't that what I did? The iron bars lock down around your heart, like teeth . . . and it's too sore to let anyone touch it.

'It hurts too much,' I say. His heart has closed down. Like mine did. He's like a tortoise, pulling his shell over himself. He thinks he's going to be safe in the dark. Shutting the gates, shutting down.

I wish I could tell him to come away back. Not to go into that dark place. Dark just wants darker, and soon he'll be locked into that tragic world of grief and rage and despair.

'Has he spoken about what happened?' Tiger asks.

'No. He does open his eyes sometimes. Stares ahead, sips some water. There is a black energy encircling him like smoke. The body, we pray, will heal,' he says, 'but the heart is angry. You are right' – he looks at me – 'it is encrusted; no energy can flow through it. Maybe the shaman will free it.'

We can see Spirit approaching, and we all follow him inside again. A small group has gathered. The women seated, chattering, the men standing by the door, arms folded. Archon takes us to sit in the far corner as Spirit approaches the bed. He gestures to a boy close behind him with a flute, and the boy puts it to his lips and begins to play. The notes speak of sadness and despair, and I feel my own tears raw as an onion, peeling away from my eyes. The music fades, and the boy steps back into the shadows.

Spirit kneels by the bed and lights some dried herbs. When he gets back on his feet, the hawk headdress swoops and dives and the rag-and-feather cloak spreads out like a ball gown.

'That was sage,' Tiger whispers. 'I think he's using it to call up the spirits.'

A sweet smoke spirals up and swirls around the bed as the shaman picks up a drum and beats out a rhythm, singing and chanting and dancing around the room. He hops forward, then twists and bends to the drum-beat. The raggy cloak swirls and lifts as he moves, ribbons spreading out like a maypole. The song has no real melody, and I can't follow the words. Sounds like he's making them up as he goes along. My granny said people often do that –chancing their arm, she said.

'It's like he's drunk,' Tiger whispers. We giggle, but Archon throws us a look, so we straighten our faces. Tiger can always do that: make you feel excellent even when you're sad.

Spirit drops the drum and picks up the bowl of smoking herbs, waving it above his head. Now it looks like the hawk is smoking a cigarette. Tiger winks at me; she knows what I'm thinking. Then, in one quick movement, he drops to his knees, opening a pretend door and drawing something out from under the bed. He's so fit. Even my dad couldn't move like that.

Spirit is waving his arm now, like a guard on traffic duty beckoning the cars forwards.

'He's releasing the disturbed energy,' Tiger whispers. Like I said, she knows everything.

The drumming starts again, more frantic this time. After a minute, just as it's driving me mad, it stops. Spirit adjusts his headdress. The hawk gazes around the room, beak disapproving, before he goes off to sit in the corner. The flute boy steps in again, playing a last sad tune.

The music stops. Everyone starts to talk, whispering first, then in normal tones. The spell is broken. Archon stretches and joins Spirit. They embrace. The hawk headdress is removed, the cloak slipped off. Underneath, a bag of bones.

'He's like a bag of bones,' I whisper to Tiger, and she claps her hand over her mouth, stifling a laugh.

Archon calls us over and we hover around, not sure what comes next.

'Is he cured?' Tiger asks.

Archon smiles, shakes his head. 'We must wait for the spirits to intervene,' he says.

I remember Nan-Nan's ointment, the one that smells like Christmas. I tell Archon about how it cured my shoulder, and he nods, eager to try any little thing.

'I'll be back in a minute,' I say as I race to the other hut to get my purple coat. The jar is in the pocket and there is something else, wrapped up. It's Nell's present to me before I left the council chamber. I tear off the paper, and underneath is a little tin of bubbles. I can share them with the children.

When I get back, Casimir is alone. Everyone is standing outside in the sun, drinking honey tea and chatting. More are drifting away. No sign of Tiger or Archon.

In the dim candlelight, I unscrew the jar and very gently spread the ointment along the scar lines. I can feel the gap under my fingers where the skin has split and is now furiously knitting together. Our bodies just want to heal; they won't give up.

I touch his hand, hold it in mine for a second. His fingers move, feather light. I lean forward – I don't know what makes me do it –and I kiss his hand.

'You want it darker,' I whisper. 'You want to turn away. Don't do it. Don't let Ramish win. Look up; don't look down. Let it pass through you.'

I leave the jar behind on the bedside table. Outside, campfires are being lit. The roasted pig is crisping over red-hot ashes, and platters of sweet potato are being prepared by the women.

Archon is moving about with Spirit while rugs are arranged in circles around low wooden tables. Tiger calls out to me, pointing up ahead through the trees where two figures on horseback are making their way down the hillside. She whoops with joy. 'It's Mitch and Poppy, Doll.'

She races along the pathway towards them, startling the horses as she chases around a corner. The two riders dismount, and Tiger wraps her arms around Mitch, rubbing his flank and making soothing noises. Poppy nuzzles into me, glad we're all back together again. We lead them back to the village and let them feed and rest.

The aroma of roast meat draws us back to the campfires. Everyone has gathered to eat and celebrate the shaman's visit. The boy with the flute has put on Spirit's cloak and headdress, and the children dance around him and squeal as he chases them through the trees.

Wooden plates are passed around with hunks of meat and runner beans. Bowls of sweet potato follow, and mugs are refilled.

The sun is slipping away over the pink horizon, and the first watery stars step out.

We sit with Archon as guests of honour. He asks Spirit about Casimir. 'Is my son lost to us? What are your thoughts?'

Spirit sucks on his pipe. 'His heart is wounded. The energy disturbed.' He places his palm on his chest. 'The heart, after trauma, it closes down.' He puts his pipe between his lips again, draws in a breath. 'The centre closes down.'

'Can we open it? Can the spirits intervene?'

He narrows his eyes, considering the question. He nods slowly, puffing out spirals of smoke. 'I feel Casimir will come home to himself.'

Archon's eyes light up like stars.

My own heart opens when I hear the words. It must be a beautiful thing to come home to yourself. You'd be happy in yourself, I suppose, not wanting to run away into another life. For the first time in my long years, I feel I am coming home to myself. Opening, not closing. Awake, not asleep.

I was like Casimir. Closed. But now I can see things I've never seen before. If I went home now, would I be different or would I topple back into the dark?

Archon turns to Tiger and me. 'Tomorrow we will arrange for your return to your families,' he says. She looks relieved, but I can't let that happen. I have to follow my map to Glenshiquin. And if I meet Ramish . . .

My mouth is dry and I swallow my drink in one go.

Spirit is talking about Ramish. 'I met him once,' he said. 'He wanted me to summon the spirits to banish his nightmares.'

'What did you think of him?' Archon asks.

Spirit shivers. 'I found a man without a soul, Archon. A man who terrorised people and enjoyed it. The smell of terror, he said, made the hair stand on the back of his neck.' Spirit sucks on his pipe. 'He despised weakness. Power was his drug.'

Spirit takes another puff. 'Terror starts in their eyes, he said to me. A pulsing on the eyelid. When he saw that, he said, his heart began to prickle with excitement.'

'His heart?' Archon says. 'He doesn't have a heart.'

Spirit lowers his voice. We lean in to catch what he's saying.

'When we met, when he embraced me, I could feel a hard object in his chest. Not a breastbone, not a ribcage. It was, I think, his charred heart – like a piece of flint protruding just under the skin.'

Tiger raises her eyebrows. Spirit looks at her. 'You don't believe me? Believe me; he has a heart of pure, liquid evil.'

'Evil isn't liquid,' Tiger says. I give her a look that says, *Do not take on a shaman.*

Spirit grabs a stick and traces three lines in the dry earth. 'Most people think there are three states. There's water, liquid.'

'Yes – steam, water, and ice. We all know that,' she says. 'Gas, liquid, solid states.'

'Now there's a fourth,' he says.

We all stare at him, and I'm beginning to think there's more than ginger and honey in his mug.

Archon looks puzzled. 'What is your point, Spirit?'

'Take blood. It freezes solid, yes. But go lower, lower, to the coldest temperature imaginable, and that solid reverts back to a type of thick liquid. Something so black, so dense that it can only be stored deep in the human heart. A human heart that has absorbed a mountain of dark energy and drawn it deep into its core.'

'So his heart is liquid evil,' I say.

'Yes, Doll, encrusted in flint. And that dark heart has to be nourished.' He takes a swig from his mug. 'By torture and terror.'

He takes another puff. Taps his nose. 'He knows all this,' he says. 'He told me himself. "When I smell fear," he said, "my black heart sings." '

Tiger's face is pale. 'I never knew of such evil.'

Spirit pats her head with a leathery hand. 'You're just a child,' he says. 'Let's hope you will never encounter it.'

I wrap my arms around my knees and stare into the campfire. No way can I travel on my own now. Fear is crawling up my legs like a jungle creeper. I'm paralysed. I'm a coward. I'm heading back. So what if I fail?

I crunch into the crispy skin of my roast pig, letting the juices run down my chin, but I can't really enjoy this wonderful feast. Wouldn't the shaman have had more sense than to scare the daylife out of us with all his talk about black hearts and torture?

Spirit cracks and crunches on a hunk of meat, licking and sucking his fingers dry as he finishes. No wonder he only has three teeth left.

Archon has barely touched his food. His brow is creased. He bites his thumbnail. 'The time has come for action,' he says. 'We cannot live like rats, waiting for the rat snake to strike again.'

The night is cool, and I pull my purple coat around my shoulders. I remember the bubbles in my pocket. I take them out, open the lid, and draw out the wand. One gentle blow, and a string of bubbles float up into the night sky. Tiger laughs. 'Cool. Can I have a go?' Some of the children run towards us and Tiger jumps to her feet. 'Come on, kids; see if ye can catch these.' She blows a cascade of bubbles into the air, and the children squeal and run after them. 'More. More.'

I notice one of my bubbles has settled on my knee, wobbling, ready to pop. Archon and Spirit peer closer and stare, and when I follow their gaze, I see something extraordinary. The bubble is the size of a tennis ball, and inside it a giant of a man with a beard across his chest is shouting and dancing about. There's a bee buzzing around his head, and that seems to send him into a frenzy. I can hear him wail, and his arms flap about as another bee appears. The man's eyes are bulging. He zigzags across the grass, staggers, and rolls into a ball, like a child hiding. More bees follow, hovering about the man's head as he struggles to get to his feet. A few seconds and then . . . *pop*, the bubble disappears.

Archon grabs my wrist, his eyes blazing. 'Who are you?' His voice is harsh.

Spirit leans forward. 'Let her go; you're hurting her. Let her speak.'

My heart lurches and slides into my stomach. I look around me. Tiger is like the Pied Piper, leading the children on a bubble train around the village.

'Earlier,' Archon says, 'when we talked' – he stabs his finger at me – 'the candle flame leaned towards you. Like some invisible magnetic force.'

Spirit looks at him from under his eyes.

'No, Spirit. It is true. I saw it. Why do you think I have her sitting here tonight, with us?'

He doesn't wait for an answer.

'Because' – he continues to point his finger at my face – 'I knew there was something about you, something metaphysical. You are not who you say you are.'

Spirit lays his hand on Archon's arm to calm him down. 'I agree with you, Archon.' He turns to me. 'There is something about you, Doll.' He nods. 'You need to tell us who you are and' – he points to my knee – 'how you came by this magic ball of truth. Or untruth.'

'Who was that man? Did you know him?'

They say it together. 'Ramish. It was Ramish.'

Spirit looks at Archon. 'A Ramish filled with terror. Who knew? Afraid of a few honeybees.' He throws his head back and laughs loudly. I can see another jagged tooth at the back of his mouth. That makes four.

His laugh breaks the tension. 'The great Ramish,' he says, 'cries like a baby.'

'Who sent you?' Archon is waiting for me to speak.

I look at the two men. How much to tell? 'Please trust me.'

I take a deep breath. 'Yes, I am on a journey. Brought here from across the universe by the Grand Mariner at the Space Agency, Nan-Nan.'

I look around, point to Tiger in the distance. 'I only met her by chance. She knows nothing of this.'

I whisper the next bit. 'I was summoned by the Council of Grand-mothers to complete a task. I am . . . I am the Child of Summer. The Manuscripts foretold my coming. Please, I can't say any more.'

I can see the campfire flames reflected in Archon's eyes.

'You're just a child. Are you telling me they sent you off into the wild, alone? What madness is that?'

Spirit strokes his chin. 'The Child of Summer from the Manuscripts? You? Nell sent you?'

'Yes. I met them all in the Cathedral of Light. It was Nell who gave me a gift of the bubbles.'

I'm blabbing too much. The Grandmothers'll kill me. 'I've said too much already.' I look at Archon. 'Actually, if you hadn't brought us here, I might have finished my task at this stage.'

He snorts.

'You'd be dead, roasted over some fire, drowned in a cage, or bleeding to death on some ancient path,' he says crossly.

Spirit looks at me. 'You are entrusted with a mission?'

'I need to find a man. Major Tom Axel. I am to travel up Glenshiquin Mountain. I can't say any more. And please, not a word to Tiger. You must bring her home safely. Tomorrow.'

'And you?'

There's a long silence. I stare into the flames. Good question. What am I to do? Afraid to travel on alone, afraid to go back and tell them I failed. That I didn't come close.

There's a woman in blue beckoning to Archon, and he straightens up. 'Wait here. I'll be back,' he says.

Spirit is looking at me. 'Are you afraid, child? You look anxious. What ails you?' His voice is low and kind. Like my dad's.

A tear snakes down my cheek. And another, and another. 'Yes, I'm afraid.' I whisper it, ashamed. I wipe the tears away. My body is shaking.

'I'm a pussycat,' I say, 'I can't go back; I can't go forward. I'm stuck. I wish I had drowned yesterday instead of nearly drowning. Some Child of Summer I turned out to be.'

'I think you're magnificent,' he says.

'Me?'

'Yes, you.' He smiles and starts to clean his pipe, knocking out the dead ash and stuffing the sweet-smelling tobacco into the bowl. He presses it down with greasy fingers.

'I believe Nell sent you. And since she did, you are perfect for the task. The Manuscripts do not lie. You must have wonderful qualities, strength, resilience. You've come so far.'

I sniffle. Brush away another tear. 'You think I could be a topper?'

'You are already, my dear girl. Everyone is afraid,' he says. 'We all have our shadow side. Fear is our lifetime companion; we can't escape it, Doll.'

He puts the pipe to his lips unlit, takes it out again.

'It's what we do with the fear that counts. How we take it on. We defeat it . . . or it defeats us.'

I feel guilty now for calling him a bag of bones. He's a wise man with a good heart.

He winks at me. 'Dry those tears.' He taps the side of his nose. 'We'll find a way through,' he says. 'Trust the Gods to lead you forward.'

Archon is back. He drops down next to us, smiling, his face lighter. 'It's Casimir,' he says. 'His wounds are healing rapidly. He's even taken some soup. He's on his way back to us. I feel it in my bones.'

He rolls a cigarette, lights up, inhales deeply.

The tattoo markings curve like tendrils around his face and scalp. They make him look fierce, but he's in a much better mood. He leans towards me. 'If what you say is true, then this ball of truth – if that's what it is – may be the answer we've been looking for.' He blows the smoke sideways. 'A way to end the brief reign of the Lord of Lords.'

Spirit nods, lights his pipe. 'Indeed,' he says. 'I see where you're going with this.'

'We'll meet in the morning again,' Archon says. 'For now, let us come back to the present and enjoy the celebrations.'

Tiger returns, breathless and laughing. She flops down next to me. 'There's plenty left,' she says, handing me the tin. 'Those kids have me exhausted.' She gulps back a drink.

'You're only a kid yourself,' I tell her, just for something to say, hoping she won't pick up on my red eyes. I feel better now as I think of Spirit's words.

Archon stands up, claps his hands, and there's a hush. Everyone looks up.

'I want to thank Spirit, our special guest, for his long journey here and his shamanic work with Casimir. Welcome also to our visitors: Doll, and I think you've all met Tiger at this stage. Now' – he claps his hands again – 'let the music begin.'

The *thump, thump* of drums fills the air, and the children leap up, clapping to the beat. Three women, their painted faces glowing in the firelight, rise and play their pipes in harmony. The sound is sweet and high, and the boy with the flute joins in. The music hovers above us, then soars like a flair across the moonlit sky. My heart follows.

Next to me, Tiger jumps up and moves to a clearing in the centre of the gathering. The children step back, making room for their new hero. She glides like a ballerina, tiptoeing gracefully, her arms stretched above her. She twirls, light as mist, weaving in and out of the children sitting cross-legged, their eyes shining. The music flows through her like a river. One of the women gives her a red scarf, and she lets it trail out behind her as she whirls. And imagine, she's my best friend. My life is brimming over.

'You're a cool dancer,' I say when she gets back. I high-five her, our palms missing each other 'cos she doesn't know the move.

My fears are forgotten. The night is magical, everyone dancing circles around the campfire, chanting and singing. Every child has their own song, Archon tells us. A song created just for them, sung at their birth to welcome them into the world. It's their Lifesong. When they hurt their knee or get sick or sad, everyone sings their song to comfort them.

Tonight, everyone sings the Lifesongs of the children without hands, and their little faces glow with pride. You can feel the love, like Heaven melting over this gentle place.

'Doll for a song?'

I get to my feet. I know it off by heart. My song, about me wishing on a star.

Everyone is smiling and clapping. Tiger high-fives me now. 'Well done, Doll.' Everyone loves my song. And here's the funny thing: it's all come true. I dreamed and wished and hoped for a new life. And a cool friend. And adventure. And a voice – well, that was beyond my dreams. But look, they all came true.

The shaman was right about fear. You can't let it win. I was afraid when Nan-Nan came. But I still jumped . . . and here I am sitting around a campfire singing, not curled up on a couch.

Maybe, just maybe, I am magnificent. Imagine if I was?

183

CHAPTER 38

SALLY

Work. Some days it's a shelter from the storm. Some days you can glue the bits of yourself back together and finish the day in one piece. When I march through those double doors in the mornings, I can morph into a different person. I'm decisive and I'm focused and a world away from the real me. The me that's in bits. The pathetic me that's spilling over and strung out. If only people knew. I'd be mortified.

The Monday morning editorial meeting is over, and the team files out of the conference room. I close the door and press my palms against it. Thank God that's over. I can peel off my happy face.

I feel a push against the door, then a knock. I nearly tip over. A blue trouser suit, blue heels. It's Terri, senior staff writer, one of my favourite people. Sharp as a tack and loves her style.

'Sorry, Sal. Oops.' She cups her hand over her mouth. 'Just wanted a quick word . . .'

We slide onto adjoining chairs at the conference table.

'Okay, what's going on? Spill.'

'How do you mean, Terri?' I really do not want to have this conversation.

'Right. I'm getting us a coffee. Wait here.' *Click-clack* heels and the door swings shut behind her.

I lean forward, rest my forehead in my hands. Two minutes later, Terri's back with two frothing cappuccinos. She sets one in front of me, hands me a Purple Snack.

'Okay, what's up, hon?'

She's not giving up. 'My head's ready to explode, Terri.'

She squeezes my arm. 'I know you're under pressure. I mean, Doll in hospital again. Jesus, Sally, I don't know how you do it.'

'It's not just that. See . . . ?' I point to my eyes, brimming over. 'Did you ever see such a mess?' I dab my eyelids dry. Why do I bother with mascara?

'I can't stop crying, Terri. It's like Doll's life is one battle after an-other. She . . . she can't . . . escape. And neither can we. We all seem to be stuck in the misery.'

It's hard to stop the tears – let them out at all, and they take liberties. Before she can answer, I'm off again. 'And Dan. There's something up with Dan.'

'You know men,' she says. 'They can't cope with any drama, and the hospital . . .'

'It's not just that. He accused me last week of actually looking for misery. We're always fighting lately. And he thinks I can't handle Doll, that I'm too stuck on the problems.'

'And are you?'

My head shoots up. 'Well, you tell me, Terri. Maybe I should forget about her and get on with my life?'

'No, I mean, you need to look after yourself. You've too much go-ing on. It's overload. Doll's despair has become yours, Sal. Come on. Maybe Dan has a point.' She takes a deep breath. 'Don't take this the wrong way . . .'

I hate when people say that.

'Maybe you need to go back to that counsellor woman? You chick-ened out the last day, remember? Take a chance, Sal.'

I open my mouth to protest, but she waves her hand. 'Wait. Let me finish.'

I get up and walk to the window. 'I know what you're saying, Terri. But I don't want to talk to anyone. Talking isn't going to change reality. Endless conversation and tears. For what? Nothing changes. Don't you see? Everything stays the same.' The tears keep leaking from my eyelids. Jesus, it's gone beyond a joke.

'How can you know that for sure?' she says. 'You've told me your-self, how you've screamed and it comes up out of nowhere. That's scary, Sal. That's not normal.'

'That's only been a few times,' I say. Why did I ever tell her that? Moment of weakness. 'Sometimes, yeah, it just erupts . . . out of nowhere . . .'

She's right, it is scary. I'm driving along, listening to the radio, and a scream takes flight inside me and . . . and the fury of it shocks me. It's like something alien, not part of me. It's not me screaming, it's someone else. And then I feel sick and my throat is sore and I'm shaking, and I have to pull over.

'But that's the thing, Sal. It doesn't come out of nowhere; it comes out of you.'

'Well, of course . . . I know that. I just mean I don't see it coming, that's all.'

'Look, it comes out of you,' she says, almost crossly. 'And you need to find out what bit of you is demanding to be heard. You need you to listen to your body.'

'Oh, for God's sake, Terri. You're beginning to sound like a therapist.'

'You know I'm right. Don't walk away from it. Stop hiding.'

She comes over to the window. Gives me a bear hug. Why can't people understand? You can't just talk it away. And if you do, it only comes back, sidling up to you, tugging at your sleeve . . . People don't get that. Maybe I am going mad?

She fetches my makeup bag. I fix my eyeliner. Pat on another layer of foundation. 'Ready for battle, Sal?' I smile brightly.

When I return to my desk, I think about what Terri said. Maybe she has a point. And is there something with Dan I'm not seeing? Some drift between us, like continents stealing away from each other? Because that's how it feels, the two of us receding from each other, caught up in our own lonely whirlpools.

CHAPTER 39

DOLL

We link arms as we pick our way back in the moonlight, giggling as we trip over a tree stump outside our hut. It's been a long day, and we're both sleepy.

'G'night,' I say, snuggling into my sleeping bag and yawning loudly.

'Not so fast, Doll.'

I knew this was coming. Tiger drops down next to me, cross-legged, arms folded. 'What's going on?' She jabs my arm.

I hesitate.

'C'mon. I saw you talking to Spirit. I saw you crying. Archon wants to know who you are. Not we. *You.*' She leans forward. 'So, who *are* you?

I blink. I don't know what to say. Or how much to say. Can I trust her? Granny always said if someone seems too good to be true, they probably are. But Tiger is the friend I always wanted. She saved my life, and I love her.

'Don't you trust me?'

How can I tell her I'm not sure, that I think she just might be too wonderful to be true? What would someone like Tiger want with me? It doesn't make sense. 'Tens hang around with tens; twos hang around with twos. That's life,' Andi once said.

Tiger shakes her head slowly. 'I saved you. I pulled you out of the river.' She hugs her knees. 'You're Little Miss Mystery, aren't you? First, you lie about your uncle.' She holds up one finger. 'Two, you tell me zero about your family. Very odd.' She jabs her middle finger. 'Three, you're having a deep conversation with Spirit . . . and you're crying. Even Archon knows there is something about you. So, Doll, I'm asking you now, and I won't let you sleep till you answer me. Who are you?'

So I tell her. Everything. I tell her about Nan-Nan, the Orb, and Major Tom. About my mission. About Ramish and the bubble. The Grandmothers will eat me without salt. And I tell her about my first life. I'm so ashamed I leave out the bits about staying on the couch and destroying my face and the darkness in my head. She wouldn't understand. To be honest, that Doll is a stranger to me now. She broke her family's heart. She wasn't very nice.

I have to answer a thousand questions, but at the finish, Tiger is silent. Wondering, probably, if I'm off my head.

'Wow, I can't believe it,' she says, after a while, fingers drumming against her cheeks. 'It's beyond exciting. And it all adds up. Or else . . .'

'Or else what?'

'Or else you're some liar.' She laughs then, like she doesn't believe I'm a liar.

'I'm telling you the truth. Promise me, not a word.'

She puts her finger to her lips, grinning. 'Not a word. I'm with you all the way,' she says, her eyes shining in the candlelight. 'All the way. Me and you.'

I have to tell her then. 'You're going home tomorrow.'

Her face drops. She opens her mouth to protest, but I tell her my mind's made up.

'And at the end of all this, what will you do?' she asks.

'I'll be sent back, I suppose. But I'm going to tell them. I'm. Not. Going. Back.'

Tiger jumps to her feet. 'I'm coming with you, and don't try and stop me.'

'But—'

'No buts. My mind's made up too.' She spreads her sleeping bag over a rug.

'But Ramish . . .'

She winks, blows out the candle. 'You have something on him, haven't you?'

She zips up her sleeping bag. 'Can't wait for tomorrow. Night, Doll.'

I lie awake for a long time. Am I really that different from the old Doll? I'm still afraid. Of Ramish. Of going to meet Major Tom. Of failing and of Almazova being destroyed. I imagine the Grandmothers shaking their heads: *What were we thinking, depending on a girl who hadn't a clue, afraid of her own shadow? Nice, but useless.* I see their tut-tutting cross faces and Nan-Nan avoiding my eye as she gets ready to bring me back through space-time. *Ah, you did your best, child.* But her *Goodbye, honey* – if you peeled off her kind face – would really mean *Good riddance.*

Who could blame them? Getting a pussycat instead of a lion. They were depending on me.

But Tiger is right about one thing: Ramish is afraid. That was Nell's message, a signpost to help us. I drift off, my eyelids heavy. The sleep sentries step back as I paddle through the gates of Dream-land, a plan already forming in my head.

*

Tiger is shaking my shoulder. 'C'mon, Doll. Archon is waiting for us.' She hands me a cup of ginger tea.

Archon is sitting at the table smoking when we arrive. He smiles and beckons us to sit. Spirit appears and joins us. He knocks his pipe against the edge of the table. 'Did ye enjoy last night, ladies?'

'It was the best night of my life,' I say.

'And mine,' says Archon. 'Last night, my boy turned a corner. Casimir is doing well. He's doing well.' He raises his mug in a cheers motion and finishes his drink in one gulp. He rubs his palms together. 'Anything is possible now.'

He looks at Spirit, gives a little bow. 'Thank you.' He turns to me. 'And your ointment, Doll? The wounds have shown a month's healing overnight.' Another bow. 'Thank you. You have no idea how tall I feel today. No idea.' He grins, smoothing his hands over his scalp. 'Now, let's see how we can defeat Ramish once and for all. Now that we know about his melissaphobia . . .'

'Who's she?' I ask. 'His wife?'

Tiger laughs. 'It's a phobia, Doll. A fear of bees.'

'The plan is,' Spirit says, 'to use this to our advantage. To draw Ramish into a honey trap.' He laughs at his own joke and strokes his chin. 'If we can expose Ramish, if he loses face with his warriors . . .'

'Yes,' I say. 'Ramish must look weak in front of his own tribe. Better again, the bees may even finish him off.'

There is silence in the room. Archon glances at Spirit.

'We must make it happen,' I say.

The candle flickers, magnetic hands draw the flame towards me. Not a word is spoken. Tiger is staring at me.

'And here's the plan,' I continue.

Archon lights another cigarette, takes a deep drag, and pulls some stray tobacco off his tongue with his thumb and forefinger.

'Go on, Doll.'

'I had a dream last night,' I say, 'and I saw it happen.'

'Go on.'

'You drink honey tea here.'

'Yes, we have a bee garden just behind the village producing seven flavours of honey and all the candle wax we need. What are you saying, Doll?'

'We need to sail upriver and bring Ramish a gift from your people, Archon.'

'You mean honey?' Spirit says.

'Yes . . . and bees. We release the bees; Ramish will panic. They will attack. You can die from bee stings, you know.' My granny told us about a cousin who had disturbed a hive of bees in an outhouse on the family farm and died in agony. In *agony*, she said.

'That's ridiculous,' Tiger says. 'There's no guarantee the bees will attack Ramish. And even if they did, his men will have our heads –or our hands – on a plate.'

Archon taps ash on the floor.

'That's your plan? Bring a bee box to Ramish and let the bees escape? Problem solved?'

'Last night I had a dream I was having tea with the Queen.'

I see their faces. 'No, listen, please, hear me out,' I say. 'She wore black velvet and a gold crown. We were sitting in the palace garden, and there were iced cakes set out on a table and servants running about. She held my hands and whispered that her army was ready to help me.'

'That'd be the queen bee, I suppose,' Tiger says, curling her lip.

Is she a little bit jealous? I ignore her.

'Then I stepped into a canoe. I was carrying a box covered in gold cloth. Later, in my dream, Ramish is shouting and stumbling into the river . . .'

'And then?' Tiger's face says it all.

'And then,' I say, turning to her, 'you woke me up.'

'It's not as simple as it sounds, Doll,' Archon says. 'The bees will be angry; they won't like being moved. Yes, they will attack, but I can't see how they will target Ramish.'

'They will. I can make it happen.'

'You're mad,' Tiger says. 'It'll be carnage. I suppose you'll be bringing the bee box upriver. Personally.'

'Of course. Ramish will be interested in me. A child he can sell on, compliments of Archon. And a peace offering. We need to send word that I am coming.'

'I'm with you,' Spirit says quietly. He turns to the others. 'She is the Child of Summer. Don't you understand? The Child of Summer has preternatural power. This is no ordinary child. She is divinely inspired by the Gods. This was a vision, not a dream.'

Archon nods and crunches out his cigarette. Twin jets of smoke trail from his nostrils. He gets up slowly. Crooks his finger. 'Follow me.'

We follow in single file through a lavender meadow, into the forest behind the village. Archon strides ahead like a mountain goat. We have to run to keep up. Through the trees, in a clearing, is a girl in a yellow dress, sitting on a fence.

'Ah, there you are,' she says, like she was expecting us. She jumps down, graceful as a deer. 'Lovely to meet you.' She smells sweet as honey as she bends to kiss our cheeks.

'Thank you, Melania,' Archon says as she leads us through a gateway to the honey house and the bee garden.

Bee boxes are stacked under the shade of pine trees. We can hear the air vibrating and a whining sound like a thin wind muscling through high branches. Bees fidget around the boxes. The sun beats down, and the sweet, sugary scent of honey hangs in the air.

Melania leads us towards a small hut. She unhooks four long-sleeved cotton tops and scarves from a nail inside the door and hands them to us. 'Put these on,' she says.

We can see the bees free-flying across the meadow.

'Will they sting us?' Tiger asks, wrapping the scarf around her head and tucking it in under her collar.

'Unlikely,' Melania says. 'They'll generally only attack to defend themselves.'

She helps me tuck my scarf around my head. Her hands are smooth as cream.

'A bee sting can be painful,' she says. 'I should know.' She winks, pointing to her arms. 'But my bees are happy and content.' She nods towards the meadow of violets and wild roses. 'They've plenty of nectar and pollen to keep them busy. You're not as interesting, trust me.'

'Aren't you afraid of getting stung?' I say.

'It doesn't happen very often,' she says. 'The bees and I have an understanding: I take care of them, they take care of me. Bees can teach us a lot. They are wise and loyal – not like a lot of humans.' She leads us towards the shade of a willow tree. 'The main thing is to keep calm. Bees understand the power of stillness. They can smell fear and sweat. And they don't like it.'

She points towards a long, low hut on the far side of the bee garden. 'That's where we harvest the honey.' We follow her finger, and we can see the bees whirling round the entrance.

'The bees gather the nectar from the soul of the flowers and convert it into soul food.' She joins her hands together like a prayer. 'My wonderful dancing bees,' she says. 'A source of light and food. Magical.'

'You make it sound as if they're your friends,' I say.

'They are,' she says, smiling. 'They help me stay calm; they distract me from my worries. They are little healers.'

'I've heard it said that humans search for truth and wisdom among the honeycombs,' Spirit says.

Melania nods. 'I have searched and found it myself,' she says, 'and continue to find it.'

Archon touches Melania's arm and takes her aside. 'He's getting the expert's opinion,' Spirit says. 'She will tell him whether the plan can work.'

We button up our long-sleeved tops, laughing as Spirit tucks his white scarf around his head like a nun. As Archon turns back towards us, Melania grabs his arm and points to the bee boxes in the shade over to our right. We all look. The background humming has stopped, and we barely register the silence. Her mouth is an oval of surprise. In Archon's eyes, there's a flicker of fear. We all stare like we've turned to stone.

A thick rope of brown and amber has uncoiled from one of the hives and begins to climb skywards. It starts to zigzag then, dipping and rising across the blue sky, gathering speed like a rollercoaster as it moves towards our little group. A soft murmur becomes a loud whine as the bees circle overhead. The noise is deafening.

'Don't move,' Melania whispers. 'Stay quite still. Don't run or wave your arms about.'

The rope rises again, dipping and swirling like a firework. The noise is even louder now as ten thousand beating wings form a horseshoe shape above me. And it's clear – when I dare to glance upwards – that it's me they want. They fidget there as if attached to my head by an invisible thread. I stand, frozen, afraid to move a muscle. And then they lift off like a skipping rope in a storm, hurtling back to their hive.

Nobody moves.

'What was that about?' Archon says.

Melania sucks in her cheeks. 'I've never seen them behave like that in my nine years here. That was not random; the formation was perfect and must've been orchestrated by the queen. She gives the orders.'

Tiger whistles, shaking her head in disbelief.

Spirit looks at Archon. His wizened face is almost hidden inside his headscarf, and I see Tiger stifle another giggle as he speaks. I give her a look.

'I think these bees recognise the Child of Summer,' Spirit says. 'They've come to welcome her. I've seen all I need to see.' He looks at Melania. 'I think, Archon, we should move on Doll's plan. The Gods are with us. What do you think, Melania?'

'I think,' she says, 'we surely have the Child of Summer amongst us. The plan has my blessing.'

In the finish, we arrange to collect the bee box before sunrise the next morning. Melania will pack some crocks of honey in a basket for Ramish. 'Only our best,' she says.

Word will be sent to Ramish today.

'The bees don't like to be moved about in the heat,' Melania says, 'so I will wrap the box in a loose cloth to keep them cool.'

She smiles at me. 'I won't have to choose which hive to give you. It's extraordinary . . . but they've already selected themselves.'

She kisses our cheeks as she leads us out through the gate. 'May fortune favour you.'

None of us talks as we make our way back to the village. Those bees scared the light out of me, but in my gut I sense the Child of Summer stirring in me, guiding me, breaking through her shell inside me.

Back in Archon's hut, Tiger wraps her fingers around her mug.

'So the plan is,' she says, for the tenth time, 'we sail to Eagle Creek, where Ramish is expecting us.'

'We? You're not coming,' I say.

She continues like I haven't spoken. Tiger can be so annoying at times.

'He unwraps his gift of honey,' she says, 'and we let the bees escape. The bees will be angry at being disturbed and will release an alarm pheromone warning other bees, who then get aggressive and join in the fighting—'

'But Tiger,' I say.

She looks at Archon, continues to talk.

'Melania said that dead bees send a signal to the others to defend or attack.' She hesitates. 'And Ramish, we know, will panic and run.'

Archon is stroking his chin. I think after what happened in the bee garden, he's warming to the whole idea.

'Even if,' I say, 'he dives underwater, Melania says bees will wait and will continue to sting.' I lean forward, facing Archon. 'I will direct them. I will make sure the bees do as I ask.'

He sucks in his lips.

'Look, the bees gave us a message earlier, right?'

He nods, taps his lips with his finger. He does that a lot. 'There's no guarantee it'll work, but it's the only plan we have,' Archon says in the end, blowing smoke out the corner of his mouth.

'It was Nell's gift,' I say. 'She was letting us see his secret fear. You saw how the bees reacted to me. It's meant to be.'

'It's meant to be,' Spirit says. 'It's meant to be.'

Archon nods. 'So be it.' He gets up, stretches his arms above his head, and yawns. 'Come on, girls, you two need some fun. I have a surprise I think you'll enjoy.'

We follow him through the village, past the children sitting in groups eating oranges. Some of them follow us, but Archon waves them away. 'Not now, children; our guests need some time to themselves.'

Through the trees, we can hear the sound of thundering hooves long before the horses come into view. There's hollering and whooping and loud applause, and as we get closer, we can see riders racing around a track. One, head bent low, is galloping past a group of boys sitting on a fence.

'Come on, Hauk. Faster! Faster!' Hauk grips the reins in his fists and jumps to his feet, knees bent, pushing clouds of dust into the air as he passes by. Another rider follows, somersaulting like a trapeze artist from saddle to flank and back again. Archon leans on the fence post, watching as the riders gallop by. We all clap, but I gasp inside.

'It's better than the circus,' I say.

'These are mustangs from the wild. Our boys have been riding since they were two years old,' he says. 'They're in the saddle almost as soon as they can walk. We are horsemen.' He taps his chest. 'It's in our blood. Comes natural, like breathing.'

'Can I have a go?' Tiger whistles as another rider passes us straddling two horses, holding both sets of reins in expert hands. She waves her arms, whistling and shouting encouragement. Another rider gallops past, swinging under the belly of the horse, then sailing back into a handstand on the saddle. My heart's in my mouth.

I turn to Tiger. 'You can't be serious.'

Archon whistles, and one of the boys runs towards us.

'Vargas, will you give Tiger a lesson? Use the harness, and no showing off.' He wags his finger. 'I'm counting on you to bring her back in one piece. Doll, how about you?'

'No, thank you.' I keep my head down.

Archon smiles and strides off. 'See you later, girls.' He turns back towards Vargas. 'Remember, look after them both, Var. No broken bones.'

Vargas winks. Places his fist on his chest. 'They're safe with me.'

He shakes our hands. He's not much older than Tiger. 'Welcome, girls. I saw you last night.' He looks at Tiger. 'Can you ride as well as you can dance?'

She blushes. 'My father was a horseman.' She pushes her shoulders back. 'He taught me to ride when I was little. Bring it on.' She jumps off the fence and follows him.

I watch as he leaps onto his horse and reaches forward to haul Tiger onto the saddle. He clips his harness around her and whispers something in her ear. She laughs, head back, eyes glinting. I feel a stab of jealousy, not for the first time. How come Tiger has it all? Will someone please answer me that? But she's *too* perfect, if you ask me.

They trot past, and she waves as the mustang quickens his pace. Tiger's not afraid to try anything either. Not like me. Can you imagine her digging her face, giving up, and throwing in the tea towel?

I watch, greenly, as Vargas leads the horse into a canter and then a gallop, gathering speed as they thunder round the track. Tiger crouches forward, hair blowing in the wind, eyes glittering. I cover my eyes, peeping through my fingers. *Keep her safe, God; keep this girl safe.*

Other riders pass by, twisting on and off the saddle, balancing on the side of the horse, their boots skimming the dust, then catapulting back into the saddle. Another hangs upside-down, head trailing the ground, legs like scissors in the air. Swinging on and off the saddle, on and off, on and off. I'm dizzy watching.

'Be careful, Tiger.' I shout it. but she can't hear me. 'Slow down, girl.'

Vargas is on his knees now, and in one quick movement, he leaps to his feet, the harness lifting Tiger onto hers, and they both balance . . . unsteadily. I can't look. I open one eye and they're still there, knees bent, swaying from side to side – Jesus, almost toppling backwards. The boys farther up on the fence stand and wave and shout. 'Atta-girl, Tiger.'

How much longer can she stay up there, showing off? It seems like an age before they're trotting towards me, the horse snorting and sweating. Vargas unclips the harness, swings off, and Tiger follows. She's gasping and laughing, and Vargas is tapping her back as she bends forward, hands on her knees, catching her breath. They're both covered in red dust.

'You're a natural, better than any boy,' he says. 'Your father taught you well. It must be in your blood.' He looks up at me. I try to smile, but I'm mad jealous. An outsider now.

'Doll, do you want to give it a go?' Vargas puts his hand on my arm.

Huh. The very idea of it makes me laugh.

'No, not for me. Thanks.'

Tiger straightens up, grinning. Vargas gives her a mug of water, and it dribbles down her neck.

'It's. The. Best. Feeling. Ever.' She can just about rasp the words out. 'Never. Felt. So. Alive.'

I can smell the sweat coming off her.

Vargas swings up next to me on the fence. 'What are you afraid of, Doll? I won't let you fall. Promise.'

Does he notice the pink scars where my face is healing? What must he think?

Tiger says, 'Go on, don't be a baby. You'll regret it if you don't.'

She treats me like a teddy bear, her little toy.

The other boys are gathered farther down, and they all begin to shout, cupping their hands around their mouths. 'Come on, Doll. *Go for it. Go for it.*' The chanting gets faster and louder.

Go for it. Just what my Dad used to say to Andi. My heart is thudding as I look from Tiger to Vargas. 'Let's go,' I say, jumping off the fence and slipping, almost falling. Ouch. What a plonker I am. I straighten up, pretending it doesn't sting.

Great start, Doll, I say to myself, following Vargas. The boys are clapping and shouting. 'Show 'em, Doll.' I smile at them, my heart turning to water. Vargas helps me mount and swings up behind. He fixes my harness around me.

'No second thoughts?'

'No second thoughts,' I say as I pray for a happy death. What in the name of Diamond Jesus am I doing?

Tiger is sitting on the fence, elbows on knees, her face still flushed. She gives me a thumbs-up. The boys, sitting farther up the corral, shield their eyes as Vargas quickens the pace, shaking the reins. 'Come on, boy . . .'

Vargas is telling me to relax, to trust him, to hold on tight. The wind is rushing past, and I can hear the rumble of the hooves underneath and see the greens and blues of trees and skies as they circle around me. I close my eyes, praying I won't be sick. I feel I'm inside a washing machine, juddering up and down before spinning dizzily. Serves me right.

'You okay, Doll?' Vargas is breathing hard, his voice rasping in my ear as we pick up speed. I stammer back a 'Y-yes,' but the breeze whips the word right out of my mouth, flinging it into the sky. My heart is on fire.

'Oh Jesus, Mary, and Holy St Joseph. It's a prayer, not a swear.' The words get tossed around like confetti. Terror is dry-blasting my mouth, and my bones are liquidising. I'm screamless and breathless. I'm jelly. I can hear the ground shuddering beneath me as my eyelids Pritt-stick together.

And then Vargas is on his knees behind me, oh merciful Granny, and he's standing now, and the harness lifts me off the saddle and I'm standing up too, and the horse is thundering around the track. I open my eyes and the wind is a whirlpool, tearing my hair off my head. Everything is trampolining up and down.

My legs slip as we turn a corner, but Vargas holds me fast. 'Bend your knees. Bend low, Doll.' And I do, crouching down and hoping I'll get the hang of it as we enter our second lap.

We're getting faster and faster. *Help. Jesus.* I can only mouth the words. *Help. Please. Help.*

I'm falling out of myself, bursting with fear . . . and then, and then . . . with colour. Like tins of paint spilling across the sky. A liquid rainbow.

A scream stirs inside me, darting around my chest like a firework. As we gather speed, it rockets up my throat, hitting off the sides before reaching my mouth. Quick, escape! My jaw is snapped open by the force of it, and it somersaults out across the fields like a song. Laughter follows, my mouth opening again and again as it tumbles like a waterfall all round me. It's like I've been waiting for this moment for years, and now in my head I can hear the roar of the wave and smell the salty foam and feel it break over me as it crashes towards the shore. The water is exhaling over me, and there's music erupting from the ground . . . the Scottish pipers are playing Granny's song about Lassie and I'm riding the wave now, skimming across the high-rolling water. I gasp. Queen Doll; here I come . . .

I was missing till now. Only a ghost. I couldn't be found. I was lost. I was hiding. I was born, but not alive. I was asleep for years, but I'm awake now. Like the Sleeping Beauty. Reborn. It's the sweetest thing, life is. The sweetest thing.

The wave carries me safely to shore and disappears back into the ocean. Everyone is cheering. 'Well done, Doll. Atta-girl.' My whole body is tingling, sweet little pin-pricks of Heaven.

When I look back, no matter what happens, they can't take this away from me. I will remember being reborn, shedding my old skin, riding over sunbeams. And someday in the future when I'm old like my granny, I'll spread these memories out like a tablecloth. And this one, this one memory, will make my heart sing. The day I came alive.

Freddie Mercury is in my head. He's telling me he's having such a good time, he's floating around in ecstasy and not to stop him now. *I get it, Freddie.*

I took a chance too. I stepped out, felt the fear like a knife in my back. But I'm winning now. I'm winning. In my mind, I can see my family – they're all smiling. *Well done, Doll. We're proud of you.* My dad is proud of me. Just what I always wanted.

'Why are you crying, Doll?' Tiger is saying. 'You were fantastic. Wasn't she, Vargas?'

How can I tell her? How can I put words on how I feel?

She hugs me close and starts crying herself, and Vargas is saying, 'You two are a right pair,' and then the three of us are laughing and we can't stop and we have to lean in on each other, lock our arms around each other, and we catch our breath. Pure gold.

Life. It's the sweetest thing.

CHAPTER 40

ANDI

Inside the main entrance, I gel my hands. First floor, Children's Unit, past the nurses' station, room ten on the right. There's a hush as I close the door behind me. Here I can sit and dream, hide, disappear for a while. I move around the bed, straightening the covers that don't need straightening.

Her cheeks are flushed, tiny beads of sweat on her forehead. A muscle on her face twitches. She calls out, a long *ooh* sound of surprise, and there's a ghost of a smile around her mouth. Makes me cry. Happy, like an angel.

'How's Doll?' I say. I don't expect she hears me. They say people can hear even when they're in a coma. I wonder if it's true. The heart monitor waves undulate across the screen. The bag of fluids drips down along a tube, slow, measured drops. Ticking like a water-clock. *Drip-drop. Drip-drop.* I sit on the leather chair. Check my phone for the hundredth time. It's been two days since I heard from Steve. Forty-four hours and twenty minutes, to be precise.

I wasn't going to mention the photo till I met him over the weekend. I'd wait and see what he'd say. Maybe it was an old photo? Chelsea was just stirring trouble? Or maybe they *are* dating and he is messing me about. When I think about spilling all my secrets on the beach on Thursday, I cringe. He must have had some laugh afterwards.

When I texted him Saturday, he didn't reply for hours, and then it was only to say something had come up and he wouldn't be able to meet me over the weekend. I should've copped it there and then. But no. Like a fool, I rang him yesterday. Twice. No answer. And he doesn't work Sundays.

I texted him then, kept it short and cold. Let him know we were done. As Stacey says, you have to have some pride. Be the one to walk away. Show him how little he meant to you, even if it's not true.

I check my phone again. Nothing. But what am I expecting? That he'll come back to say he needed to finish it with Chelsea and wants to start over with me? I should be concentrating on Doll instead of stressing over Steve. How selfish is that?

Should I call round, though? Maybe his gran is ill? Maybe he's in some kind of trouble. He'd tell me, though, wouldn't he? I just don't want to face reality.

A nurse waddles in, closes the door carefully behind her.

She smiles and nods towards Doll. 'Poor wee mite.' She checks her temperature and oxygen levels and writes something on the chart at the foot of the bed.

'It must be tough on you all. Draining, I'd say.' She reaches up to adjust the drip, her blue tunic straining over her ample middle.

'More so my mom,' I say. 'She's here day and night.'

'Oh, I know. I've met her. A nice lady. She's holding up well. And your dad. It's not easy' – she looks at Doll – 'with herself so poorly.'

'Poorly?'

She swings the bag of fluid around at an angle. Checks the levels. 'I mean, you know. Herself not responding. God love her. It happens. We see it every week. Some infections grab a hold.' She clenches her hand into a fist, grits her teeth. 'And they won't let go.'

My heart flips over, and it's nothing to do with Steve. 'But isn't it just a matter of time?' I say. 'I mean, she'll recover.'

'Where there's life, there's hope.' She moves to the sink and washes her hands. I stare at the gushing tap as it sprays over the front of her tunic. She grabs a paper towel, runs it down her middle. 'I'm always doing that,' she says.

'Are you saying she mightn't recover? Is that a possibility?'

She rolls her eyes as she dries her hands vigorously. 'It's not for me to say, pet, and that's the truth of it.' She tosses the paper towel in the swing bin at her feet.

'Mr Davis is meeting your parents in the morning, far as I know,' she says, making for the door. 'He'll fill them in with all the details.' She looks flustered, pursing her lips, like she's sorry she opened her mouth. 'You call me if you need anything,' she says, giving me a thumbs-up and closing the door softly behind her.

I stay rooted to the chair. I feel as if all the air has been sucked out of my lungs.

I sit looking at Doll. My legs feel wobbly. What did that nurse just say?

It's what she didn't say, though, that worries me. She knows some-thing we don't. I lean over the bed, push a strand of damp hair off Doll's forehead. Is this her goodbye? Only eleven and already checking out? *Some infections grab a hold* . . .

I trace my finger along her cheek; feel the hollow of her scar, almost invisible now. Undisturbed skin healing quietly. A tear lands on her arm, and I brush it away. Her skin is warm. I place my finger in her palm. Do I imagine it, or does her hand close over it for a moment?

'Doll, can you hear me?'

She doesn't move.

'Doll.' My voice sounds alien. 'I know you hated your life, Doll . . .' My face is very close to hers. 'But Doll . . . don't give up.'

I stroke her face.

'You're so loved, you know. I wish they loved me like they love you. Come on, it isn't all about you. You've got to think of everyone else . . . so fight it and come home.'

I can feel her hand move lightly over my finger. A message, sister to sister.

'Anyway,' I say, 'you have to be my bridesmaid. It's a long way off, but you have to be there as I walk up the aisle. Is that clear, Doll?'

On the locker, there's a card. A crayon picture of a pink house and a rainbow and a scrawl saying *Love Ruby xxx*. In crayon-land, life is always wonderful.

I stay there on the bed for a long time, my finger held in her hand. I let the tears drip down – quietly, so Doll can't hear – and I say a prayer to Granny.

There's a knock on the door. A whisper. 'Cup of tea or a coffee, love?'

'No thanks.' I blow my nose, wash my face. Head for the bus.

On the way home, I'm thinking maybe there *is* something up with Steve. I might have been a bit premature sending that text. I take a detour and skirt along the river path. It's dusk, and there's a light on in the hall of number 3 Brandon Terrace. I slip across the road and swing open the gate. I'm just about to knock when I hear raised voices coming from inside. Steve is saying, 'Leave it, Gran.'

I can't make out what Joanie is saying, but another female voice is saying, 'Please, he's mine. I want us to make a go of things . . .'

My fist is frozen pre-knock. I turn quickly away, and I'm glad of the dark closing in and the quietness of the river path, where no one can hear me crying.

At home, I go straight to my room and shower. When I go downstairs, Mom and Dad are having dinner in silence.

'I've already eaten,' I lie.

'How is she, love?' Mom asks as I fill a glass of water.

'Her temperature is up and down, but she's the same. No change. It's dragging on, isn't it? She's in nearly a week now.' I don't want to face the table in case they spot my red eyes. 'A nurse says the consultant is around in the morning to talk to you both.'

'That's right,' Dad says. 'I'm meeting him at lunchtime tomorrow. I'll report back to your mom.'

'Your dad is going on his own,' Mom says. 'I'm not much good in these situations. I can't handle . . .' She trails off. 'You know what I mean.'

My phone pings. I nearly drop my glass. It's Steve. We need to talk, babe.

'Leave the wash up, Mom. I'll do it. Go in and sit down, and I'll bring you a cuppa.'

She smiles and glances over at Dad. 'Well, if you insist, Andi.'

'You too, Dad.'

I need the kitchen to myself so I can dance around it. I'm not getting my hopes up. It mightn't be what I want to hear, but just knowing that I'll be meeting him again is enough for now. Like that nurse said: where there's life, there's hope.

CHAPTER 41

DOLL

Through a gap in the doorway, I can see the sky. The moon is white as a dinner plate. We're ready before Archon taps on the door, and we tiptoe along behind him, making our way silently towards the river. It shimmers silver in the moonlight, and our canoe rocks gently at the water's edge. Melania introduces us to our two guides, Damon and Vitaliy. I recognise them from our first night here. They're placing the bee box carefully in the middle of the boat, tucking the gold cloth underneath. Melania puts her arms around us and kisses us. She hands us a crock of her best honey for Ramish to sample.

Last night Spirit burnt sage in our honour and called on the spirits of his fourfathers to bless us and guide us. Imagine having four fathers; Tiger hasn't even got one. Life is just not fair.

I turn to say goodbye to Archon. He hunkers down so his face is close to mine. In the bright moonlight, his tattoo whorls make him look like a demon. He grips my shoulders. 'Are you sure about this?' he says. 'There's still time . . .'

'To turn back? No way.'

He looks up at Tiger. 'You?'

'Not a chance.'

'May the Gods protect you.' He whispers it, placing his palm on his heart as we move off, like we're his soldiers heading into battle. Which we are, I suppose.

'Are you scared?' I ask Tiger as we glide upriver.

She shakes her head. 'No. And you know why? Because I trust the Child of Summer.' She circles her hands towards the sky. 'It's written in the stars, Doll.' She trails her hand in the water. We can hear a soft murmur from the bee box sitting between us. Ramish thinks the box holds six large crocks of heavenly scented honey. Vitaliy and Damon paddle us upstream, the rhythmic *slosh-slosh* sound drawing us into a drowsy numbness.

The air is clean and sweet as a newborn baby. We sit in silence, listening to the *yip-yip* of night birds calling to each other across the forest. Slowly, slowly, the sky pales and the sun appears on a red horizon, melting into the water. There's a hush, like a pause before the new day begins. We watch dark forests and lofty cliffs float past, a mighty world hidden in the gloom – bark and rock and shadowy leaves. Trees lean forward, wetting their bony elbows in the water. I never saw these things before. Too busy in Misery Street. Yesterday I was born. I'm alive now and wide awake.

And the day is waking up too. Birds chirp and squawk. Insects hover over the water, singing in circles. A frog plops in from the bank for an early-morning swim. Crickets hiss in the mossy green as the sun climbs in a hazy blue sky. I see it all; I hear it; I feel it. It touches me. My beautiful, wonderful life.

An orange bird lands on the boat, a tail of blue feathers fanning out like a summer skirt.

'It's a kingfisher,' Tiger says. 'Isn't she beautiful?' The bird stares at her, making a *cack-cack*ing sound. Tiger reaches her hand towards her, but she spreads her wings, sailing into the sky and swooping back down to snare a fish.

'The kingfisher is a good omen,' Tiger says, tapping the side of her nose.

She trails her hand in the water. 'I dreamt of my father last night,' she says, without looking up. 'We were riding through a dark forest. But I wasn't afraid.'

I think of my own father and how easily I walked away from him and Mom. Something squirms inside me, some eel of guilt.

I can see she's crying, quiet tears sliding into the river. I rub her hand.

'I miss him.'

'He's up there, Tiger,' I say. 'He's watching over you, and he sees how strong and beautiful you are. Like a star, the brightest star in the universe.'

The tears slip down, one after another. She doesn't brush them away, just keeps staring into the distance.

'And he knows you're the berries, Tiger, and he's so proud . . .'

She mouths *Thanks, Doll*, brushing tears off her face with the back of her hand.

Vitaliy turns back towards us, cups his hand to his ear.

'Shhh. Listen.' The sounds of the forest have given way to distant drumming. I sit up straight. The jelly hero is shivering. An ice-cream heart.

Damon shades his eyes. 'They can probably see us approaching.'

The drums get louder.

Boom, boom. Shaka boom, boom, boom.

Under the gold cloth, the bees begin to fidget.

'They won't last much longer without ventilation,' Tiger says.

'We want them agitated,' I say. 'We need them angry.' We're so close now, and the whole plan is getting real-er in my head. But could it be the end for us all?

'This could be the end for us all,' Tiger whispers, frowning.

'But it won't be,' I say. 'I'm the Child of Summer, remember? Do you hear me, bees?' I turn to the bee box. 'We've got to make this work, lads. It's all down to you.'

Vitaliy points up ahead. The forest has turned blue, a sea of zigzag faces and blue feathery headdresses. The forest sways and chants:

Aro-ami aro-ami aro-ami
Chay-chay-chay
Aro-ami aro-ami aro-ami
Chay-chay-chay

I can hear my own heart beeping like a car sensor.

'What are they saying?' Tiger asks Vitaliy.

He holds the paddle in mid-air. 'It's a war chant, a show of strength and a celebration of who they are.'

'Ramish wants to impress us,' Damon says, spitting into the water.

Tiger cups her hands around her eyes. 'He thinks we're coming with a peace offering from Archon. Is he pleased, do you think? Or suspicious?'

'He's not suspicious. He truly believes Archon would not dare to deceive him,' Vitaliy says.

Damon nods.

'He has a big ego, so he's celebrating Archon's submission. He's pleased to receive gifts. Makes him look good.'

Vitaliy says, 'You're right, Damon. Two children and a gift box of prized honey. But the real prize is in humiliating Archon. Remember, Ramish has tried to slaughter his son, he's mutilated five of our children, and he's killed and wounded our men. He has Archon on his knees . . . or so he thinks.' He smiles. 'Ha, he's in for a shock today.'

'He's a wild animal,' Damon says, slapping the paddle against the surface of the water, 'and today he'll pay his dues.' He hesitates. 'I hope the plan works – if it doesn't, we're all finished.' He makes a cutting motion across his throat. Vitaliy looks back at him, frowning.

Nobody answers. We all know full well it's true. I hope the bees are listening.

Within a few minutes, Vitaliy is guiding us towards a wooden pier. The tribe are gathered behind the trees and fall silent as we step off the canoe. A stocky figure emerges, each step slow and deliberate. The blue feathers fall back. And there, standing like a bull, is the man Spirit called liquid evil. I can smell him. A stench that comes at me in waves. There's a rat tattooed on his chest, and you can see protruding – just at the animal's teeth – the shard of bone that Spirit told us about, encasing his black heart.

Ramish smiles.

'Welcome, my girls.' His voice is thick, like oil. He bows, and when he shakes my hand, I can feel my fingers crunch under his. 'How lovely of you to come visit me.'

I bow. 'You're welcome, Your Majesty.'

He laughs at that. I can hear the bees murmuring and pray that Ramish can't. Damon moves towards the canoe, but Ramish says, 'Wait, sonny. You can bring my gift in a moment. First I want to talk to my girls.'

He pinches Tiger's cheek. 'Good and strong,' he says, placing his finger underneath her chin. 'Look at me when I speak, child.'

He pats my head. His breath is foul. 'Charming little girl, I'm sure.' He cups his hand around my neck, and I flinch. 'I can see why they wanted to get rid of you, child.'

He turns to his warriors. 'Wasn't Archon very kind, sending these gifts to me?'

Painted faces nod, murmuring agreement.

'Very, very kind. A sensible man.'

They nod again, like clockwork dolls.

I offer my sample jar of honey. 'There are six flavours of honey in the crate,' I say, pointing to the canoe. 'This is the clover honey, the best of—'

He shushes me, finger to his lips. He takes the jar and lifts the lid. Scoops up two fingers full and sucks the sticky liquid. He closes his eyes, savouring the sweetness. He scoops up another fingerful and runs his tongue across his lips.

'De-lish-us.' He cleans the honey off his gums with his tongue. He's hooked on the taste.

'Archon has packed thyme-scented and leatherwood flavours.'

He closes his eyes. 'Don't speak till I tell you to.'

'Yes, Your Majesty.' I can hear my knees knocking.

'You!'

I think he means Tiger.

'Stand here beside me.'

Tiger does as he asks.

'If you move,' he says, without looking at her, 'I will slice your throat open, are we clear?'

Tiger stares straight ahead.

'Are we clear?'

He shouts this time, and she whispers, 'Yes. Yes, Ramish.'

'And you? Look at me when I'm speaking to you!'

I look up at his dead brown eyes. He is savouring our terror.

He snaps his fingers, and one of the warriors steps forward. His belly is level with my face. I can see an axe hanging from the belt around his hairy middle, and I can smell his sweat, trickling down from fuzzy armpits.

Ramish looks at Damon and Vitaliy.

'The canoe stays here; you can hoof it back to Archon.' He grins. 'I'm being generous. I'll spare you this time.' He runs his tongue over his front teeth. 'Call it gratitude for the gifts. And tell Archon I'll be looking for more.'

He takes another scoop, licking his fingers.

'This won't last very long, I can assure you.'

He looks at me. 'Now, you . . .' He shakes his head, like he's sad. Sad is scarier than bad.

'You . . . I'd like to hear you scream.'

'I will,' I say. 'I can do that. No problem.'

Loud guffaws all round. Ramish throws his head back.

'Your little hands will decorate our boat nicely.'

Tiger staggers, and one of the blue women catches her as she falls.

I get it now. Oh Diamond Jesus.

The man with the belly draws out his axe. I can see my reflection in it; my face looks fat and very white.

'Wait.' Vitaliy is leaning against the pier. 'Thank you for sparing us, Ramish. Archon won't forget this. You'll get a regular supply of honey, I'll see to that.'

Ramish grunts.

Vitaliy points to the canoe. 'Just try the spicy leatherwood and thyme-scented honeys before we go, Ramish.' He points to the bee box on the boat. 'If you tell us your favourite, we'll bring you a whole case of it tomorrow.'

Ramish snaps his fingers. He can't resist. 'Bring it to me now, boy.'

Damon and Vitaliy step towards the canoe.

'Just one of you,' Ramish says.

The man with the axe runs a stubby finger along the blade. Behind him, way up in the sky, I see the Headscarves hover and swoop in the distance, like all the flags in the world strung together. As they dive closer, we can hear a wall of sound, like a choir of archangels. Everyone looks up in astonishment. Ramish is off his guard.

Vitaliy lays the box at Ramish's feet.

The Headscarves twist and swoop higher, and Ramish turns his attention to Vitaliy. 'Hurry up. Don't waste my time.' Vitaliy reaches down to unhook the mesh door.

Ramish still doesn't get it. 'What are you waiting for? Open the damn box, boy.'

The bees begin to murmur and circle outside, checking their bearings with the sun's position.

Ramish is confused. It takes him a few seconds, and then he roars in horror as thousands of hot, angry bees exit the bee box. He kicks at the box with his sandalled foot, sending it tumbling towards the edge of the pier. Big mistake, Ramish.

'Get this out of my sight!' The bees continue to swarm, and the Headscarves descend again. Some of the warriors run towards the forest, screaming and disorientated. The noise is frightening. Twenty thousand wings flutter from the bee box as the Headscarves tumble through the air, shrieking and singing, their scarves flapping about their faces. Ramish charges at Vitaliy.

'Get them out of here!'

The bees are enraged. Ramish is hollering, running towards the river. The blue faces are shocked, arms flapping, running in circles, frightened by the stinging army of bees and the fury of the Headscarves. Some plunge into the river to escape.

Tiger and I watch, staying perfectly still. We can see a thousand bees circling Ramish's head. They're gorging on the honey around his mouth, stinging his face and scalp. He screams, thrashing and writhing, as he plunges headfirst into the river.

Melania told us how the message of attack is sent from bee to bee. As Ramish surfaces, the bees hover, like bullies at the school gate. He disappears underwater. Seconds pass by and he rises again, treading water. His face is swollen, and he is howling in pain and terror. The bees circle him purposefully, buzzing loudly.

'No, please, have mercy.' I approach the pier. The bees form a circle over my head. Ramish is crying, sobbing, pleading. I nod to Damon, and he and Vitaliy exchange glances and swim toward Ramish. The circle of bees follows. The water reaches Vitaliy's chin, but Ramish is out of his depth.

'He shouldn't suffer like this,' Damon says. The two boys circle Ramish. 'We won't see you suffer, Ramish.'

He nods his head, grateful, still sobbing like a child. A few stray bees swoop in under his tongue. He squirms, slapping his face.

I call to Vitaliy, and he nods, dragging Ramish under, holding his head in a tight grip. Legs thrash, arms flail, muscles strain in his face. The bees hum restlessly.

Damon says, 'Need a hand there, brother?'

Vitaliy shakes his head. Seconds pass. The only sound we can hear is the *pop-pop* of dark bubbles as they gurgle up and break the surface. The smell is vile.

Ramish is still, his body sinking into the mud. Black liquid oozes to the surface. Vitaliy raises a clenched fist, like a matador. The bees disperse, flying into the forest.

'Sleep well, Ramish,' I whisper to myself.

Now there's only silence, like the quiet clean that follows heavy rain. Drums are discarded; headdresses flutter in the breeze. Even the Headscarves have disappeared.

Vitaliy points to the scattered sea of blue. 'They are grateful,' he says. 'They loathed Ramish. To them, we are heroes.'

Damon shakes the water from his hair and carries the bee box back to the boat. No one speaks as we all climb back in.

Vitaliy pushes us off and we paddle downriver, skimming the water, Tiger and me holding hands. We watched a man die. *We killed him.* Where is he now? We're all silently replaying the movie in our heads, knowing how close we came to not making it home.

Damon breaks the silence. 'Mission accomplished.'

Vitaliy stops paddling, lets out a roar. 'We did it! Ramish is dead.'

Tiger frowns. 'It was damn close, though. Oh, Doll, when I saw the axe . . .' She shudders and squeezes my hand. 'Archon will be so pleased.'

We go back over it again and again as we glide home: 'Do you remember when . . . ?' 'Did you see Ramish . . . ?' 'Did you notice . . . ?' 'What about when . . . ?' We can't stop talking, releasing all the terror we've been holding in our bones.

'The bees are the real heroes,' I say. 'Melania said they would come back to the hive. Where are they now?'

Damon points to the horizon. There's a swarm flying across the water towards us. They circle overhead, then swoop down and straight into the bee box.

'Home sweet home,' Tiger says, and we all laugh. We give them a round of applause as Tiger closes the hatch.

We're nearly home. But it's not my home. Tomorrow we move on.

Ahead, there's a crowd waving from the riverbank. A rainbow of colours. The sun is sinking into the water, drowning in orange. Smoke is rising from campfires, reminding me I haven't eaten since morning. We can hear singing in the distance. We all stand together as we approach, thumbs-up.

They're all singing my song, and it brings me back. The orange cushion, the telly, the couch. Who was that girl? The one who refused to live? That otherworld ghost-girl?

'Doll, you're miles away,' Tiger says. 'What are you thinking about?

'Just a girl I knew once,' I say. And I'm only realising this now – a girl who was surrounded by love. I think of my mom, and my heart crumples.

Everyone is waving. I come back to the present. I can see Melania. I smile and blow her a kiss.

On the riverbank, there's a boy standing between Spirit and Archon. Standing tall. Tough as a tree. I recognise the wolf tattoo. It's Casimir, and he's waving. Oh, happy day. Happy, happy day.

Life. It's scary, but for sure, it's the sweetest thing.

CHAPTER 42

DOLL

The wood is crackling and spitting as we sit cross-legged around the campfire. The stars are out. The bowl of charcoal chicken on my lap tastes like Heaven. Tiger passes me a hunk of pineapple cake. 'It's a feast,' she says, her mouth full. 'Make the most of it, 'cos tomorrow it'll be bread and water.' She laughs and shovels another pineapple piece into her mouth, points towards the clearing on our right.

Archon is up dancing again, the light of the moon bouncing off his head as he whirls to the music.

'Come on,' he shouts over at us. 'Dance. We're celebrating tonight!' Tiger jumps up, her mouth full again, and joins him.

Casimir is sitting next to me. He laughs at his father's antics.

'I've never seen him so happy,' he says. 'Ramish's death is an answered prayer.'

'It's not just Ramish,' I say. 'Your recovery is another answered prayer. He loves you so much, it broke his heart to see you so near death. Didn't it, Spirit?'

Spirit touches Casimir's shoulder. 'You are the light of his life, sonny. And Ramish dead? That's a bonus.' He sucks on his pipe, puffing circles of smoke from the corner of his mouth.

Casimir's brown eyes shadow over.

'I know that, Spirit. My father and me, we are very close.'

He turns to me. 'I remember you, Doll,' he says. 'I could smell the ointment as you put it on and what you said; it was like you could see inside my heart. Like you knew the grief and the guilt. Coming home without Lani . . .' He shakes his head. 'What happened that day – I can't understand or forgive.'

'I heard what happened,' I say.

'You were right. I needed to shake off the things I saw. Put them in a casket, set fire to them in my head. And I did that. And my heart escaped.'

211

He kisses my hand. 'Thank you, Doll. I salute you.' He turns to Spirit. 'And you.'

He bows, and Spirit catches his hand, locking it in his own bony fingers. 'Remember, all suffering has a purpose, Casimir,' he says. 'It tears open your heart, but you learn. You grow, you become a man.'

'You were a comfort for my father and a true friend,' Casimir says. 'You will always be welcome here.' He sees Spirit's empty mug. 'Here, let me get you a drink.'

Spirit winks at me. 'Thought you'd never ask.' He shouts after him, 'Fill it up, like a good lad.'

Spirit shakes his head. 'Casimir is a fine boy. And I love Archon: he's like a son to me.' He puffs on his pipe, closing his eyes. 'Tomorrow I must be gone. Time to move on.'

It starts me thinking. *Tomorrow.* It's a big word. It keeps creeping up on me tonight, like a shadow. Tomorrow I need to set out and find Major Tom Axel. I've delayed long enough. Tiger is coming with me, and I'm not arguing. Truth is, I feel safer with her. Two's company.

'Tomorrow I must move on too,' I say.

He opens his eyes. 'You won't be needing the horses,' he says. 'The terrain is too rough on Glenshiquin. You can collect them here on the way back.'

'On the way back?' I shiver. 'Do you think we'll make it back, Spirit?'

'Do you?'

'How do I know? Anything could happen. I only know Major Tom Axel's involved in the mine. Will I even find him?'

'You've no plan?'

'How can I have a plan, Spirit?'

'Do you believe you can do it? That you can succeed?'

We both look at the dancers. Archon and Tiger are spinning in circles, and everyone is clapping. The pipe smoke curls up around our silence.

Several minutes pass. More dancers join in, and now they all make a large circle, their faces lit up by the flames. Eyes shine. Bursts of laughter. The fiddlers slide their bows over winding tunes. *Clap. Clap-clap. Clap-clap-clap.* The *ting-tang* of the guitar, the whistle-call of the pipes.

'Do you believe you can do it?'

I'm still thinking about the question. On the one hand, it's ridiculous what they've asked me to do. Putting me at risk, seeking the impossible. Tom Axel is a lunatic, and I'm to take the Orb and disappear with

212

it; how the Jesus am I supposed to do that? I'm only a child. What's the chances?

'What's the chances?' I say.

'You tell me, Doll.'

The music is getting faster, and the children are whooping and giggling, trying not to be the one to break the circle. 'Come on, Doll,' one of them shouts over, but I smile and wave them away. I'm too busy thinking.

Didn't I get to Almazova and the Grandmothers didn't doubt I was truly the Child of Summer? Didn't I nearly drown but get saved? And I've seen the candle flame follow me.

What else?

Didn't the bees clearly choose me? Look, I even rode a horse standing up. And Jesus forgive me – I'm sure he will – but I helped to push Ramish into the next world. When you think of it like that . . .

'What are you thinking, Doll?'

I have to shout to be heard. 'I think I can do it.'

'You do?'

'Yes. I think there's two ways of looking at it. And I prefer the second way.'

'Which is?'

'Which is that I *am* truly the Child of Summer, and it's okay to be afraid, because it's what you do with the fear that counts. Like you said, Spirit.'

He chuckles. 'You learn fast,' he says. 'You're a topper. And what will you do with it? What will you do with the fear?'

'Put it in a casket, set fire to it in my head?'

We both laugh. 'That's the girl. It worked for Casimir,' he says, 'so I reckon, Child of Summer, it'll work for you too.'

He wags a skinny finger at me. 'Fear is our life companion, so we just need to know what to do with it when it gets too big for its boots.'

Casimir comes back with Spirit's refill. Spirit takes a sip and splutters. 'That's strong stuff.' He wipes his mouth with the back of his hand. 'Just what the doctor ordered.'

There's a scream. Spirit looks up in alarm. The music stops. The laughter dies. We all hear it. A loud voice says, 'Quick. Down by the river . . . hurry.'

We make our way along the path to the river. I push my way to the front. My heart lurches. The water has all but disappeared from the

213

river. Fish twist and turn, flapping madly, gasping, their silver scales like tinfoil in the moonlight. Crabs stagger. Even as we watch, horrified, a mottled trout at our feet flips over one last time, gills stilled, glassy eyes, forlorn, staring at the moon.

'It's the Orb,' I whisper to Tiger, and she nods. Her brow furrows. Archon stands next to me. He watches as some of the boys jump down onto the riverbed, their sandals squelching in the mud.

He cups his hands around his mouth and roars, 'Get off the riverbed, boys. Make your way home.'

Even as he's talking, there's a rushing sound. A giant wall of water hurtles back, filling up the riverbed. Everyone starts running toward the campfire, back to safety.

'This is Major Tom sending another message, Tiger,' I whisper. 'He's letting the Grandmothers know the power he can unleash.'

'The river is our livelihood,' Archon says, as we walk back to the village. 'We can't survive without it. What madness is in the air?'

Archon moves about, making sure no one is missing, telling everyone it's a minor tsunami, nothing to be afraid of. The river is flowing gently again, like nothing happened. But the party's over. Mothers bring the children home to bed as the men stand around, arms folded, talking about what happened.

Back in Archon's hut, I show Casimir my map. 'He knows the area better than anyone,' Archon told me.

'The mine is between Inchiquin and Glenshiquin Mountains, here.' Casimir marks it with an X and traces the best route for us. 'There are watchtowers.' He marks an X again. 'Keep out of sight as far as you can. And it'll be cold, so wrap up.'

Tiger says, 'At least we don't have Ramish to worry about.'

'You're right,' Archon says. 'The mountain will be safer now. His father will take over again, and he's a good man. There will be no grief at his son's loss.' He shakes his head. 'You raise a child. You have such hope, you dream your dreams for him, and then . . . you realise you've raised a monster. *Your own son.* It makes you weep.'

'That is the truth,' Spirit says. 'Ramish has brought only despair to his family.'

Like me, maybe? There's a knot in my chest. Didn't I bring despair to my family? And was I a monster for walking away?

We head back to our hut. Melania has sent new rucksacks with parcels of food and warm clothes and boots. Archon will wake us at sunrise.

I lie in my sleeping bag. Mom and Dad keep flashing into my mind. I think of my bed, safe, cosy. I think of my couch, my hair combed, being kissed. I think of my new pink coat and the ice-cream birthday cake I wouldn't eat. I think how cold my heart was, freezing them all out. I was so angry then. So mean. I was so mean. I hope that's not how they'll remember me. If it is, who could blame them?

CHAPTER 43

DAN

Mr Davis checks his watch. 'Good afternoon, Mr Redmond.' He consults his notes as I step into the cramped office space. The desk is strewn with a profusion of files and clipboards and Post-it notes. How can people work in this mess?

He gestures towards the chair just inside the door and peers at me from over his glasses. 'You're the father. Is Mrs Redmond here?'

'No, my wife is working.'

'I understand. Quite.' He perches at the edge of the desk, pushing aside some papers.

He doesn't hold back. 'I'm afraid your daughter is quite ill,' he says. 'We are concerned.'

I didn't expect this, this bald expression of concern. It spells trouble. 'You're concerned?'

He nods. 'Pneumonia is a strange one. You don't always know what you're dealing with. Whether the patient will respond to this or that antibiotic. It's a serious illness. You're aware of that?'

'Yes, of course. But she's come through before.'

'This time, I'm afraid, finding the right antibiotics is proving challenging.'

'What are you saying exactly?' His words feel like finding a worm in an apple.

'So far, she's not responding. Her heart rate is still elevated, and she's running a fever.'

'Not responding?' I swallow. 'Can't you give her something stronger? Damn it, in this day and age.'

He pushes his glasses up the bridge of his nose and leans forward, his palms resting on his thigh.

'Her white cell count is raised, and at this stage, we're worried about carditis.' His face is grave.

'Carditis? Jesus, what's that? Something to do with her heart?'

He looks over his glasses again. 'Yes, inflammation of the heart. Pneumonia can cause all manner of complications.'

'So what more can be done?'

'We've called in a bacteriologist, and . . .'

'And?'

'And we suspect now that she may have a strain that's resistant to antibiotics. It's hard to identify.'

I can't believe what I'm hearing.

'Hard to identify? You have scans and blood tests and x-rays. Twenty-first century medicine, and you're telling me—'

He raises his hand. 'I know how difficult this is, but please, bear with me.'

I drag my palms over my face, trying hard to focus.

He folds his arms, shifts a little on the desk. 'Severe pneumonia can lead to sepsis, and that can be very serious. The infection can spread rapidly.'

'Christ. Sepsis; I've heard of it. Is it treatable?'

'We have her on powerful antibiotics now. And steroids.' He adjusts his glasses. 'We are monitoring her carefully, Mr Redmond. If she worsens . . .' He stops and strokes his chin. 'If she worsens – and she may not – we might consider a ventilator to help her breathe.'

'Jesus.'

'Can I ask?' he says then, interlocking his fingers.

'Yes?'

'Do you want us to go all the way?' He looks at the gold band on his finger, waiting.

'All the way? How do you mean?'

He steeples his hands. 'I'm sure you're aware' – he picks his words carefully – 'that there are situations where we may not intervene beyond a particular point.'

I know what he means. 'Are you saying, do not resuscitate?'

If he pushes those glasses up one more time, I will hit him.

'Precisely. It might be something you might want to consider.'

I can't believe he's saying this. There must be a law against it.

'Are you suggesting we just let her go? Is that it, in plain language? What happened to do no harm, eh, Doctor?'

He leans back, folds his arms again.

'Oh, I'm not suggesting that at all, Mr Redmond. I'm merely saying it may be something you might want to discuss with your wife.'

I feel like punching him.

'I think you're out of order there,' I say, trying to keep my voice calm.

He raises his palm. 'I'm sorry. I can understand your upset. But it's my job to ask. Parents are often grateful for the space to bring this up. For the opportunity to discuss the issue.'

'No discussion required,' I say, calmly. 'We want you to go all the way, as you put it. End of.'

He straightens up, buttons his suit jacket. 'Of course. Please understand, I have to ask. Sometimes' – he waves his hand towards the corridor outside – 'lives can be brutal, often intolerable. We see such suffering.' He looks at me. 'What would you want, if it was you?'

'I don't know,' I say. 'But isn't that the point? How can we know what someone else would want? We're not God.'

He nods, reaching for his car keys. 'We'll do our best,' he says. 'This week will be critical. In the meantime, Matron will keep you updated.'

He shakes my hand. There's nothing left to say. He moves off down the corridor, swift as a dancer, his shoes barely making a sound on the tiles.

She's quite ill. She's quite ill. She's quite ill. On the journey home, the wipers swish hypnotically to the rhythm of the three words I can't get out of my head. *She's quite ill.*

The rain is still bucketing down as I shove my key in the front door. The familiar smell of home hits me, that comforting mix of laundry, cooking, and wood smoke that wraps itself around you like a blanket.

'I was trying to contact you,' Sally says, coming down the stairs. 'Well?' She follows me into the kitchen. 'Do you want some soup and salad?'

She takes two bowls from the dresser.

'How's Doll? What did he say, Dan?' She starts chopping tomatoes. 'Get a bowl there and tip some lettuce in for me, Dan, will you?'

Cliff Richard is on the radio singing 'Living Doll'. I flick the off button.

'The antibiotics are kicking in now, I'd say. I thought she was improving last night.' She pushes her hair behind her ear. 'Did he think she was improving?'

'Sally.'

'It's been a long week, but I think she's getting there. I thought—'

'Sally, listen.'

218

She keeps chopping. 'That nurse Rachel is lovely. Did you meet her yet?'

'Sally. Stop it!'

She looks up sharply. 'What? God, you're grumpy.' She slides the tomatoes into the salad leaves and tosses the knife into the sink. 'Sorry, Dan . . . go on.'

'I've spoken to the consultant.'

'Mr Davis. What did you think of him?'

'Sally, he brought me up to date on Doll . . .'

'And?'

'She's quite ill.'

'Well, we know that already; they always state the obvious.' She wipes her hands on the tea towel, leans against the worktop. 'What else did he say?'

'I think she's fighting for her life, Sal.'

'You *think*? Did he actually say that?'

'He said she's not responding to the first- or second-line antibiotics . . .'

Her face is pale. 'It's too early to tell, surely?'

'Listen. They can't call it. She's quite ill, that's what he said. It could affect her heart. They've started her on more powerful drugs, but sepsis is a possibility.'

'Sepsis. Jesus Christ, Dan. Sepsis is lethal. She needs . . . they need to . . .' Her hands fly to her mouth.

'Sally, they know what she needs; they're doing all they can. We have to wait. And hope . . .'

'Hope?' She pulls out a chair and sits at the table, ashen.

'Hope that the meds will work, that her heart will be okay. The next few days are critical.'

She smiles then. 'Dan, don't be so dramatic. Did he actually say that? You know what these guys are like; they cover their arses. Right? You said so yourself.'

I don't know what to say. I bring the salad to the table. Pour a glass of water for her.

'Dan?' She takes a sip. 'What are you saying?'

I sit down opposite her, take her hand. 'We have to hope that she'll fight like she always does. That she'll pull through. Nothing's certain.'

'My poor Doll.' She closes her eyes and shakes her head. 'We won't say anything to Andi for now,' she says in a flat voice. 'I think she's upset enough as it is. Will you let Will know? He rang me earlier.'

'Sure, I'll talk to him.' I turn off the soup and pour hers, but she waves it away.

'I'm not hungry.' She gets up and takes her coat from the closet in the hall. 'I'm going to go to the hospital now, Dan.'

I put my arms around her, and she leans in. We stay like that, swaying slightly, for a long time, just holding on. I can feel the tension through her sweater.

My mobile vibrates on the table. 'Take that,' she says, releasing herself and kissing my cheek. 'We'll talk later.'

It's Joe from work.

'Yeah, Joe?'

'I thought you should know, Dan.' His tone is off colour.

'Know what?' I can sense his hesitation.

'Regional Office was on. Did they contact you?'

'No. About what?' The hairs on the back of my neck start to prickle, like sensors.

'Well, don't say anything if they ring you, okay? You weren't talking to me.'

'What's going on, Joe? You're sounding like a secret agent.'

'The regional audit manager is coming tomorrow to have a look at the books.'

'Frank McKenna? You're joking!'

'They want to see the files on Rob Colbert's accounts.'

I can feel my heart dislodging, moving a centimetre to the side. 'What? Who does?' My stomach muscles begin to knot.

'Lorraine authorised it. I just wanted to tip you off.'

'Thanks, Joe. Appreciate it.'

'Is there something you need to be telling me, Dan?' He lowers his voice to a whisper.

I hesitate. There's only one reason they're investigating Colbert Bakery's account. But how the fuck did they know?

'Well, Dan?'

'I authorised zero interest on Rob Colbert's loan, Joe. Under the circumstances. Just a short-term arrangement while Joanne is off.'

'Dan, Dan, you can't do that. You know the rules. Are you mad? Why didn't you pass it on to them for approval? The rules . . .'

'Someone must've tipped them off, Joe.'

'What are you saying?'

'I'm saying, how would they know to look? Someone said something.'

There's a silence. I'm thinking of Friday night and Shirley's face as I was leaving. The chill in her voice slithers through me now. *Nothing happened, Dan. Get over yourself.*

She never would, though, would she?

'Is Shirley in today, Joe?' I knew she rang in sick yesterday with a bug.

I can hear an intake of breath down the phone. 'No, she's out for the week with flu.'

Am I putting two and two together and getting five? There's a long silence.

'Bit of a coincidence,' Joe says. 'Did you piss her off?'

When I don't answer, Joe whistles. 'You did. And no, Dan, you don't have to tell me . . . look, tread carefully. If she's sticking her knife in . . . well . . . watch yourself.'

'Bit late now,' I say. 'Anyway, thanks for the heads-up. I'll be in later.'

I can hear the hesitation again. 'They'll want you out of the way for a day or two, Dan; you know the drill. Especially if they call in the audit team. Which they usually do.'

'Fuck.'

'Lorraine will be in touch, I'm sure, if she hasn't been already. I'll keep you posted anyway, mate.'

I scroll through my emails. Lorraine's message is there, short and polite:

> *The Regional Operations/Audit Manager, Frank McKenna, will conduct an audit with particular reference to the Colbert accounts. Head Office auditors will follow up with a wider investigation if required.*

I'm suspended pending the outcome of these investigations.

There's also a missed call from Lorraine's office.

I have to sit down. Jesus, this is serious shit. What was I thinking? I have no defence. This could mean my job, my career. And my reputation. One mistake. I broke the rules; I'm going to pay. I've seen it happen – the bank takes no prisoners. One strike and you're out.

I sit at the table, staring at the congealing soup. It feels like a sinkhole is yawning open under my chair and I'm tumbling down into it. I'm trying to grasp the walls, but my hands slide off and I'm hurtling towards the darkness.

And fuck it. The worst thing is, I've only myself to blame.

CHAPTER 44

DOLL

Morning is breaking open like an eggshell. Spirit and Archon have come to wave us off. 'Keep the sun off your eyes, child.' Archon jams my straw hat on my head. 'And don't forget, you'll need something warmer up there.' He points to the shadow behind us. 'See the snow on top of Glenshiquin?'

I know he's worried about us, and his kindness touches a spot. It's hard to fight the tears.

'Good to go so,' he says, rubbing his palms together. The four of us embrace in a little circle like folk dancers.

Archon spreads his hand across his heart. 'May the spirits protect you and guide you.' He stands back, feet apart, arms clasped behind him. 'Go now. Bless you.'

We set off. Tiger leads the way across the meadow and up onto the steep forest path we need to follow. In the distance we can hear a bell tinkling, some wandering goat or sheep across the valley. A mist hangs in the air like a ghost, and I shiver.

The mountains frown down on us like giant gorillas, swallowing up the brightness of the day. Archon told us that thousands of years ago, Inchiquin and Glenshiquin were beautiful twin sisters who fought with a local witchdoctor. Legend has it, he said, that in revenge, he turned them into twin peaks, forever imprisoned in the baked earth.

The sun climbs higher above us, and underfoot the path is uneven. More than once I stumble and fall.

'Wait up, Tiger!'

She stops and falls into step beside me. We clatter along in the heat. My throat is sore.

'How do you think he'll react when he meets us?'

'Who?'

'Who do you think, Doll? Major Axel, of course.'

'We'll have to find him first.' I stop to take a breath. My chest feels like a bag of stones. 'I'm hoping, when we do, that he'll see sense.' The thought of what's ahead, the weight of it, makes my knees buckle.

'How likely is that? Be realistic.' There's a sharpness to her tone I haven't heard before. She takes a long drink of water and passes the bottle to me. 'He's a criminal, so he's more likely to kill us than see sense.' She marches ahead again.

Part of me wants to grow wings and fly back to Bluebell Grove, where I was loved and safe. It wasn't all bad. Sometimes, when you look back, you see things differently. It's like time changes the angle of a thing.

'You can still turn back,' I shout after her, stumbling again, angry. Why won't she slow down? 'If you're afraid . . .'

She spins around, rolling her eyes. 'How many times have I told you, I'm not afraid?' Her eyes flare. 'You're the one who seems to be afraid. And you're supposed to be the Child of Summer. *The chosen one.*'

She's right. I *am* afraid. The day, the whole journey, is starting to sour on me. What am I walking into? It's like being in one of Will's computer games – but this is real. And that worm keeps crawling around in my head: Can I trust her?

'It's a bit strange,' I say, struggling to keep up, looking for a fight.

'What is?'

'You wanting to come with me. Why're you so interested, Tiger?'

She spins around, breathing heavily, hands on her hips. 'How do you mean?'

'You're risking your life. You'll be in so much trouble when you get back. *If* you get back . . . and you don't seem that bothered.'

Her jaws clenches. 'What are you trying to say?'

'It's just a bit strange, that's all.'

She thrusts her chin forward. 'I like danger,' she says. 'Does that answer your question?'

'Why are you mad with me?'

She kicks a stone and it sails over the edge, clattering onto the rocks far below. 'You don't trust me. You think I'm the spy in the camp.'

'Well . . .'

She waves me away. 'Oh grow up, Doll.' She walks on ahead in silence.

I've never felt less like the Child of Summer. She's vanished like a spark, and here I am again, my old self, stumbling along. By the time we stop for lunch, my head is on fire. Melania packed banana bread and yoghurt for us, but I'm not hungry.

Far, far below, I can see the river like a glittering necklace, circled by matchstick pine trees. From up here, the valley is a buttercup carpet under clouds that change their shape like smoke. The air is sweet-scented. Despite all the beauty, my energy is only ankle high, some dread-weariness pulling me under. It's like the colour has melted off the rainbow and now it's dripping grey. Tiger is quiet, eating silently, the glow dimming between us.

It's getting colder and we press on, leaning forward on all fours as we pick through jutting rocks and soft bog. The farther we climb, the louder and sharper the wind, its teeth biting through our clothes and sucking the skin off our faces. I'm grateful for the warmth of my purple coat. Up here every step is a squelch, every breath hurts. My fingers are yellow-white numb.

We're amongst caves now, damp, drippy mouths dotted between the scrubby oaks and bracken. Casimir has marked where we can shelter. 'The light's fading. We need to stop for the night,' I shout to Tiger.

She consults Casimir's map and turns back to me for the first time since lunch. 'We're close to the pass.'

'Pass? I'm going to pass out,' I say, 'if we don't stop soon.'

She nods and points to a large cave set back against the rock face up ahead, partially covered in scrub. 'I think this is the one Casimir told us about.'

We shrug off our rucksacks at the entrance. I only want to close my eyes and sleep.

There's a stack of small logs and some candles on a shelf just inside the cave entrance. Tiger coaxes the wood alight. Heat is medicine. A honey drink warmed in the pan over the fire gives me hope. I peel off my socks and squeeze the muddy water out.

Tiger shovels warmed rice and thick chunks of bacon into her mouth. The drink is heating my bones, and the ointment lightens the weight in my chest. We spread honey on our bread rolls, curl into our sleeping bags.

I know my dark mood is affecting Tiger. I say, 'I'm sorry, Tiger, for thinking . . . you know . . .'

'Forget it, Doll. I'm sorry too. I shouldn't have reacted like I did.' Her face glows in the firelight.

'We're still best friends?'

'Best friends forever,' she says, bringing her face a little closer to mine. 'Doll, you look yellow. I'm worried about you.'

'I'm good.' The fire crackles and sparks fly, and we watch drowsily. Bit by bit the flames die down and the embers turn to ash. My eyelids close, and I drift off into a deep sleep.

It's still dark when I hear it. My heart hammers as I nudge Tiger awake. 'Did you hear that?'

'What is it?'

'Listen.'

Footsteps and whispers. We daren't move. Tiger fumbles to light a candle.

'No lights, Tiger.'

She ignores me, as usual.

A boot comes into view, a leg, a pair of eyes. I scream, and the sound curdles the night.

'Who are you?' Tiger's voice is steady.

The boot steps forward, and a boy blinks and shades his eyes. Tiger holds the flickering light up to the shaven head. A boy in an oversized jacket. He hunkers down, the jacket spreading out around him.

A girl with curls leans over his shoulder. 'My name is Layla,' she whispers. 'C-can we come in?'

Tiger gestures them inside.

The girl's hand is frost-cold in mine, her face ghostly in the dim light.

I pass them some water and honey biscuits. 'Are you coming from the mine?'

They look at each other.

'We didn't expect to find two girls up here in the dead of night,' the boy says. 'What's going on?'

'We're looking for someone,' Tiger says.

Layla wipes some crumbs from her mouth. Her eyes narrow. 'Who?'

'We'll come to that in a minute,' I say. 'Just tell us how you got here.'

Layla takes another bite. 'We did escape from the mine. There was an incident.'

'How do you mean?' Tiger looks across at me.

'Last night,' the boy says, 'the river got sucked up.' He clicks his fingers. 'It just disappeared.'

Layla nods. 'They were running all over the place. The water started spinning away, and then the river filled back up. So strange.'

The boy takes another drink, wiping his mouth with his sleeve. 'Today, everyone was rattled. They think it was a warning from the Gods.'

'How many are there in the mine?'

'There are fifty-two children,' Layla says. She stops to count on her fingers. 'And there are seven, no eight, adults. Some more come and go.'

'Security?' Tiger asks.

'Yep. There's a fence with two gates. And watchtowers,' Layla says. 'The gates are locked in the evenings.' She looks at the boy. 'But tonight, with all the chaos,' she says, 'they were left open, and Yamen here, my brother, said we should go for it. There's going to be murder in the morning when they find out.' She bites her lip. 'That's why we need to be gone at first light.'

She chews the inside of her mouth.

'I don't think we're the priority, Layla,' Yamen says. 'They're afraid the river will disappear again and come back and swallow the mine. They're wondering if they should think about getting out themselves.'

'How did you end up there?' I whisper.

'Same as everyone else,' she says. 'Ramish.' She says it like Archon does. *Rameeesh*. 'He organises the labour. You can't resist.' She makes a chopping motion on her wrist.

Yamen nods. 'Ramish is a monster.'

Tiger says, 'Ramish is dead.'

Layla's eyes widen.

'Dead as a dead duck.'

'How?'

'Stung by bees. He died roaring,' I say.

Yamen looks to Tiger. 'Are you sure?'

'We saw it with our own eyes.'

Layla claps her hands. 'That changes everything, don't it, Yamen? The whole valley will be celebrating.'

He beams and nods his head slowly.

She joins her hands in prayer. 'Thank you, Gods.'

Yamen rubs her shoulder. 'So what brings you here?'

'Major Tom Axel. Do you know him?'

Yamen nods. 'Yeah, we know him. Tall, shaven head, big hands.'

Layla says, 'He used to bring us chocolate and sherbet when he visited. He often stopped and talked to us.'

'What did he talk about?'

'He'd tell us stories. About the army. Do you remember, Yamen? And he could make a coin disappear.'

Yamen nods. 'He's the kinda guy you wouldn't mess with, though.'

Layla taps her lips. 'You're right. I heard him argue with Grinder more than once—'

'Who's Grinder?'

'He's the boss.'

'What would they argue about?'

'I couldn't hear much. The major's job was getting the load transported out. He was a big gun.'

Tiger leans closer. 'How did it work?'

'The diamonds were packed and winched aboard a helicopter once every ten days. Major Tom was always there that day, guaranteed,' Layla says.

'Was? Did something happen?'

'Well, that's the thing, Major Tom is long gone. He's not coming back.'

No one says anything. I can hear the *drip, drip* of water at the back of the cave. My mouth feels like sawdust.

'How do you mean, not coming back?' Tiger says. 'When did you see him last?'

Yamen looks at Layla. 'Maybe three weeks, maybe four.'

'Are you sure?'

'It was four weeks ago,' Layla says. 'Major Tom and Grinder were arguing. We could hear them from the dorm. The major stormed out of Grinder's office, shouting over his shoulder.'

'And?'

'And that was it. He took off the next morning, and we haven't seen him since.' She smiles. 'We missed the chocolate. And the stories.'

'Are you sure he hasn't been back?'

'No. He's not coming back. Grinder told us. No more sherbet, he said. He thought that was funny.'

Tiger looks at me. 'I can't believe it. After all this.' She looks at Yamen. 'Do you know where he might have gone?'

'Sorry. Haven't a clue.'

Layla shakes her head. 'You're too late.' She looks at Yamen, yawning. 'Better get some sleep.'

Yamen nods, pulling the collar of his jacket up and leaning against the wall. 'We'll be gone in a few hours,' he says. 'Looks like you need to turn back and start again.'

Tiger nods slowly. 'You're right. We need to rethink, right, Doll?' She sighs.

Layla yawns. 'I hope you find him.'

'We'll find him,' I say, looking straight at Tiger. 'If it's the last thing we'll ever do, we'll find him. Isn't that right, Tiger?'

She pretends not to hear and blows out the candle.

I stare into the darkness, lights dancing in my head.

*

When I open my eyes, Layla and Yamen are gone. Tiger's in her sleeping bag, her hands laced behind her head.

'You were coughing all night,' she says.

'I'm fine. What now?'

She closes her eyes. 'We go back. What else?' Her voice is flat.

'Go back . . . where?'

She turns to me. 'Back to Archon. Back to the horses. Back home.' She sighs. 'I suppose back to the cathedral for you.' She leans up on her elbow. 'Or have you got a better idea?'

'We can't just go back.'

'So have you got a better idea?' Her voice is sharp.

I close my eyes for a second. I feel like a beaten docket. A fool. I dig my face with my thumb till it hurts. 'Maybe the mine is still worth checking out?'

She makes a sneery sound. 'Nice one. Especially after those two,' – she jerks her thumb at the entrance – 'disappeared last night. They'd say, "Welcome, girls. Right place, right time." '

I know she's making sense, but I can't go back.

'I hope,' she says, 'this isn't all one big joke, Doll. That someone isn't sending you on a wild-goose chase.'

I dig at my face. 'Don't be ridiculous. The Grandmothers authorised this. You can't get higher than that.'

'Doll?'

The cave is closing in, and someone is plastering cement around the walls of my heart. I miss my mom. I want her back. I want to go home. Why did I come here? I'm not a hero, just a dummy with a screw loose.

'Doll. Listen.' Tiger is sitting up, eyes wide.

'What?'

'I've just . . .'

'I'm not going back,' I say.

'Shut up for a minute and listen.'

'What is it?'

'The bubbles. You didn't leave them behind?'

I rummage through the rucksack, panicking till I feel the metal canister.

Tiger unscrews the top for me. She blows a string of bubbles through the wand, and they sail up, floating out into the grey mist. Nothing.

'Give it to me.' I dip the wand in the liquid. *Please, Nell; give us something.* I take a rattling breath and blow. A cascade of bubbles floats pinkly across the cave. One shimmers, wobbles, and comes to rest on my sleeping bag.

An image is starting to form. We hold our breath, afraid to move the still air and disturb this circle of knowledge.

It's a stone building with a bell tower on a lake island. From behind a tree in the foreground, a fox appears. He looks straight at us, then turns and trots back towards the lake, disappearing into the undergrowth. The image fades, and the bubble pops.

Tiger jumps up and does a little dance.

'Don't bump your head, Tiger.'

'I know that place. I recognise it. We did it in history.'

'Where is it?'

'It's Inchiquin Monastery. They started restoration work on it years ago. It's one of our ancient holy sites, going back over two thousand years. That's Loughfada Lake. Legend has it that it's a bottomless lake.'

I clap my hands and feel a stabbing pain in my chest. 'Do you know how to get there, Tiger?'

'Well, that's the thing. Not really. But I know we have to descend from here, then cross the waterfall to Inchiquin. After that . . .'

'I think the fox will guide us,' I say, rubbing ointment on my chest. I think about digging my face earlier. I must remember that I am the Child of Summer. These images work only for me – so I am powerful. That old Doll, I hate to say it, is never far away. She's like a ghost trying to bury the new me.

The mood has changed. We're back on course. Hope has rescued us.

'So we need to find the fox,' Tiger says, smiling and rolling up her sleeping bag.

'Or we need to let the fox find us,' I whisper.

*

Our spirits go up as we inch our way down. By early afternoon, the sun is warm on our backs, and we take turns singing songs we know, stopping to fill our water bottles from one of the streams. The breeze nudges us forward as we cross the open plain from Glenshiquin to Inchiquin. The sun is still high in the sky when we stop for lunch under a cypress tree.

'We're actually on Inchiquin Mountain now,' Tiger says, pointing to a rough trail that disappears into a pine forest. She wipes a sleeve across her forehead. 'Beyond that wood, we may need our Mr Fox.'

'He'll turn up,' I say, pulling out the last of our supplies.

Me and Tiger are okay again. The creeping suspicion has been put to bed. We finish off the biscuits with cheese and stretch out in the shade.

Tiger says the cypress tree will restore me. It's home, she says, to sacred ancestral spirits. The thought of them watching over us as we sleep comforts me, and I pull my hat over my face and surrender to sweet oblivion.

Andi comes and sits next to me on the grass. I'm surprised to see her here. She pushes her hair off her face, rubs my cheek. 'How's Doll?' She always says that – *How's Doll?* Even though I never respond. Never even try to catch her eye.

'Hi, Andi.'

She jumps back, her hands covering her mouth. 'You're talking! Oh my God, you're talking, Doll.' She drops onto her knees. 'Go on, talk to me.'

I've never said a word to her, and now that I can . . . I don't know what to say.

'Talk to me, Doll.'

I touch her hand. It feels warm. Purple nail polish with gold stars. Cool.

'Andi?'

She squeezes my hand. 'Wait till Mom and Dad hear you.' Her eyes glitter in the sun.

'I'm not going back. Will you tell them for me?'

'Of course you're coming back. We miss you.'

'You've no idea, do you? How could you? With your Insta-perfect life. I don't blame you. I got the short straw; you got the haystack.'

'Don't talk like that,' she says, her face cross.

'Sorry. I just want you to understand. So you can explain.'

'Explain what, love?'

'That lying on a couch is not a life. That eating cardboard is not a life. That sitting on a plastic horse in a merry-go-round is not a life.'

Her hands fly to her cheeks. 'Stop it! Do you think I don't know that?' She shouts the words. 'Do you think I need reminding? I've been watching you since I was five.'

'I want a real life,' I say. 'Like *you've* got. I don't want people's pity. The way they look at you. The relief in their eyes that I'm not *their* child. Andi, it's not that hard to understand, is it?'

She tries to catch my hand, but I pull it away. She needs to hear this. 'It was a fake life. What was it all about? Remember Granny's song?'

She cries when I mention Granny. 'Granny loved you,' she says. 'We all loved you, but it wasn't enough, was it?'

'It wasn't enough,' I say.

'You can't just give up,' she says, blinking, tears falling.

'I'm not giving up. Just leaving for a nicer life. I was dead, Andi; I'm only waking up now.'

She wails when I say this. 'You were very much alive, Doll.'

'Not in any way that mattered.' I fold my arms. 'I don't want to be somebody's cross.'

She rubs her panda eyes. Her mascara is streaking down her cheeks. She looks like a witch.

'You look like a witch,' I say, laughing. I hand her a tissue from my rucksack.

She laughs. 'Can I tell you something?'

'Go on,' I say, sorry for upsetting her now. It's not her fault she's the golden girl.

'I've always been so jealous of you.'

'Oh, really? Yeah, right.'

'No, listen. You're the centre of their lives. I'm the one on the side-lines.' She blows her nose. 'I was always jealous of that. Still am.'

'That supposed to make me feel better? I might be all they think about, but not in a good way. I'm the stone in their shoe, the broken child they didn't ask for. They're stuck with me. Andi, why do you think I cry?'

'It's not all about you, Doll.'

'How do you mean?'

'You're so wrapped up in your own life, you can't see beyond it. We all have to pay, don't we? You want to make sure we all pay.'

'That's not true. How dare you! Even if it was true, who could blame me? You don't get it, do you?'

I'm starting to shout now, so I have to move away. I'm shaking. She doesn't follow me, and when I turn around, she's already fading into the distance.

I wake slowly, the past cycling backwards away from me. Andi is still wrapped around my mind like a shawl. I think about what she said. It surprises me, and a sliver of guilt gnaws at the back of my skull.

It's not all about you, Doll.

She's a bitch. Easy for her to say.

But I can't shake off what she said. That it wasn't all about me.

CHAPTER 45

ANDI

From the reception window, I watch him approach the hospital entrance. His hands are deep in his pockets, his blond head bent, leaning into the wind. He looks like a male model on a breezy catwalk. I want to run to him, feel his fingertips on my cheek. I want to hear him whisper in my ear that he cares, that it was all a misunderstanding.

I've got to face it, though: he might be telling me we're finished. *We need to talk, babe.* He said he'd be in the city tonight and he'd drop in to the hospital. He wanted to explain everything. But I'm going to play it cool. I'll listen; I won't cry. Boys hate that. Clinging. I read it on Missy. ie. They like the chase. They love what they can't have. Maybe that's the problem: I've been too available. Too transparent with my feelings. Spilling too much. Maybe I should've been more . . . aloof. The ice queen.

A woman in a wheelchair stops him and gestures that she's looking for a light. He shakes his head, smiles at her, shoulders and palms raised. He must've said something funny, because she laughs and waves goodbye. That's Steve. A charming boy. People respond to him. Look at me, hooked from day one!

He stops at the *Patient Safety* sign and places his hand under the sanitizer.

When he spots me, he smiles, gives me a wave. The butterflies inside me escape and fly in formation across the reception area – purple, red, yellow, and blue. He takes my elbow and kisses my cheek. I can smell Pour Homme. My hand is limp against his chest. 'I missed you, girl.' I almost forget to breathe.

The butterflies skydive. My backbone does a side-slide. *Andi, remember, cool.*

'How's Doll?'

'They're not telling me much; what's new? But . . . it doesn't look too good.'

'Oh, I'm so sorry.'

He pulls out something from his pocket and places it in my palm. His fingers are cold.

'It's a Little Nell medal. Not a saint yet, my gran says, but a miracle worker all the same.'

'I never heard of her,' I say, grateful for something neutral to talk about.

'Put it under her pillow. It can't hurt.'

'I will. Tell your gran thanks, Steve.' I put it into my jeans pocket.

'She has a novena going too,' he says, smiling. 'Don't ask. Prayers said over nine days. Has to be a full moon.'

'A full moon?'

He grins. 'Just joking about that bit.'

He takes my hand, squeezes it. Our fingers lock together. A perfect fit.

'Can we go for a Coke? I need to tell you things.'

He's going to spill about Chelsea. But at least he's coming clean; that counts for something, doesn't it? It's over with her, he'll tell me. He needed time to sort it all out, but it's done now.

I steer him towards the Coffee Dock, and he orders two Cokes. We sit at a plastic table under the glare of fluorescent lights. He cracks open his can.

'What's going on, Steve? I've hardly heard from you in nearly a week.' I sit back, fold my arms, and wait. My mouth is dry, and I sip my drink, not tasting it.

He leans back, looks straight at me.

'Well?'

'I needed some time out.' He looks down at his Coke.

'If you don't want to see me again, Steve, say it. Don't make excuses. I can't stand that.' My heart is thudding; can he hear it?

His eyes shoot up. 'It's not that. Are you crazy, girl?'

My heart exhales.

'Then what . . . ?'

'You don't need this shit,' he says, running his hands through his hair. 'Not now. Not with your sister, you know . . .'

'Are you in some kind of trouble?'

He shakes his head, swallowing. 'My mother's back. From London.'

'Okay, so you've been too busy to call me?'

'It's not that. She wants me to go back there and live with her. A new start.'

234

I'm thinking ahead. Ryanair flights, a part-time job. If I couldn't see him again . . . then my life is over.

'And?' I hold my breath.

'And if I don't, she says she's staying here with me and my gran.'

'And are you . . . ?'

'And my gran said no way. Over her dead body.'

'I called on Monday. I heard arguing . . .'

He sighs. 'Yep, that was my mam.' *So it wasn't Chelsea.*

'But isn't that good?' I say. 'She wants to get to know you again. She wants to, I don't know, make amends for walking out.'

He rolls his eyes. 'I told you, my mam is a heroin addict. She's a wreck, Andi. Her boyfriend's walked out, and she's gotten some notion now that she wants to play happy families.'

He shakes his head.

'If you saw her, babe, she's like a corpse. High as a kite half the time. She's been checking out where she can score around town. Gran is mortified. She's too old for all this shit.'

I lace my fingers through his. 'Oh God, that's awful, Steve. You should have said.'

He rubs my fingers absently, scattering my concentration.

'Last night, she had a few friends round. Pals, she said, from the old days, but Gran said she wouldn't give them the time of day. Wasters, she said. She was right. You know yourself.'

'Maybe she'll get help. Her wanting to be with you must count for something.'

He makes a face. 'I wouldn't hold my breath. To be honest, my gran is my real mam. That'll never change.' He shakes his head again. 'We didn't know she was coming, Andi. She just arrived on Friday, and it's been a shit-storm since then. I had to be there for my gran.'

'And Chelsea?'

He looks puzzled. 'What about her?'

I tap my screen, show him the photo, and tell him about her calling to my house.

'Ah, fuck it, Andi. You should have told me.' He looks mad. 'That's an old photo taken one night when we were all in Luigiano's.'

'So there's nothing . . . you're not . . . ?'

He furrows his brows. 'No. I told you. And I told her to back off.' He clenches his jaw. 'Leave her to me, babe.'

I say a silent prayer of thanks.

'Andi.'

I look up. My mom is beckoning to me.

I call her over. 'Mom, this is Steve.'

'Hello, Steve.' She hardly sees him. Her eyes are red rimmed, and she looks wrecked. 'I'm heading home; you can travel with Dad if you like.' She fishes her keys out of her handbag. 'Will is coming home. He'll be here tomorrow.'

'Will is coming home? When was that decided?'

'I only got his text today.' She shrugs. 'It was his own decision.'

I look at Steve. 'See what I mean? My brother's on his way home from Ethiopia, and I'm the last to know. What does he know that I don't?'

Mom takes a step back and rolls her eyes. 'Andi, don't make a drama out of this . . .'

I scrape my chair back. 'I'm going to the loo.' I look at Steve. 'I'll be back, babe.'

I blow my nose; check my face in the mirror. *Don't make a drama out of this.* Give me a break. Will's coming home, and no one tells me? What's going on?

I march back out to confront my mom, but she's gone.

'That was a bit harsh, Andi?'

'Don't you start,' I say. 'They're shutting me out of things.'

After the conversation about his mother, I regret my outburst.

'I'm sorry, Steve.'

'Your mam is doing her best, like.' He sighs. 'What I wouldn't do to have a mam like that. You're a lucky girl.'

'I'm lucky to have *you*,' I say, reminding myself he's mine. Chelsea is out of the picture. Just knowing that is a lifebuoy. 'Come on up and meet Doll.'

We walk hand in hand up the staircase and along the corridor to room ten.

Dad's perched on the leather chair. A silent question mark in his eyes when he sees Steve.

'How is she, Dad?'

'Same, love. Will's home tomorrow. Your mom left a message on your phone earlier.'

'Yeah, she just told me.' So she did text me. I feel stupid now for causing such a fuss. 'Dad, this is Steve.'

'How's it goin', Mr Redmond?'

'Hello, Steve.' My father nods, doesn't get up. He's such a snob.

'Steve's gran gave us a medal.' I walk around Doll's bed and slip it under her pillow. 'It's Little Nell.'

'I've heard of her,' Dad says. He smiles. 'Who knows what might work, son. Thank your gran for us.'

The three of us sit in awkward silence.

'Will she get better, Dad?'

Just as he's turning to answer, the heart monitor starts beeping and flashing. Two nurses race in. A doctor in green scrubs barks orders to a woman behind him.

We're ushered out. 'Please leave it to us.'

The door slams shut. My father paces, his hands laced behind his head.

'I'll go,' Steve says, brushing my cheek with his mouth. 'I don't want to be in the way.'

I wave him off, mouthing *thank you* as he disappears down the staircase.

We sit, me and Dad, in a grim silence, and he reaches out – *thanks, Dad; it means an awful lot* – to pull me towards him. I sink into his arms. I inhale his aftershave. I'm his girl. I'm four again, and I'm safely home.

CHAPTER 46

DOLL

As we move off, Tiger takes a handful of nuts from her rucksack and circles the tree, scattering them underfoot. 'For the spirits,' she says, brushing her palms off each other. 'It's to honour them and thank them for their protection.'

There's a flicker of movement from behind the tree. I nudge Tiger. A face appears between two trunks. Green eyes stare. The fox walks towards us, then turns and trots off along the trail, looking back now and then. *Follow me.*

'There goes our guide, Child of Summer,' Tiger says, smiling.

We fall into step together. My mind is away over the hills, thinking about what lies ahead. 'Tell me again about the island. Will it be easy to get to?'

She shrugs. 'I don't know, Doll. We'll figure something out.' She grins. 'We're a team, aren't we?'

An almighty roar drowns out my answer, the sound of ten thousand horses thundering by.

'It's Blood Falls,' Tiger says, as a huge waterfall tumbles into view. She whistles. 'I've read about this, but it's amazing to actually see it.'

I gasp in terror. The water is crimson, surging over the cliff like a giant's heart, pumping and spilling a never-ending supply of blood.

'It's not real blood, Doll. Something in the rock dyes the water. Isn't it magnificent?'

We both stop and stare at the roaring scarlet wall. 'Legend says that the monks turned the water red as revenge on some local chieftain who wouldn't allow them to build their monastery on Loughfada.' She stops, rests a finger on her lips. 'Which means . . .'

'Which means,' I say, 'that Loughfada can't be far away.'

'Exactly.' She gives me a friendly punch. 'Come on, let's walk faster.'

We follow our fox along the trail, speculating on what we might find once we reach the lake. Will we discover an empty monastery? Even if we find the major, what then?

'What do you think will happen?' I ask Tiger.

She grins. 'We'll find the Orb, shove it in our rucksack, and get back on a boat. We'll make our way down the mountain, back to Archon . . .'

'And then?' I'm enjoying this.

'Then we go back and restore the Orb to its rightful place in the Cathedral of Light.' She waves her hand like a magician. 'And then the heroes will be welcomed by all.' She makes a wide circle with her arms and takes an exaggerated bow, blowing kisses to imaginary fans.

We both whoop with laughter.

She clicks her fingers. 'Just like that,' she says. 'Mission accomplished. "Thank you, ma'am." ' She bows again. ' "You're welcome, Your Majesties." ' She curtsies, almost keeling over with the weight of the rucksack. ' "It was no trouble, ma'am. Isn't that right, Lady Doll?" '

Tiger is so excellent. She'll always lift your spirits.

'But then,' I say, not wanting to think about it, 'you'll go back home. I might never see you again.'

She nods. 'And you, Doll? Will you go back?'

I stare ahead. 'Maybe I could stay with you, Tiger?'

'Doll, I don't think . . .'

'Forget it. It's a silly idea.'

'It's not that, Doll. The Grandmothers would never allow it. There are rules around deep-space travel, you know.'

'Sure. Forget it.'

She pulls a face, slaps my shoulder. 'Let's not think about that now,' she says. 'One step at a time.'

We walk along in silence.

'There's also the possibility . . . ,' I say.

'Yes?'

'. . . that you and me won't make it back.'

She rolls her eyes. 'Don't think like that, Doll. Let's focus on the Orb.'

I know she has more to lose than me. 'If you want out now, Tiger, I wouldn't blame you. You don't have to do this.'

'Shut up, Doll.' Her eyes flash. 'How many times . . . ?'

We've reached Blood Falls now, and the spray is like a broken artery, showering us in red droplets. I hope it's not an omen, a warning of blood to be spilt. I think of Ramish and shiver. I'm so glad when the falls are once again a distant roar.

We trudge on. Stars are appearing now as the sun glows in the west. Up ahead, our fox trots to the top of the ridge and waits on a narrow ledge, a thin shadow silhouetted against the sky. I'm flattened. My chest hurts, and I stop to catch my breath. There, below in the valley, the sun is drowning in the waters of Loughfada Lake. In the middle of the lake, the ancient walls of the monastery glow in the sunset. It's a breathtaking sight.

Tiger points to a small wood skirting the lakeside. 'We'll get there before dark if we hurry.'

We zigzag downhill. I pull out my purple coat as the temperature drops. By the time we reach the wood, the wind is whipping the surface of the lake and slate clouds are scudding across the sky.

'Weather's changing,' I say, grateful for the shelter of the trees.

Our fox has disappeared. 'His work is done,' Tiger says, stretching as she tosses off her rucksack.

We spread out our sleeping bags under the canopy of an oak tree. I pull out our last supplies of fruit.

'I'll get water,' Tiger says, grabbing her drink bottle. She peers through the trees and the lake water beyond. 'We're so close,' she whispers. 'So close to the prize.'

'I'll go with you,' I say, but she shakes her head.

'I'll be fine; you peel the oranges. And don't move from here.'

'As if.'

A bird *yip-yip*s on the water. There's a splashing sound nearby and I scream.

Tiger puts her finger to her lips. 'Shh, Doll, not a sound. I won't be a minute.' She runs like a cat through the trees, melting into the shadows.

Alone now, I can taste fear on my tongue, like metal.

I sit on my sleeping bag trying to peel an orange. Do I hear footsteps? I freeze. No. It's me being silly. The clouds are moving fast now, the wind like a collie herding sheep across the sky.

There's a howl in the distance. I definitely heard it. A wolf? Jesus, are there wolves up here? My nerves are tinkling up and down my spine like a mad piano. I see a pair of green eyes in the dark. I clamp my hand over my mouth to stifle a scream.

Is it a wildcat?

The eyes disappear.

What's keeping Tiger?

My heart is hammering. I reach for the sweets that Nell gave me, shovel three into my mouth. Courage, I need courage. Fast. I'm jingle-jangling.

Night has gathered in like a crow. Overhead, the trees groan and crawk, their arms clawing at the sky. They sound nervous.

What's keeping Tiger?

I peer through the murky shadows.

What if she's hurt? Or drowned? What if she doesn't come back? What if I'm only dreaming and I wake up in Bluebell Grove? Now that'd be a nightmare!

One, two, three O'Leary . . . The song is spinning around in my brain.

Still, I'd be safe at home. There's a lot to be said for safety. A lot to be said for a mom and dad who love you. That's only hitting me now.

Raindrops plop and crackle against the leaves overhead and slither down my face. I put on my hat.

Where's Tiger?

> *Tyger, Tyger, burning bright*
> *In the forest of the night* . . .

I can hear Andi reciting, her back to the fire, exaggerating the sounds to get the diction perfect:

> *What the anvil, what dread grasp*
> *Dare its deadly terrors clasp?*

The words have come alive and are merry-go-rounding in my brain.

> *And when thy heart began to beat*
> *What dread hand and what dread feet?*

I close my eyes to shut out the poem. I can hear the lake waters sigh and hiss and moan, complaining, restless, uneasy. The waves crawl ashore, their *swish-swish*ing sound like whispers in the dark.

Or is it Tiger whispering? Calling out for me?

I button up my coat; it takes me ages. Where is she? I wish I had some rosemary beads.

What do I do?

My fingers close over the bubbles in my pocket. Maybe . . . I take the wand out and blow. One circle lingers, lit from within, like a Christmas bauble. I peer closer. There's a man in a black shirt, the top two buttons open. It's Major Tom. He's talking to someone. They embrace.

I stifle a scream. It's Tiger! Her hands are clasped around him. The image fades. My stomach heaves. I retch.

I'm a fool, always was. Always will be. Not right upstairs. It's all true. Child of Summer indeed. I pour my face into my palms. There's snow falling inside me, compacting inside my chest. Feather-falling, filling up my throat. I can't breathe. I try to cough it up, but there's a blizzard inside me. I'm fifty shades of white. Too cold to cry. Glassy fingers close around my throat.

'Tiger!' I shout out her name. Snow sprays from my mouth. Like sugar.

'Tiger, where are you?'

I hear footsteps. Heavy breathing.

She's back. She'll explain all.

'Tiger?'

The silence raises goosebumps on my skin.

From the corner of my eye, a swish of shadow, a hooded cloak, a gloved hand, the glint of an eye.

My legs wobble. The sweets haven't kicked in yet . . . Time stops. My mouth freezes over. The glove removes my hat and glides a fat cloth across my lips, pulling it tight behind my head. Raindrops fall like bullets.

The silent figure ties us together, wrist to wrist. We move towards the lake, me stumbling, trying not to fall. I'm wailing on the inside. Drowning in fear.

I can smell the lake, a fishy, damp scent. The flicker of light from a lantern throws up the shadow of a small boat. My wrist is untied, and I'm nudged on board. The figure pushes us off and jumps in, taking both oars and rowing expertly across the lake. Push, pull, push, pull. No word is spoken. Is it Tiger? Is it Nan-Nan?

The rain is falling in slanting sheets. The wind is a roar. I can hear the Headscarves, a faint melody at first and then getting louder and louder. They swoop towards us, rising and falling in the wind. Their singing is a wall of melody, their harmonies rising far above the whine of the wind. They're singing about a showdown happening tonight, and I silently hum the ELO song inside my head.

They're so close I can see their faces bunched up together, their toothless mouths moving in unison, their scarves askew. Wispy hair is blown back, tangling in the wind. Their eyes are closed, the music sweet and strong. All around, invisible violins soar like birds.

242

A shadow at the edge of the group peels away and swoops towards us, her liquid face hovering over me, fingers pushing back the wet hair plastered across my face. When I look up, I recognise her gentle eyes – it's my granny. And I know now I'll be safe. My captor shrinks back but keeps rowing, panting and heaving as the boat lurches and slaps against angry waves. The figure doesn't even look up as my granny leans in and kisses my face before the wind pulls her back to the others. She whirls towards me again. 'Doll, Doll.' It's a whisper, like she's too weak to shout, like she's using all her strength just to stay near me. 'I'll keep you safe . . .'

The wind tugs at her, and she sweeps back to join the others, singing now, defiant, directing her song towards the hooded figure.

The music fades, and the Headscarves are swept back into the mist and the rain.

Having seen my granny again, I feel a surge of courage. She's my protector, my champion; she'll mind me. The boat lurches and hits off a small wooden jetty. I'm thrown forward. The monastery looms overhead.

My captor slings a rope around the post. Gloved hands hitch up the dripping cloak, and the silent figure leads me up steep steps cut into the rock. We spiral left, then right, then left again. Up and up and up. Rivulets of water gush down, and my companion almost slips twice, saved only by the rope handrail.

At the top, sheets of rain push us across a courtyard towards an arched door. Light leaks through a coloured window.

The figure turns the handle, and the door swings back. Inside, there's a flagstone floor, and warmth. The gloved hands untie my gag. My mouth is numb.

In the far end of the room, there's a fire blazing, huge logs hissing in the flames.

The figure kicks the door shut behind me, tosses off the cloak, and discards the gloves. The mask follows, and my captor unties a hair band and smooths out a mane of silky hair.

I gasp, steadying myself against a small table. A pool of water is forming around my sodden shoes.

'*You*,' I whisper, pulling myself up to full height. I don't know where I get the courage. Probably Nell's sweets. 'You are disgraceful!'

From behind a fireside chair, a deep voice booms out.

'Welcome, Child of Summer.'

Valda glares at me as she dries her face with a towel. She scrapes her white hair back from her forehead with a comb. Her eyes narrow. 'Close your mouth, child.'

She laughs. 'You're surprised?' she says. 'I thought the Child of Summer would've detected a traitor in the Grandmothers' camp.' She gestures to the water pooling at my feet. 'Get that coat off, and here' – she throws the towel at me – 'dry yourself. You're making a mess.'

Up at the hearth, the major has risen from his wingback chair. A big man, blue-green eyes. A wide, warm smile. 'At last we meet.' I walk towards him, and he leans forward to shake my hand as if I'm a guest in his country house.

'My pleasure, Doll,' he says, gripping both my hands in his. 'My name is Tom, Tom Axel. Also known as Major Tom Axel.' He bows slightly, one arm across his middle. 'At your service, miss.' He clicks his heels together.

'I know who you are,' I say coldly.

He gestures for me to sit.

'You're soaked to the skin,' he says, pushing a chair closer to the fire. 'Terrible storm out there. I'll fetch you some hot chocolate. You'd like that, wouldn't you?' He takes a glass of amber liquid from a small table by the fire, takes a sip, swirls it around his tongue.

'There's another one out there,' Valda says, still standing inside the door. 'I'm going to get her now.' She jerks her thumb towards the window.

'She's probably gone,' I say. 'You won't find her now . . .'

She ignores me. The seahorse tattoo glows against her white face.

'I won't be long, Tom,' she says. 'We can sort things out when I get back.' She reaches for a dry cloak from the hook behind the door, tying the hood under her chin. She slips on her boots and stuffs the mask, still wet, into her pocket.

Major Tom gives her a soldier salute. 'Be careful out there, Val.' He nods as she prises the door open. The wind is howling like a wolf. 'Good job. Well done.'

He reaches for a tartan rug. 'Here, I'll get your drink.' He returns with a tray and sets it down on a table in front me. I can smell brandy off him. There's a plate of toast and cheese, and I eat as he pours my hot chocolate. He retrieves his drink. 'Cheers,' he says, raising his glass, and I raise the mug. It's what you do, I suppose.

The liquid warms my bones. This kindness is not what I had expected.

I smile brightly, wiping the crumbs from my mouth. 'Thank you. That was nice.'

The courage sweets are kicking in, and I feel in control of the situation. Yes, confident, I would say, very confident. Major Tom is a good man underneath; even Kurt said that. 'You know I was sent to find you,' I say.

'I certainly do.' He smiles. 'Even though I found you first.'

'The Orb,' I say. 'The Orb is the thing.'

He nods. 'Yes, Doll, the Orb is the thing.'

There's a carved chest next to his chair, and without a word he lifts it up and places it on the table next to my tray. He raises the lid carefully.

'I don't leave this out of my sight,' he says. Slowly he lifts out the Orb, like he's lifting a newborn baby, and when he sets it on the table, I have to shade my eyes. The Orb swirls and dazzles; whorls of blue and gold spin in layers under a cloudy mist. The major stands back to admire it.

'Don't stare at it too long,' he says. 'You'll damage your eyes.' He leans forward and runs his hand around the surface.

I can't take my eyes off it. A ball of pure magnetic energy, and I can almost feel the tug, like an invisible thread, drawing me to it.

He hunkers down so his eyes are level with it. His face glows.

'You're looking here, Doll, at the very birth of creation, the matrix of life itself. Isn't it divine? A thing of beauty.' He takes another drink.

'It is beautiful,' I say. 'And pure.' I can feel the power, the waves of energy coming off it. I reach towards it, but he wags his forefinger. 'Don't touch.'

I can't peel my eyes away. Now that I'm in its presence, I understand I must have it.

'It's a priceless thing,' I say, 'and—'

He raises his palm. 'And that's why, Child of Summer, you cannot have it.' He stands up and puts one hand in his pocket. 'If you must know, I take no pleasure in your defeat – or your demise.'

My dim eyes? The cheek.

He sighs. 'In war, Doll – and believe me, this is a war – there's something called collateral damage. Did you ever hear of that?'

I shake my head. What's he talking about?

'There's always going to be someone caught in the crossfire, you know?'

I nod, not sure what he's on about.

He sighs again. 'It's inevitable, but . . . it's for the greater good.'

The great or good? I don't follow. Who are they?

'Anyway,' I say, 'the Orb must be returned. It's written in the Manuscripts, and you can't change that.'

He laughs, a rich sound, like Christmas cake.

'You haven't a clue, child, have you?'

'Well,' I say, sitting up straight, 'I know the Orb isn't yours to keep.'

'Oh, who owns it, then?' His voice has a new edge. 'Who does own it, eh?'

'The people of Almazova, of course. Its home is in the Cathedral of Light. Why do you want to destroy that?'

His eyes flash, and he drains his glass. 'Why am I even talking to a child? It's ridiculous.'

He puts his empty glass on my tray and takes a seat opposite me. 'Okay, little Doll, let me educate you.' He rests his elbows on his knees, fists under his chin. 'The possibilities of the Orb are unknown. Did you know that?'

I don't answer.

'I thought so.' He leans closer and purses his lips. 'What can the Orb teach us? How can we extract more of its power?' He caresses it again with one hand. 'But it's not just all about power. It's about pushing out the boundaries of knowledge and understanding. Asking what more can the Orb do for . . . civilisation.'

He stands up and begins to pace. 'We need to examine how the Orb is constructed, its intelligent core, maybe even duplicate it . . .'

I try to interrupt, but he keeps talking.

'We need to be bold; we need to be . . . disrupters. To disrupt the status quo. To experiment.'

He stops to stroke the Orb again, like it's a favourite cat.

'The Orb's ability is limitless,' he says. 'The secrets of living forever, disease prevention, expanding the mind, time travel, unravelling the origins of our world, becoming divine – these are all secrets that it could unlock.'

'What about special knees?'

He's not listening. 'We know' – he taps the side of his nose – 'that the Orb can speed up time, slow it down. We could manipulate life, disrupt the ageing process. We could become masters of the universe.'

'I don't like the sound of that,' I say. 'Living forever would be a nightmare.'

'Take diamonds,' he says.

'You've certainly taken enough of them,' I say.

He ignores the dig. 'Mined diamonds take millennia to grow. By manipulating time in a lab, we could grow them in weeks. How exciting is that?'

'No more kids napped.'

It's as if I'm not there. His eyes glitter in the Orb's stunning light. He refills his glass from the bottle by the side of his armchair.

'Even if what you say is true,' I say, 'this isn't the way to do it. The Orb is delicate. It's . . .' I try to explain what Jasper told us. 'It's like a weighing scales, balancing the seasons, the flow of the oceans, the pull of the moon – you can't upset that harmony! The damage you could do, meddling with the Orb, in your quest for . . . for . . .'

'For progress, Doll.'

'For power,' I say. 'You want control. The Orb controls everything; you want that power. Admit it.'

His eyes glint. 'I'll grant you that. The Orb is power. Yes, that exhilarates me, but are you not paying attention? This is about expanding the boundaries of life itself, child. It's bold, it's dark, it's dangerous, but it's a future of unknown possibilities. Why can't you see that?'

'You and Valda are playing God,' I say. 'And you don't even know what you're talking about.' No more than I do, I'm thinking. 'You're a soldier, not a scientist.'

'Correction. Was. Past tense.' He stares into the Orb.

'Mind your eyes,' I say, but he ignores me.

'Valda was a professor when I was a student at university. She was my mentor. An extraordinary research scientist. She has the vision; over the years she's tried to persuade the others to experiment with the Orb, to take risks, to question, to investigate the workings of the matrix. But' – he shrugs – 'they didn't have the courage. Too stuck in the old ways.' He sits down again, facing me. 'Valda needed a partner, someone bold, someone who could share her dream.'

'So she persuaded you?'

He nods, refills my mug. Replaces the Orb in the chest.

His tone changes. 'My dear Child of Summer, I didn't think you'd find me. We thought you'd lose the scent. How could you possibly succeed?' He looks puzzled. 'But now, here you are, and I can't let you return.' He smiles. 'But you knew that, didn't you? And your friend?' He jerks his thumb towards the door. 'Her too.'

I swallow.

'I am sorry. Truly.' He removes a small gun from his waistband. Lets it lie on his lap. 'Just two bullets,' he says.

I nearly collapse. 'And if you miss?'

A log shifts, sending a shower of sparks onto the hearth.

'I never miss.'

I feel the energy drip out of me, like a leaky tap.

So this is how it ends. I never really saw it coming. Stupid, I know. I got carried away. Never thought when I sailed out that window with Nan-Nan that it would all end with a bullet in my head. I believed the hype, or tripe, as it turned out to be.

I did my best, though. I'm proud I took the chance and jumped. I did really live for a while, and I don't regret that. It's been magic. Unswappable.

'It'll be quick, I promise. You deserve that.' A look of impatience creases his brow. 'Where is that damn woman?'

He puts the gun back in his waistband.

I feel strangely calm. They say that happens. I saw it on the telly. Before you die, you surrender to the strange; you embrace the strange. You know you have to go, so you're not going to put up a fight. What's the point? My chest feels heavy again.

But Tiger. A tear slides down my cheek. She'll never become the space traveller she dreamed of. Blown away by a madman who thinks he's bigger than the universe.

A thought comes to me. 'Does Nan-Nan know any of this?'

He looks at me. 'Nan-Nan walked away from me many years ago,' he says. 'Shut me out. I don't blame her. I did enough damage in her life. Believe me, she wouldn't want anything to do with me now.'

'You're pathetic,' I say. 'You're not right upstairs. You're just a crazy soldier who's lost his way.'

He stares into the fire.

'All for what, Major? Cheaper diamonds and life everlasting?'

The door swings open. Valda is back. She bundles in a drenched figure. Tiger's arms are bound, her mouth hidden behind a gag. I had hoped, by some miracle, that she'd escaped.

'She's a fiery bitch,' Valda says, untying her. Tiger's hair is plastered across her face, and there's blood on her chin.

Valda throws off her cloak and mask, smooths her perfect veil of hair.

Major Tom rises. He turns to face Tiger. 'Welcome, girl. And who have I the pleasure of meeting?'

'What's your name? Answer the major!' Valda says, drying her face. She throws a towel at Tiger. It falls to the floor. 'Did you hear me? Tell him your name.'

Tiger folds her arms.

'It's Tiger,' I say. 'Her name is Tiger.'

Major Tom stares at her and turns to me.

'No, seriously, it is her real name.'

'We need to sort these two out,' Valda says, tossing her boots in a corner. 'That's your department. And no need for any of these damn . . . niceties,' she says, pointing to the tray. 'With respect, *Major*, we're wasting time.'

Major Tom hasn't moved. I can see a nerve in his temple jumping. He brings his fist to his mouth.

Tiger rips off her khaki jacket and kicks it away from her. She sweeps her hair off her face, tucking stray bits behind her ears.

She looks straight at the major and spits on the floor. 'Don't think you've won,' she says. 'You're a bully and a criminal.' She puts her hands on her hips. 'It's not going to end good for you,' she says. 'Or your . . . hag-helper.'

'She's one of the Grandmothers,' I say. Tiger's eyes widen.

Major Tom drags his hands over his face.

'Tiger.' He says it in a whisper. He coughs, clears his throat. 'My lost girl?'

Nobody moves. I look at his blue-green eyes, the handsome face and perfect teeth. I look at Tiger. How did I not see the resemblance?

'Dad?'

Their eyes lock.

'You're my father?'

He nods, fists clenched at his sides.

'I thought you were dead. They said . . .'

'She wanted it that way, Tiger. It was easier. I wasn't a good man.'

It's like all the hard stuff has gone out of his body and only the blood and skin are left. His hands tremble. He turns to take another sip from his drink. Granny said brandy steadies your nerves. And she'd know, my dad said.

'You walked away from me.' Her face begins to crumple like an old tissue. 'I waited for you. To come home. To come back to me. Even though you were dead, I dreamed about you.'

Silence.

'But you were alive. You could have come back. You could have come back to see me.' Her hands slump to her sides. 'But you never did.'

'I wanted to. Believe me, Tiger . . .'

'But you didn't, Dad.'

Major Tom stares at her.

'Tiger . . .' His voice is like ashes. 'It was the hardest thing I ever had to do.'

She starts to sob. 'I missed you. Every day, every night.' Her voice is just a whisper. 'I missed you, Dad.' She wipes the tears away. 'I loved you. I thought you loved me. You were my hero. Look at you now.'

'I did love you. I do. I've never stopped. You were my golden girl. Losing you was the tragedy of my life.'

Valda makes an impatient sound. 'Come on, Tom. Pull yourself together.' She looks at Tiger. 'I'm sure it's very touching to meet your long-lost papa, but' – she glares at the major – 'this doesn't change anything.'

Major Tom looks like he's just woken from a dream. 'This is an unforeseen circumstance, Val. For crying out loud, give me a break. I've just met my daughter.' He raises his voice to an angry shout. 'This is my daughter, so don't tell me this doesn't change anything.'

'Don't be a fool, Tom.' Valda almost spits the words out. 'You hardly know her. Anyway,' she says, 'it's a wise man who knows his own child.' She snorts.

I think if she was closer, he'd have hit her. His eyes flash, and she backs away.

'We need to talk.' She says it quietly. 'I'm going to change.' She disappears up a narrow spiral staircase, and we hear a door banging loudly above.

Major Tom steps closer to Tiger. He opens his arms. She hesitates. Then she walks towards him and into the curve of his chest. They stand there together for an endless time. Tiger sobs quietly. I can see her arms wrapped around his back. No way is either of them letting go.

CHAPTER 47

SALLY

His phone goes straight to voicemail. I leave another message. The sun is unseasonably warm, and I buzz down the car window, letting the breeze dislodge the hospital cobwebs. After four or five hours in that stifling room, you need sunlight and air. I punch in the bank landline. Laura answers in her usual breezy voice. 'He's on leave, Sally. For a week, I think.'

I recover quickly. 'Of course. I forgot.' I pull into the hard shoulder quickly, my legs shaking. *On leave? He left for work this morning.* 'Can you put me through to Claire, please, Laura?'

'Sure, Sally. Just a moment.'

Claire comes on straightaway. 'Hi, Sally. How's Doll?' Claire is an angel, a good friend and Dan's right-hand woman. I know I can trust her.

'We're waiting on the new meds to kick in, Claire. It's hard to say how things will go.'

'That's tough going. Please God she'll pull through and soon.'

'Claire, what's going on?' There's a pause.

'How do you mean, Sally?' I hear a door being closed.

'Dan is on leave? He never said anything to me. I need to know if . . .'

'You should talk to him yourself, Sally. I don't have the full story.'

I keep my voice composed. 'Is he in some kind of trouble? I need to know, Claire.'

She takes a breath and lowers her voice. 'The auditors are here. Dan has to step aside while they're investigating.'

'Investigating what?' I'm grateful to be parked up and sitting down.

'I don't know for sure. They've asked to see some specific accounts.' There's a long silence. 'My guess is it's all a misunderstanding. This is just procedure . . .' She trails off and then adds, 'You could've done without all this.' Kindness colours her tone. 'Talk to him, Sally. I'm sure he just didn't want to worry you – you know what he's like.'

*

The Volvo is in the driveway when I get home. Dan's in the kitchen making coffee. His expression is unreadable.

'Early lunch?' I say lightly, checking the clock.

He doesn't look up from filling the carafe. 'I'm heading to the hospital for a few hours.'

'Why not take the day off, Dan? Or the week, even?'

He looks up then and almost smiles. 'Not a chance.'

'Why not? They couldn't do without you, is that it?'

He takes two mugs from the rack. I can't believe he's still saying nothing.

'On the other hand, you might be in the way?'

He's in the middle of pouring two cups of coffee. 'Sorry?' He looks up, trying to read my tone. 'How do you mean?'

I fling my car keys on the table and fold my arms to keep them from shaking. 'I mean the auditors might not want you under their feet.'

He holds my gaze for a moment. His expression is grim. My heart turns over in my stomach.

He sits down heavily and puts his face in his palms. His shoulders sag, and there's a pause before he says, 'So you know.' His voice is flat.

'I had to find out from Claire. What the fuck is going on, Dan? Why didn't you tell me?'

There's a long silence. Then he says, looking up, 'I didn't want to worry you.'

I can feel myself boiling inside. 'I'm your wife. Why go through the charade of pretending to go to work? Why shut me out?'

He runs his fingers through his hair. 'Look, Doll is very sick. You had enough on your plate.' He waves his hand. 'This may all blow over.'

I sit down opposite him. 'God, Dan, what did you do?'

When he tells me, it's a relief.

'That's hardly a crime, is it? Supporting a client through tough times? I mean, it isn't like you stole money, is it?'

His face is grey. 'They don't see it like that, Sal. I broke the rules. The decision wasn't mine to make. I knew that.'

'Is it serious?'

'Yes.'

'How serious?'

He pushes his coffee away and massages his temples. 'I could lose my job.'

'Whaaat?'

He shrugs. 'You know what the bank's like. One strike and all that.' He purses his lips. 'Remember Kelvin Cotter? He had to resign. That was the end of his career.'

'Jesus, Dan, he was creating fake accounts, stealing cash . . .'

'It doesn't matter, trust me. I fucked up. That's how it'll be seen.'

'So what happens now?'

'They'll go through everything with a fine-tooth comb and report back. There'll be a meeting with Lorraine . . .' He trails off and shrugs again.

'Jesus.'

I want to reach for his hand. I want to say, *It's going to be okay, Dan; we're in this together. Everything will be fine.* I want to wrap my arms around him and kiss him. I want to murmur words of reassurance, tell him that whatever happens, he's a decent human being and that's what counts, when everything is said and done.

But I can't. The space between us is a shadow, and there's an undercurrent of something, something unsaid, some unspoken suspicion, and I can't put my finger on it. I know he needs me, but I'm holding back, and I know he's holding back. And I know he senses the tension, though his expression is blank.

'When will you know?'

'Next week maybe.'

A thought occurs to me. 'How did they find out, Dan? About Colbert's?'

'I don't know that.'

'Well, someone must have reported it. How would Lorraine's office have found out? They must've got a tip-off.'

He hesitates.

'Well?'

'It's nothing. I've no proof.'

'Who'd have it in for you, Dan? After all this time?'

'I told you I don't know.' His voice is angry now. 'Can't you leave it? What does it matter? The damage is done. I don't need the third degree, Sal.'

'I'll find out, Dan. I'm not letting this go.'

He gets up, pushing his chair back noisily. 'I told you. Drop it, Sally. It's got nothing to do with you.'

'You're hiding something. What are you not telling me?'

He pauses at the door to grab his keys from the hook. 'I'll see you at the hospital.'

I can hear the engine revving loudly, and then he's gone. The house is silent. I sit at the table and stir milk into my lukewarm coffee. A wave of panic rises like bile in my throat. Doll's life is hanging by a thread. *Hanging by a thread.* Some flimsy, tissue-thin fibre will decide her fate. And now, from where I'm sitting, our marriage is hanging by another thread. And if Dan loses his job, that's his reputation ruined. Mud sticks.

I rest my head on the table. I want sleep to swallow me. And when I wake, Doll will be better and Dan's reputation will be restored. And the sun will shine and I'll have the energy to fight for my husband and he'll fight for me, and we'll pull through this and get back to where we used to be once upon a very long time ago.

CHAPTER 48

DOLL

I'm thinking disgraceable thoughts. I'm thinking maybe Major Tom is right. I often heard the monjunior at Mass say that pride is one of the ten deadly sins. *Deadly.* 'The clue is in the name,' he'd say, his voice thundering from the pulpit as Granny pursed her lips and rolled her eyes. Pride meant you were too big for your boots.

But I am the chosen one. Everyone is saying it. So maybe I need to think about what the Orb can do for me. I mean, what did the Grand-mothers ever do for me?

The lid of the chest is ajar, and the light from the Orb is leaking through the crack. I can't peel my eyes away from the golden glow. I never thought it would be so *powering.*

What if the stuff the major said is true? He has a way of making things sound . . . promising.

And maybe he is right – that the Grandmothers are too stuck. Too old. Too safe. Maybe it's time to delve in and dream and discover new things. My heart is fluttering at the thought, the deadly thought that . . . *I could stay here with Major Tom and Tiger.* He wouldn't send me back like the Grandmothers would. I could actually have a future if I stayed with him. And I don't want to go back to my sleepwalking life, do I?

Anyway, what were the Grandmothers and Nan-Nan thinking, sending me off on my own into danger? I nearly drowned – a lot they cared. What about health and safety? I could've broken my neck on that mustard horse, and I almost had my hands axed by that wild animal Ramish . . . and I nearly caught my death, out in all weathers, sleeping in caves, and what kind of adults would let that happen to a child? Es-pecially a Child of Summer like myself. It's very unresponsible is what I think. But they wanted the Orb and I was colloseral damage. As Tom said.

Hey, I could be the Keeper of the Orb, making sure Valda's exper-iments don't go too far. Me and Tiger – we'd be the new Protectors.

It's a good plan, and someday the Grandmothers will understand. And Nan-Nan too. I feel a ripple of guilt, but only a ripple.

'Doll.'

I snap out of my daydreaming.

The major's face is softer. He takes the gun from his waistband, lays it on the mantelpiece, and pulls up a chair for Tiger. He throws another log on the fire. 'We need to get you warm, my love,' he says, sitting down next to her, taking her hand. 'Now I need to figure out the next step, Tiger.' She looks at him, smiling. Her eyes are like stars. 'Dad, you're coming back with us.' She glances up at the gun. 'This is madness. Do the right thing, Dad. Everything will work out.' She turns to me. 'Won't it, Doll?'

He frowns. 'It's not that simple, Tiger.' He stares at me, his eyebrows furrowing. 'She'll have to go.'

'Go?' Tiger looks alarmed.

He rakes his hands over his scalp. 'You hardly know her, Tiger. She's from another universe. A bullet may send her back there. I don't fully understand the laws of universe transference, but it wouldn't surprise me.'

I shudder. What's he saying?

Tiger looks horrified. 'Are you crazy?' She rolls her eyes. 'That witch upstairs has got to you.' She looks at me. 'He doesn't mean it, Doll.'

'Maybe we could stay here,' I say. 'Your father has some very good ideas . . .'

She smiles. 'Don't be afraid, Doll. Deep down, my father is a good man. He'll do the right thing. Won't you, Dad?' She squeezes his hand, linking her fingers through his. She follows my gaze. 'Is that the Orb?'

Major Tom gets up and opens the chest, places the Orb on the table in front of her. Tiger shields her eyes as she watches the gold-and-turquoise glitter ball sparkle and shimmer and pulse with life.

'Wow. Blow me down!' Tiger whistles and arches back. 'Is that smoke coming off it?'

'It's water vapour, keeping the Orb cool, we think – like a protective layer.'

She points at the mist wafting towards me. 'It's like the candle flame following you, Doll.'

Major Tom looks puzzled. He leans forwards and moves his hand to disperse the vapour flow, but it still drifts in my direction.

Tiger's eyes light up. 'It's so intense. This is so exciting, Dad. I can feel its presence.'

'As I feel your presence . . .'

We all look towards the icy voice on the stairs. Valda steps into the room. She's wearing a black pantsuit, her white hair flowing. A bag is slung over her shoulder.

' . . . and I've had enough of it.' She glowers at Major Tom. 'Let's have it. What's your plan?'

He sounds like a man used to giving orders.

'The children stay here tonight,' he says firmly. 'We will discuss it in the morning.'

Her eyes narrow. She places one hand on her hip and walks towards us.

'Certainly not.' Her eyes swivel towards the mantelpiece. 'This is a complication too far.'

'What do you propose, Val?' The major stands up, towering over her. He folds his arms. 'That I shoot my own daughter? Don't be absurd, woman. Get a grip on yourself.'

'Well, you need to get rid of *her.*' She points at me. 'She's the dangerous one. Get. Rid. Now.'

'I told you—'

She cuts in, her eyes twin jets of fury. 'You're compromising us. No one knows they're here. We are safe in this remote place. I can ensure that. But' – she spits the words out – 'you must dispose of her. She is dangerous.'

The major hesitates, considers for a moment. '*I'll* decide what happens next, Val. I suggest' – he gestures towards the stairs – 'you get some sleep, and we'll talk in the morning.'

I breathe out slowly. Looks like I will live to see another day.

Valda clenches her teeth. She leans close to me – I actually think she's going to slap me – but instead she snatches the gun from the mantel. She steps back, aims it at Tiger.

'Give me the Orb.' She bares her teeth, like an animal.

Tiger's eyes blink.

Major Tom takes an in-breath. Unfolds his arms. His voice is a whisper.

'Put that down, Valda. Please, Valda.'

She holds the gun with both hands, still pointed at Tiger's head.

'Please, Valda.' His voice is steady, kind, appealing.

'You've got a count of three . . .'

'Val . . .'

'One . . . two . . .'

There's a click, a catch turning. Nobody breathes.

'Give it to her, Tiger. Now. That's an order.' His voice is a command.

Tiger lifts the Orb with both hands. It dims for a second, then flares again, light radiating through her fingers.

'Good girl. Leave it here.' Valda points to her feet, and Tiger lays it gently on the floor. Valda slowly hunkers down and slips it into her bag. It hisses and sparkles, the vapour trailing down over the sides towards me.

The major's voice is low. 'What are you doing, Valda? Think, woman. Don't be hysterical.'

She smiles grimly.

'Don't follow me.' She backs towards the door, grabbing a cloak from the hook without looking round. She drops the bag and pulls the cloak around her. 'You've made your choice, Tom. Now I'm making mine.'

'You used me,' he says bitterly. 'And now you have what you always wanted.'

She slings the bag over her shoulder. 'I've waited a long, long time for this opportunity. You could have been part of it, but you let your heart get in the way.' She purses her lips. 'Big mistake, Tom.'

She opens the door. Behind her the rain is coursing down and the wind snaps at her cloak. 'Do not follow me.' She shoves the gun into her pocket, and the door slams shut behind her.

Major Tom sprints forward like a panther.

'Dad, she has a gun!'

But five long strides and he's wrenched the door open and is calling after her. 'Valda, Valda, don't be insane.'

Tiger and me follow him out into the storm. Through the driving rain we can see a Valda-shaped figure snaking down the narrow steps to the jetty, her white hair falling forward as she negotiates the treacherous stairway. Clinging to the rope handrail, she slips and steadies herself. For an old Grandmother, she's some mover.

'There's a faster way down,' Major Tom shouts, the wind whipping his words as he leads us to a steep cliff path.

Lightning flashes across the sky, and thunder rolls like the drums of war. We zigzag along the muddy trail, scrambling and slithering, sending loose stones scattering far below into the darkness.

'Careful, careful. It's dangerous here.' Major Tom is ahead, swearing every time he slides on the mud and crouching sideways as the wind dives and shrieks above us. It's a long, long way down, and I can hear my blood pounding in my ears. One slide too far and it's 'Goodnight Irene'. Another jagged bolt of lightning rips through the sky, and we can see the lake below, churning and boiling, waves rising like claws ready to tear us apart if we tumble in.

When I stagger and lose my grip, Major Tom turns to haul me upright. I can feel his strong hands on my shoulders. 'Mind yourself.'

I don't get him; one minute he's planning to shoot me, and now he's keeping me safe. I remember Kurt's story, how the major wouldn't leave him behind. A hero. I stop for a moment to cling on as the wind tears at our clothes. You can do bad things, I suppose, and still be a good person.

Rain falls like needles. I must think only of each next step, my fingers gripping the wiry grass. *Just hang on. Don't look down. Don't skid. Don't fall. Don't die.*

The sky flashes, and the thunder roars like an animal waking from a long sleep. I can see Valda below us, making ground. She's hunched over, her cloak billowing around her, the bag swinging from her shoulder. You have to admit she's a tough old bird.

We reach the path at the foot of the cliff as Valda reaches the jetty. Major Tom races ahead over the shingle, but Valda has already untied the boat. Another crackle of lightning and she's scrambling aboard, her bag swinging forward. I watch, horrified, as the Orb falls out and rolls along the jetty towards the water. She races after it, scoops it up, and dives into the boat. One of the oars slips into the water, but she pushes off with the other one, rocking unsteadily from side to side. Major Tom races towards a second boat, struggling with the moorings. Valda is using her oar to paddle away from the pier. She sways from side to side, screaming, 'Don't follow me! I warned you, Tom.'

Her face is like a mask, the seahorse tattoo luminous in the Orb's glow. She topples forward. Steadies herself and scans the jetty for movement. When the lightning flashes again, she pulls the gun from her cloak and fires. The bullet zings past my ear. Valda staggers backwards but holds her balance.

'You meddling bitch.' I crouch down into the shadows.

Another fork of lightning erupts, and I see Tiger, bent low, running towards me. Major Tom shouts, 'Get down, Tiger! Get down!' A shot rings out as he hurtles himself after her. Her head crashes onto the rain-soaked jetty.

'Tiger!' I scream her name. *Please, God, I swear I will go back. I'll stay forever on my couch. I will do anything; just save her. Don't take her. Please, not Tiger.*

But Tiger isn't wounded. She leaps to her feet, races to the figure lying on the jetty. 'Dad, Dad. Come back, Dad.' She's screaming and sobbing. 'Doll, do something. Where's the ointment? Fix him. Doll, fix my dad. Please.'

The blood is puddling under his head. Washed with the rain, it gushes over the sides of the jetty into the lake. *Blood falls.* Major Tom is looking skyward. The rain splashes into his eyes and trickles like tears down his face. He looks surprised. Frozen in time, like a spell was cast over him.

I put my hand on her shoulder. 'Tiger, he's gone,' I say, but she's not listening. She's holding his bloodied head in her lap, kissing his forehead, cradling him like a baby. 'Come back to me, Dad, come back to me.' She's hysterical. *And it's all my fault.*

Valda's boat is twirling away into the angry waves.

The major is dead. The Orb is gone. Tiger is inconsolable, and *it's all my fault.* Hell won't be too hot for me. I caused all this chaos. *Too big for my boots.* I drop onto my knees, beat my fists off the ground. I'm hysterical myself now. I'm screaming for my lost years. I'm screaming for the family I walked away from and for my broken-hearted friend. Tiger, Tiger, burning bright. And I'm screaming for Major Tom, the wounded soldier who lost his way but ended up saving the life of his golden girl.

It's not fair. Nothing is fair. Why didn't Granny protect me like she promised? You can't trust anyone. What's it all about? All the sadness and loss . . . for what, in the end?

I'm still screaming as I scramble onto the second boat. I grab the oars and start to row. If it's the last thing I do – and it probably will be – I'm following Valda.

Thunder growls and another bolt of lightning scars the horizon. I see her then, like a mad sea dog, standing astride, her cloak clinging to her thin body, hair hanging like wet ropes about her head. She laughs when she sees me, her eyes glittering.

My boat plunges into the waves, rising again like a fairground ride. I can only hang on; the oars are too heavy for me to fight the swell.

Our boats are tossed together, and I can hear her laughing again. 'You're a joke. A pitiful creature. Give up, you fool.'

The lights from the monastery grow smaller and smaller. The rain sweeps across the lake. Valda is out of sight. I can feel the water slapping and swirling around my legs. I crouch and wait. Hopeless wins again.

I've screamed all my rage out, and now nothing really matters. Not anymore. My life was no more than a birthday candle, bright for a few moments, then lights out. When it's time, you must blow yourself out and just go.

'Go? What are you saying, child?'

My granny is sitting at the other end of the boat, and her face is set straight. 'Remember who you are, Doll. Don't be a chicken.'

I can only stare.

'You're the Child of Summer. You always were. Don't you understand that yet? That's your gift.' She looks cross. 'The Child of Summer was inside you, always. She is inside you now, Doll. Listen to her. Release her.'

I start to cry. Granny leans forward and takes my hand. 'Valda has no power, child. Her heart has closed. Use your power; that's what heroes do.' She points to the figure paddling furiously in the distance.

Dawn is humming like a prayer. The boat rocks as I get to my feet. I know what to do. I can feel it fizzing up inside me like shaken 7up, a rage, radiating from my heart. One last pulse of life-force skidding through me. My fingertips are tingling.

A fork of lightning crackles through the sky, and I reach up to capture it, to lure it to me. The lake lights up like a stage. Twin bolts of lightning surge through my hands, orange sparks burning my fingers. I scream, summoning up all the light inside me to redirect the fiery rods towards Valda.

The prongs are a merciless force, slicing though her boat like a pirate blade. She staggers backwards, smoke pouring from her chest. Her arms circle like a mad clockwork toy before she plunges back into the waves. Her white hair floats on the surface amid the smoke and the matchstick remains of her boat.

'That's the style,' my granny roars, clapping her hands. 'That's the style, Doll.'

I watch, awestruck, as the Orb rolls along the surface of the water, light flickering, before it descends into the waves. I don't stop to think. I leap into the freezing water, thrashing towards the yellow ball of light. Down I go, down through the murky depths, desperately searching for the glow. I can see the Orb slow-falling beneath me through the silent waters.

I need to remember that the Child of Summer is inside me, powering me. I need to believe it and focus on her.

Far below, the Orb stops, suspended in the dark. Then it begins to reverse, and gathering speed, it starts to whoosh towards me, like a comet, trailing vapour. It crashes into my arms with a soft thud.

For a dreamlike moment, the water blankets me, sucking me down and pushing gently against my mouth as I slow-motion into the depths. Such quiet, such green silence. And then, like an explosion, the Orb is shooting towards the surface like a rocket. I can feel the heat of it in my arms, the dazzling light pulsing and vibrating, and I know the Orb is life itself, captured. I am feather-light, a speck of stardust.

Granny-hands stretch out and drag me into the boat. As I lie there, shivering, she rows towards the lake shore. The wind has died. The water is calm, the sun a sliver of pink on the horizon, and the Orb is a baby in my arms. I gaze up at the disappearing stars and the chill beauty above me. The Headscarves float into view, their scarves like sails on the ocean-sky, and they're all singing, '*Will you go, Lassie, go?*' And just before I close my eyes, I see them beckon to my granny, and she smiles and floats up to join them.

In my mind, I can see the blooming heather and the girl called Lassie running through the fields, happy because summer is coming.

CHAPTER 49

DOLL

I'm hot. Smoking hot. My head hurts, and my throat's on fire. I'm upside-down. Flying upside-down. Oh, I get it. I must be on the road to hell. I'm getting hotter. That'll be the flames. Hell and dalmation . . .

The words go together like . . . like bacon and cabbage, or jelly and ice-cream . . . I'd love an ice-cream now. Strawberry or lime. My lips are stuck. Glued together. Anyway, I couldn't eat an ice-cream upside-down, could I? Upside-down ice-cream, upside-down cake. It makes me want to laugh.

It's so boiling. But what do you expect when you're in hell? Granny said hell was for wicked people. Andi didn't believe in hell. It's only a story, she said, to scare children so they'll behave, but Granny was having none of it. 'It's as real as that fire there,' she'd say, pointing to the hearth at home. 'Hotter, even.'

'How come people don't turn to ashes so?' Andi still wasn't convinced.

'Oh, they do, they do,' Granny said. 'Their hearts are ashes; they can't feel. And when you can't feel, well, you know you're in hell.'

But right now I *feel* thirsty . . . and I *feel* hot . . . do those feelings count? And I feel sad, and I hate myself. They're all feelings, aren't they?

I open my eyes. It's like there's knives stuck in them. Or teeth.

I see blood, hear it gurgling. So much blood. They never said there'd be blood in hell. Maybe it's to remind you of the people who died because of you. And that you didn't complete the mission.

What was the mission again? Oh yes, the Orb. Where is it? Gone, lost. I failed. And now it's payback time. There are hot coals nestling behind my eyes. Pride comes before a wall. I mean a fall. It's a sin. You have to pay for your sins. Everyone knows that. I hear a sound. A *flac-flac-flac* chopping sound. A loud whirring. Is it a ghost train? I hear voices. Orders barked out. Is it the devil? I'm flying now, the wind shrieking, tearing at my face. My head is throbbing. *Wuppa wuppa wuppa.* Round and round, blades in my head, round and round, slicing me up.

Granny was wrong. You *can* feel in hell. You can feel like hell in hell. That's why it's called hell. It's meant to be—

Diamond Jesus, I hear Nan-Nan's voice. Will she hold my hand and call me honey? Honey, lavender honey, clover honey. Oh Jesus, Ramish will be here, lurking, waiting for me in the shadows, plotting revenge. I'll be running away like Goldilocks, forever running and running . . .

My heart is juddering. *Bang. Bang.* The major died. Gone in a heartbeat. Like a candle snuffed out. Someone – who? – is broken-hearted. Ah, poor Tiger, sobbing her heart out in the pink rain.

'Ah, don't cry. Don't cry.'

A hand on my forehead. Cool. Soft as a marshmallow. There's a clink of glass against teeth. Water trickles past cracked lips and a furry tongue, dribbling down my desert throat. I'm sipping back to life.

There's a cloth over my eyes, damping down the flames of hell. *Another sip. Please, one more.*

Ramish. *Is he here, waiting for me?* I wail. I seem to spend my life wailing. I wish I was back on that mustard horse, galloping through the wind. *Don't stop me now; I'm having such a good time . . .* I was something, wasn't I? And when Tiger danced around the campfire like a butterfly, her red scarf floating behind her . . . I was happy then.

Life is little squares of happiness like that, stitched together with little squares of misery. A quilt-life. If you're lucky, you get more happy squares.

I remember, now, sitting on my couch after a Saturday bath, smelling of coconut. Sipping hot chocolate and listening, all of us, to Granny's harmonica and everyone singing.

. . . and we'll all go together to pick wild mountain thyme

That was another little patch of happiness. When you think about it, I suppose it wasn't all black, back then.

I open my eyes. I'm in a bed. It has dark wooden beams rising up to a curtain canopy. The quilt is blue, and the sheets are lacy at the edges. Might be Heaven. A window looks out over a garden with purple, pink, and white flowers, like sprinkles. I blink, in case I'm dreaming. The sky is a heavy blue, a single cotton-wool cloud drifting from a snowman to a wolf to a chair. A bell tinkles in the distance.

There's a smell of roses drifting in the window. I lace my hands behind my head and feel a stabbing pain in my chest.

'Well, hello, sweetheart, You're awake.' Nan-Nan comes over and sits on the edge of the bed. I can see her red shoes as she stretches her legs out, crossing her ankles. 'How are you feeling, honey?'

'Sore. Where am I?'

'You're in Nell's house.' She lifts a glass to my mouth. 'Here. Drink this.'

The water melts the glue on my lips. I mouth a *thank you*. When I move, it's like a scissors is sticking into my chest. My bones rattle when I cough.

'Take it easy, Doll.' She props the pillows up around me. 'You've had a very high fever.'

'What happened?' My voice is croaky. She gives me another sip, purses her lips. 'Valda is dead.'

'I know. I remember.'

'You very nearly drowned, but you were close to the shore when Vitaliy saw your boat, half-submerged.'

'Vitaliy?'

'A lovely young man, I must say.' She puts the glass back on the bedside table. 'Archon heard from the mine children. How they had met you and how Major Tom was no longer there.' She folds her arms. 'He decided to set out to find you and bring you back. He was worried about you, out on the mountain with very few supplies and a storm coming.' She shifts on the bed.

'How did they find us, Nan-Nan?'

'When they didn't meet you on your way back to the village, they thought you might have followed the Inchiquin trail. They know every inch of that mountain, but they had help.'

'Help? Was it our friend the fox?'

She raises her eyebrows. 'A fox? No, it was the Headscarves.'

'The Headscarves?'

'Yes, they led Archon and his group towards Blood Falls and down to Loughfada lake. By then, the storm was ferocious and there was no boat, so they waited at the shore. Archon, Casimir, Vitaliy, and Damon. Fine, honourable men.'

She refills my glass from a blue jug on the bedside table.

'They saw how you summoned the lightning; they saw Valda going down. And they watched you dive into the lake to retrieve the Orb. They swam out to help you get the boat ashore. You were shivering and delirious.'

'And the Orb?' I hold my breath, and it hurts.

She beams. 'The Orb is safe.'

I'm trying to soak it in. My heart feels like a dust mote. My bones are singing.

'The Headscarves alerted us too. Archon carried you back to Blood Falls, and Earl had a chopper ready to winch you to safety.'

'And Tiger?'

'Tiger is safe and well.'

'Where is the Orb now?'

'In the Cathedral of Light, where it belongs.' She smiles. 'Doll, you are our hero. You showed courage and such determination. Only you could have done this. The Manuscripts never lie. You've saved Almazova. You've done everyone proud.'

I done them proud. I roll the words around my head in wonder. Me, Doll, the beaten docket. They're proud *of me.*

If my family could see me now. *Look at me, Dad. Look, Mom.* If they could just see me. They'd be smiling. And clapping.

'Tiger told us what happened at the monastery. A dreadful business. Valda was an evil woman. I never trusted her.'

'Tiger found her dad, Nan-Nan, and then she lost him. He's dead, isn't he?'

'Yes. He's dead.' She moves off the bed and crosses to the window.

I remember the photograph I found in her house. 'Did you love him, Nan-Nan?'

She rubs her finger under her eye.

'It's a long story.' She lowers the blind slightly, fidgeting with the cable.

'Tell me some of it.'

She stares off in the distance, as if something very important has appeared on the horizon.

'The major and I . . . well, Doll, I loved the bones of him, plain and simple. A long, long time ago.'

She looks over at me. Her eyes are glassy. 'There was something about that man. He was heroic. A lonely man. But he was damaged.'

'Like a cracked cup?'

She smiles through tears. 'Yes, sweetheart. Just like a cracked cup. Tormented.'

'Like me,' I say, remembering my couch life. 'Tormented.'

'Yes, like you, Doll. And me. And anyone who's worth anything. We're all broken or cracked somewhere. Maybe that's what makes us real.'

266

'Tiger is tormented too,' I say.

'I know. Poor girl. She can't be consoled.'

She smooths the quilt, tucks the sheet up around my chin. 'Get some sleep, Doll, and we'll talk again. Sleep is medicine.'

I close my eyes.

I hear her footsteps *clack-clack*ing across the wooden floor.

'Nan-Nan?'

'Yes?'

'Will they let me stay?'

The footsteps stop. Silence for a beat.

'Nell will talk to you soon, honey.' The door clicks shut. I drift off.

There's a hooded figure standing at the top of the crowded room. A crooked finger beckons me closer. Everyone stares at me as I pass by, whispering. The figure lowers the hood. It's Nell. She turns to me.

'The people have spoken,' she says. 'I sentence you to life on earth . . .'

'Wake up, Doll,' I tell myself. I push the dream away and sit up. I feel stronger, and my head is clear. Still, I know my future is dangling on a thread. I must convince Nell to let me stay. I've done my job; now it's payback time.

That's it. That's what I'm going to tell her. It's payback time.

Someone has left some orange juice on the bedside table, and a little bowl of porridge. I'm thinking I'm like Goldilocks, but this Goldilocks won't be running anywhere. I hum to myself as I eat. Life is getting exciting – it's the berries, actually. Life is the berries, and everything's coming up roses.

CHAPTER 50

SALLY

I push the accelerator as far as I dare. Raindrops pound on the roof of the Honda, and the wipers thud back and forth. I flicker my lights at the driver in front, who's slowing down at the amber. 'Keep going, you idiot.' I slam on the horn, but he stops anyway. A careful joe. Just my damn luck.

'Take it easy, Mom; we're not going to get there any faster. Do you want me to drive?'

'Thanks, love. I'm good . . . no, you're right, it's just that I'm a bit rattled.' I glance across the passenger seat. 'It's good to see you, Will. We didn't want you flying halfway across the world, but you know, I'm glad you're here now, son.'

He squeezes my shoulder. 'I wanted to be here with you lot. We're all in this together.'

'She loved your present, Will. Nan-Nan was a big hit with her.'

'Present? I didn't send her a present, Mom.'

'The doll you posted?'

My phone glows on the dash and pings a message. It's Dan.

'What does it say, Will?'

'Just not to delay. Hurry back.'

'What does that mean? Your father doesn't panic . . .'

I step on the pedal. There's a drumming in my ears, and I don't know if it's the rain or some warning system inside me.

'We're almost there, Mom. Don't get yourself into a knot. You know Doll; she'll come out of this. She won't give up that easily.'

'I know. You're right, love.' But I'm thinking, *You still came home, son.*

A few minutes later I swerve into the hospital entrance area and abandon the car on a double yellow. We sprint across the rain-soaked tarmac.

Andi is waiting for us in the reception area. She throws her arms around Will. 'Welcome home, bro.'

'How's Doll? Did something happen?'

'Don't worry, Mom,' Andi says. 'Her heart monitor went off, there was a bit of panic, and they kicked us out. But she's stabilised.'

Upstairs, in room ten, Doll is peaceful, her eyelids flickering. Dan gets up to meet us, giving Will a bear hug. 'How's the man. How was your flight? Good to see you, son.'

'Is she . . . ?' I need to hear it from him.

He gives me a thumbs-up over Will's shoulder. 'She's fine, Sal. Her heart rate went crazy, but she's stable again.'

'They haven't said any more? We just wait?'

'Exactly.'

Will takes Doll's lifeless hand in his and kisses it. He rubs her hair. 'Take Mom down for a coffee, Dad. Me and Andi will stay here with Doll.' He looks at me. 'Go on. You'll only be three minutes away. We'll catch up later. You both look as if you could do with a bedside break.'

He grins at Dan. 'You better park up Mom's car first though, Dad. She abandoned it at the entrance.'

We head downstairs to the café, two strangers walking side by side. Dan is more silent than usual, and there are dark circles under his eyes.

'Give us your keys, Sal; I'll move the car before they tow it away.'

'Thanks. I'll get the coffees.' Everything so polite. What's happening to us?

It's late, and most of the visitors have drifted home. There's a hush – I've often noticed it. A sort of lunar calm that seems to descend on hospitals at night.

Tears are pooling behind my eyes. Was I so tangled up in my own barbed-wire misery that I didn't see the signs? I should've brought her to the hospital sooner. If I did . . . if I wasn't so slow to react . . . My thoughts are needles pricking my skin.

There's only a vending machine, and I slip the coins in, grateful for something mechanical to do. Something that requires action. Stops you from getting quietly, politely distraught.

I empty two sugar sachets into the black liquid. The crystals settle on the surface for a few seconds before sinking and dissolving into sweetness.

She might slip off in the night, like a cat burglar; we mightn't even hear her go. She might disappear on us. *Please God, no.* Because, you know, we never got to really know her.

There's a copy of *The Echo* on the chair next to mine, and I take it and pretend to read it.

She was locked in all these years. And now, at just eleven . . . I want to get up and smash my fist through the table. I want to hurl the stupid plastic chairs across the tiles. I want to fire my coffee at some random passerby. *Good enough for you*, I'd shout. *Tough tutty.* And then I'd scream. And I wouldn't bloody stop.

And people would stare, or look away, whispering to each other. *Mental*, they'd say. *That poor woman is off her head.*

I turn to page three.

Tourists good for Ireland's economy . . .

It's engrossing if I concentrate properly.

Did she know we loved her? Is it too late now? The print blurs a little.

And does she *want* to go? I wonder. A match strikes in my head. A thought lights up and glows: *She wants to go.* From day one, that's what she's always wanted.

I turn the page. *Doll, have you given up? Did you love us at all? Did we fail you, daughter?* Teardrops wrinkle the ad for Lidl specials.

I must not cry.

I sit up straight, catching the tears with a tissue before they run amok. We weren't enough. I should've had more courage. Instead of falling down. And crying like a child.

I must not fall down.

She was calling out. *Mind me.* Didn't I hear her that first day?

And I did mind her, didn't I? As best I could.

I can't put a name on the choking feeling in my chest. Like the walls are collapsing like sand, spilling down.

I think of her little life, a house of desolation. I wander through the rooms, opening doors. I see the child sliding from the womb and the static silence and the clock ticking, hammering on the white wall of the delivery room.

Page five.

The Bank of America will set up headquarters in Dublin . . .

Wow. Incredible.

I remember pearl buttons on a cardigan. A pair of crochet socks, threaded through with pink ribbon and tied in a little bow against a fragile white ankle. And the hospital building racing backwards in the car mirror.

There's another memory drifting in. We're on the beach. It's winter. Her pale-blue polka-dot coat is buttoned up. Some kids are building a sandcastle, and she's watching them shovel and dig. They arrange shells and stones on the castle walls, fixing a feather on top like a victory flag. They're laughing, their faces flushed from an east wind blowing. I can't forget the look on her face. Standing there, watching them, her tiny shoes sinking into the sand near the water's edge.

I must not cry. I must not fall down. I must not smash up the hospital café.

Page nine.

Tom Jones is coming to Cork next summer. . .

Life goes on. Sand keeps falling.

I don't think she understood, though. That day at the beach. The bleakness of it. I don't think she felt that. No, no, it went over her head. Please God it did anyway. My mother said it probably did.

I feel myself slipping through my fingers.

A funny memory bubbles up. It was Doll's christening. Father Reilly was sipping a glass of red. 'Just one. That's my limit, Sally; no, I mean it. Oh, go on so . . . just a drop, mind.' He's chatting to my mother and me. Then he points to the cradle and whispers, 'Via Dolorosa.' He shakes his head morosely.

'Via Dolorosa?' my mother answers, quick as a flash. 'It's Valpolicella, actually.'

We all got a good laugh afterwards. But . . . he wasn't far off, was he? *The Way of Sorrow.*

Dan scrapes the chair back and sits down heavily. His hair is glistening wet, and the rain is dripping off his jacket. He takes a sip of his coffee, makes a face.

'I forgot to tell you I had an umbrella in the car . . .'

'No worries.' He stands up, restless. 'Do you want a snack?'

'No thanks.'

He pulls some coins from his pocket. The vending machine clatters and whirrs, and the chocolate falls into the chamber underneath.

He sits down again, slides the wrapper to half-mast.

'Why don't you head home, Sal, for a few hours? No point in us all being here.'

'No, I'll stay. I wouldn't sleep anyway.'

'Me neither.'

He takes a bite.

'Will looks well,' I say. 'It's tough for him coming home . . . to this.'

'Yeah, it's good to have him home, though. He was lucky to get that cancellation.'

We skirt around the small talk, stepping away from the boulders.

'Dan?'

'Yes?' He takes a sip of coffee.

'What's wrong?'

'How do you mean?'

'You look worried. Did they tell you something earlier there? Is she . . . ?'

'No, Sal. You know as much as I do.' He shrugs. 'It's just the work situation. I could do without it right now.' He gives me a watery smile. 'Nothing I can do about it, Sal. And we've more important things to worry about.' He sighs and keeps his gaze fixed ahead.

'Did you meet this guy, Steve?' I say, knowing he wants to change the subject.

He nods. 'Andi's friend? Yeah, I met him. Why?'

'More than a friend, Dan. She's in love with him.'

He looks surprised. 'I hope not. He's not exactly what you'd want for Andi, is he?'

'He's good-looking – a heart-breaker, I'd say – but yeah, definitely from the wrong side of town.'

'Mom, Dad.'

Andi appears at the table, her eyes pale in the glare of the fluorescent light. I jump, startled.

'Jesus, love, you gave us a fright.'

'You need to come quickly. The doctor wants to talk to you.' She marches ahead of us.

I free-fall up the stairs three steps at a time. There's a muffled sound of glass breaking. It's my heart splintering into tiny shards.

CHAPTER 51

DOLL

I can see my face in the polished brass doorknob. If I lean back, it looks long and skinny. Like a horse. When I lean forward, it looks round and fat in the middle. Cool. I'm sitting here on a velvet chair, waiting to meet Nell. Waiting for that shiny brass handle to move. Waiting for Nell to say, *Come in, child.* Not long now, I'd say. I've gone over and over what I'm going to say. She'll see things my way, I'm sure of it. She's a good woman. Everyone says it. I gaze at my new black patent shoes. I can tie the buckles myself no problem to me. I have a new red skirt, and when I twirl, it swishes out. Tiger put my hair in plaits, white bows at the ends. Nan-Nan says I look a picture. A picture of what? She didn't say.

Poor Tiger. Her eyes are red as a puppy's tongue. What can you say to someone who's just lost her dad? What can you do? Only hug them. Hold on to them as they wail for what they lost. When you wail, you let out some of the hurting inside. Wailing is what you do when you have no tears left.

I saw her mother and granddad yesterday. I watched them from my bedroom window, wrapping her in their arms, whispering consolations. The granddad was whistling. Sweet as a bird.

Watching them, I felt a slab of guilt. I mean, here I am, choosing *not* to go home, *not* to see my family – I mean, who would *do* that? But if I go home, I'll never find out what I could've been. My life here is waiting for me. Just as soon as Nell gives me the green light. And I know Nan-Nan will take me back home to visit. She surely will.

Tiger said she'd cross her fingers for me. I explained it all to her. She knows I can't settle for a half-life. Not now.

There's a sound of footsteps on polished wood. My heart squeezes up. I sit back in my chair, smooth my plaits, straighten my skirt, place my feet neatly together.

The doorknob turns. Nell appears, patting a comb back into her perfectly coiled hair. She's starched to her chin, but her watery blue eyes are smiling. 'Thank you for waiting, my child.' She steps back to let me pass and motions me towards a long, long polished table. There's a vase of pink roses in the middle and their scent fills the room. She comes and sits opposite me, her claw-hand resting on the table. She takes a small box out of the pocket of her black dress, places it in front of me.

The room is quiet as a chapel. Faintly, I can hear a clock.

'How are you feeling, Doll?' Her voice is low and gentle.

'Very good, thank you, ma'am.'

Nan-Nan said to call her *ma'am*.

'I'm delighted to hear that. A few days ago you were all in. A wretched fever.' She shakes her head.

'I can't remember much of that,' I say.

'Sleep is medicine, child.' She leans forward. 'Please know that Almazova is utterly indebted to you. You completed the mission. You demonstrated fortitude and determination. You refused to give up.'

I sit up a bit straighter in my chair.

She pats her comb into place again.

'You are a plucky girl. You saved our planet. We are, and will always be, indebted to you.'

'I had a lot of help.'

'You did indeed. But you were the force propelling the engine, so to speak.'

I smile at her. 'The bubbles were magic.'

'Only for you, Doll. None of us had the ability to access that magic, only the Child of Summer.'

'And the courage sweets. They gave me strength.'

'Courage sweets?' Her brow furrows. 'They were just sweets, child. The courage, if you found it, was all your own.' She pauses. 'You look surprised to hear that, Doll. I think you underestimate your qualities. You should be very proud of all that you have achieved.'

She takes something from the box in front of her and pushes it towards me. It's a medal on a thin silver chain.

'Keep this as a reminder of your honourable contribution to Almazova.' She bows slightly.

'Thank you, ma'am.' My fingers close over it.

'Now, is there anything you want to ask me? Before we leave. Jasper is on his way.'

'Leave? Are you going away, Nell? I mean ma'am?'

She looks at me.

'Tonight, Doll, you will return to your corner of the universe.' She pauses. 'It's time, child, to go home.'

There's a ringing sound in my ears.

'Oh, I don't want to go back, ma'am.' I smile what I hope is a winning smile. 'I want to stay here.'

She shakes her head. 'I don't think that will be possible.'

'I won't be any trouble. I'll pay my way. I'll . . .'

'No, Doll.' The words are like bullets.

'I'll earn my keep. Please. It'd be cruel to send me back . . . it wouldn't be fair.' My voice is cracking.

'That won't be possible, child. There are protocols.'

I know I can get around her. She owes me.

'Couldn't you turn a blind eye? Leave me with Nan-Nan. Or Tiger, maybe?'

'It can't happen. Please put it out of your mind.' She's not even listening to me.

'I've done a good job. I found the Orb, and you're still sending me back to that life?'

'It can't happen, my beloved child. I'm sorry.'

I pull out my final card. It's a bit saucy, but I say it anyway: 'You owe me. You *do* owe me.'

I can hear myself shouting now, but I don't care. 'It's payback time. You owe me.'

Nell leans forwards, looks into my eyes.

'What do I owe you, child, do you think?'

Do I have to spell it out for her? Amazing when people get what they want, they just spit you out. My granny was right: eaten bread is soon forgotten.

'I was the one – you said it yourself – I found the Orb. I saved Almazova. I risked my life.' Tears of anger start to fall down my face. 'Didn't I? You can't deny it. What's it to you anyway if I stay or go? You're just playing it by the book. What do you care? You got what you wanted.'

I pull a wet sleeve across my eyes. I never want to smell roses again.

'Please, ma'am. Swear to God, I'll be no trouble.'

She doesn't answer. Crosses to a desk by the window and brings back some paper hankies for me.

'Dry your eyes, Doll. It hurts me to see you upset. You poor girl.'

I sob. Tears fall on my red skirt.

'My lovely Child of Summer.' Her voice is soft as a feather. 'Please trust a wise old woman. I can see further than you. This is for the best.' She reaches out to touch my hand. 'Doll, your family miss you – they are waiting for you.'

'Who cares? I won't be able to talk, or think straight, or do anything.' I rub my eyes. Bawl like a baby. So embarrassing. But this is the worst news. I can't believe she's doing this. My dream-life is melting away.

'Doll, you were given a life. A unique path that you and only you must follow. Life expects it of you, child.'

I blow my nose. It's not fair.

'You are the master of your soul. A challenge rips open the soul, Doll; that's how we expand and grow.'

The words are like fingernails scraping along my gut.

'I don't want my soul opened – I want a life. A proper one.'

'You can have a life, Doll. You can live it your way.'

'How? On a couch? Don't make me laugh.'

'That is your choice, child. To decay and decline or' – she flips her good hand palm down, then palm up – 'or find a way to triumph.'

Talk is cheap, my granny always said, and she's right.

'I have special knees,' I say. 'Was that my imagination?'

'What I'm trying to say, Doll'– she hands me another hanky – 'is that you can break through the ropes that bind you. You can be invincible, Doll. You can untie every knot and fly—'

'Huh, fly? I bury my head in my hands.'

She gets up and comes round to my side of the table.

'There are many ways to fly, love. Come here.' She wraps me in her arms, rubs my head with her thumb. 'Don't fight with life, my love. It's there, waiting for you. I promise. You are precious and loved. You just have to break through the skin of despair and step into a new story.'

She makes it sound so easy. What would she know?

There's a knock on the door. Nan-Nan comes into the room.

'Hello, Nan-Nan. Will you meet Jasper when he arrives? He'll be here soon, and I have some things to attend to before we leave.'

'Are you coming too, Nell?'

She nods. 'Indeed I am. I want to give Doll a good send-off. Tiger can accompany her.' She looks at me. 'Doll, gather what you need and get something to eat. We'll be leaving by and by, so be ready, child.'

The hall is a blur. I can taste the mould of despair furring my throat. I make for the gardens.

I'm falling into the dark. It's time to suffer again, and I'm sick.

Across the valley, way off in the purple distance, I can see Inchiquin and Glenshiquin. The sky is bright blue and there are pink flowers at my feet. I can taste the summer, like sugar on my tongue. My Almazova life. The sun is warming my bones, and for a moment I forget my fate and stretch my arms up in glee. Oh, the miracle of shiny new me. But now all of this is being snatched away. I must walk away, back to my other life. A life as flat as the wheel of a scrapyard pram. Invincible, me? No, I don't think so. Tears fall like stones.

I had a thread of hope, but it's been snipped good and proper. I slump onto a bench. Above, a weeping willow leans over me, keeping me in the shadows. Story of my life.

'Doll.'

I look up at Tiger. Her face is streaked with tears.

'Nan-Nan told me. I'm so sorry.' She sits next to me, puts her arm around my shoulder. 'I'm allowed to come to the Space Station with you.'

'I'll miss you, Tiger.'

She kisses the top of my head. 'We're a team, Doll.'

'I'm so sorry about your dad.'

She wipes a tear away. 'He saved my life, Doll. I know he was a criminal and my mom didn't want me to find out, and . . .' She bites her lip; her eyes fill. 'But he was a good person deep down, Doll.' She sniffles and rubs her eyes with the heel of her palms. 'Danger was a drug to him, Nan-Nan said, and I think she's right.'

'He was a topper,' I say. 'A hero in the military. Be proud of him.'

'I am, Doll. I'm proud to call him my father. I'm glad I got to meet him, and I know now that he did love me. He always loved me. Like your family loves you. That's what counts.'

It's time to go. I pack my things, rolling my purple coat into my rucksack with the tin of bubbles. The window is open, and I can hear the Headscarves off up amongst the trees lining the avenue to Nell's house.

Imagine! They know Elton John's 'Rocket Man.' I race to the window to see if my granny is still with them. I want to shout out to her. Too late – they're off like a flock of colourful geese, flying into the horizon.

I see the chopper landing. Time to go. Tiger and me take our seats behind the pilot. Nan-Nan is there too, in her white shirt and navy skirt.

The Almazova sky is streaked orange as we take off, but I'm neck deep in loneliness. There's a lump of ice in my throat, and it just won't budge.

Nan-Nan says, 'You know the mine has been closed, girls? It should have happened long ago. There's been a big clear-out.' She chatters on, trying to keep our spirits up. 'And I heard about Ramish,' she says. 'Well done – it was a cracker of a plan.'

She nudges us and leans back in her seat. 'Look. You can see Inchiquin and Glenshiquin.' We strain forward and can see a dusting of snow on top and the river far below, dark as liquorice.

My thoughts drift towards home. Soon I'll see my mom and dad. And this time, maybe things *will* be better. And what about my bed in Bluebell Grove . . . and the telly . . . and Andi and my mom singing? Still, I think it might be a hard life. That's all. That's what I think. It'll be hard.

The sky is darkening, a navy velvet muscling away the orange glow.

'There's the Space Agency HQ,' Tiger says, craning to get a better look. Her eyes glitter. 'It looks amazing. Look, Doll, all the glass domes, like bee-hives.'

'One day,' Nan-Nan says, 'you may be one of the leading space scientists here at the agency.'

'I'd love it,' she says, 'that's my goal.'

My blood runs green.

Lights wink and flash. We're skimming over the trees. I can see a gated entrance with glass steps leading to double doors. People in pale suits glide up and down glass elevators, along corridors. Like a slow-motion army.

We land inside a circle of yellow lights and follow Nan-Nan and Jasper through the main entrance. She punches in a code, and we take a lift to the fifth floor. Halfway along a glass corridor, we stop at room ten.

'Here we are.' Nan-Nan's voice is cheerful, but she doesn't look at me. Inside, a small group is seated on rows of silver chairs. Under a table, four pairs of laced-up shoes stand to attention. There is a burst of applause as we enter.

'Stay where you are,' Nan-Nan tells us as she takes a seat beside Earl and Tiger's mom and granddad in the third row.

Everyone is smiling. Except me. What have *I* got to smile about?

Nell motions for silence. The other Grandmothers, Kitti, Mauran, and Ki, take a bow.

'Ago-ye. We are gathered here tonight to bid farewell to our magnificent Child of Summer.' Nell's voice is quiet.

Someone coughs. I swallow. Tiger slides her hand into mine. My heart leaps when I see Hanni and Kurt, jazz hands waving from their laps.

Nell continues.

'She has travelled across the universe to come to our aid, and she has served us well.' She bows slightly. 'On behalf of Almazova, thank you, Doll.'

Archon is nodding, exchanging smiles with Casimir and Spirit. Melania, the honey girl, winks at me.

'The Orb is now safely back in the Cathedral of Light. The mission has been completed successfully.' Nell glances at Tiger, shakes her head.

'We did suffer some loss. Major Tom Axel lost his life. But he lost it saving his daughter, a noble act.'

Tiger squeezes my hand.

'We do not condone his treachery, but we will remember him as a man of many facets.'

'Hear! Hear!' Hanni gives Kurt a nudge, placing a finger against her lips.

Nell glances at a page in front of her.

'Valda too has died. Out of respect for her family, I will say but this: her outrageous deception has put our very planet at risk. She has taken a life, a most grievous crime. She has undermined the highest office of the land. But we will recover, regroup, and learn from these events.'

She looks around the room. 'I'd like to thank Vitaliy and Damon' – she nods in their direction – 'and you, Archon and Casimir; you are exemplary citizens.' She bows. 'I salute you.' There's a burst of applause.

'And you, Tiger, are a strong and fearless girl, and I commend you. You've played a pivotal role in all of this.' She smiles at Nan-Nan. 'Tiger will make a wonderful scientist someday, and if she becomes half the woman you are, Nan-Nan, she will do well. None of this could have happened without your expertise and planning. You are an asset to us and a credit to this Space Agency.'

Nell takes a seat and Kitti rises. She still looks scary, with her bald head and red lips, but today she's in a good mood.

'You've all helped Doll, in your unique way, to complete her mission. Everyone here has played their part – and this is no hyperbole – in saving the future of Almazova.' She steps forward to shake Tiger's hand, then mine. 'Thank you.'

In this moment, I'm ten feet tall. I'm somebody. *Invincible.* I look around at all the faces. They're clapping and cheering. Everyone is smiling at me. I want to hold on to this. The ice cube in my throat starts to melt. *Invincible.*

They all shake my hand, whisper their thanks. 'Here's a toast,' Nell says, raising her glass, but none arrives.

Nan-Nan takes me to one side. She points to a door at the far end of the room and presses a remote. It slides open. 'We have to go,' she says. 'Are you ready, sweetheart?' She sees the tears welling in my eyes and hunkers down, puts her face close to mine. 'Can I tell you something?'

I nod.

'I shouldn't – it's against the rules – but . . .'

'What is it?'

She cups my ear, looks left and right. '*You will be back.*'

Every cell in my body starts to fizzle.

'How do you know?'

'Shhh! I don't know when, but you're definitely coming back.'

I'm wondering if this is just some fairytale to keep me happy.

'How can you be so sure?'

She hesitates for a second. 'I've seen the Manuscripts. The Child of Summer returns. I read it myself.' She taps her nose. 'Confidential . . . so not a word, okay?'

I nod. She's throwing me a lifeline. I must grab it and hope it's the truth. My heart has become elastic, stretching the length and breadth of my chest.

I throw my arms around her and smother her with kisses. I love Nan-Nan.

We turn towards the open door. Beyond, there's darkness and a thin wall of light, thin as Archon's cigarette paper. Even as I watch, the light begins to expand and curve into a tunnel shape.

Tiger steps forward. We cling to each other before she releases me. I put my hand in Nan-Nan's. It's like a magnet, and I couldn't pull it away even if I wanted to. We step towards the tunnel of light.

'Look straight ahead, Doll.'

The light is dazzling, and I have to shield my eyes as we walk to-wards it. Then the wind – I hear it coming like the scream of a train – catches us and hurls us forward. We're spinning, out through the night sky, through the milky-white stars, through the holy silence, somersault-ing home.

We're floating now, through the raw air. Lights wink and tremble in the distance. A lighthouse blinks into view. Streetlights like a string of pearls guide us safely home. We're falling, falling like snowflakes, tiptoe-ing back, screamless and breathless.

I half open my lids. Is it a painting? There's a girl bent over a tiny screen. A woman sleeps on a leather chair. A man and a boy stand to-gether, deep in whispered conversation.

There's a cloying smell. I'm lying on clammy sheets. A radiator gur-gles and sputters. A machine *beep-beep*s behind me. My heart rattles, tum-bles from my chest and clatters across the tiles. *Thump, thump.* I feel my bones collapsing like a folding tent. I squeeze my eyes shut. *I'm back. I'm back. I'm back.*

After a while, I open my eyes and let out a long, low wail.

CHAPTER 52

SALLY

Mary Winters' waiting area is a narrow room off reception with three forlorn chairs sitting in a row. I'm ashamed to be here, and I'm grateful it's empty today.

After Doll came round that night, we all cried with joy and relief. We'd held our breath for so long; now we could exhale again. Our prayers were answered, and now we could move forward. Doll was back with us. We could manage everything else. As Andi would say, what's not to like?

It started about three days after she came home from hospital. I had dropped Will to the airport before heading in to the twice-weekly editorial team meeting. Terri was going through how we'd support the December road safety campaign, item four on the agenda.

'Happy with that, Sal?'

It felt like someone crouching behind my chair had reached around and closed his fist around my heart, squeezing it like a clamp. Waves of fear crashed through me. I had to run before I exploded across the board-room. I remember grabbing my jacket, frantically thinking how I might make my exit look natural.

'Is everything all right, Sally?'

A chorus of concerned voices said, 'Carry on, no problem, do what you have to do, talk later.'

I remember stuffing my laptop into my bag with slippery fingers. 'I'll be back. Just forgot to . . . turn off the cooker.'

I took the stairs three at a time, my heart a squelching pink mess sloshing around inside my mouth. I was being hunted like an animal. I remember randomly taking a left, hurrying past the deli, past the pharmacy, silently screaming onto Strandside South and down onto the prom. I was gasping and grateful for the mist wrapping people into their own interior worlds. Too cold, too damp to notice me. I could not handle a conversation. *How's Doll now? Thank God she's better. 'Twas rough there for a while.*

The soothing crash of wave after wave slowed my pounding heart. The hunt was over. I had outrun the monster inside me. And no one suspected.

A blonde head appears round the waiting room door. 'Dr Winters will be with you in five minutes, Sally. Apologies for the delay.' I nod my thanks.

I Googled it afterwards. *Panic attack.* Convinced myself it was a one-off. When it happened again two days later, I did think I was going to die. It was just after dinner. I was watching *Fair City* when I felt the fear hurtling towards me like a train, and I had to get out of the way before I was run over. This time, I couldn't run. I was paralysed, my shoes glued down. I just stood there, smothered in terror, gripping the table, begging the sweaty attacker to retreat.

Panic. Attack. It's a perfect word combination to explain how it feels, like a knife scoring your skin and then twin blades of anxiety and terror plunging through you, leaving you sapped and shredded.

Dan had just walked in. 'What's up, Sal.'

I had to tell him – though I didn't want him to know. I knew I was shutting him off. I was angry with him. Not about what he did for Rob Colbert. It was more of a diffuse anger, unspoken hostilities rising like histamines in the bad blood between us. It was breaking my heart, and I couldn't fix it.

'You need to go to the doctor,' he said, when I'd done my best to explain. 'Why are you fighting it?'

'So he can give me anti-anxiety drugs? No thanks.'

You can't be medicating for everything, can you? Drugs are not the answer. I read ten per-cent of the population is on antidepressants. Does it solve anything? I doubt it. My mother said there was no stress in her day. Now everyone is stressed. It's pathetic. *I'm pathetic.*

Dan made the appointment with Mary Winters in the end. I protested, but I couldn't think of a good enough reason not to go. And I needed to find a way through these panic attacks.

So here I am, and at least I have something concrete to talk about. Panic attacks are real. I can describe them. They have a shape and symptoms. I Googled it; I know other people get them. Dr Winters has to have come across them in her practice, so she'll have the formula that works, and I want to hear about that. Shouldn't take long.

The receptionist is back. 'Sally, you can go through now.' I follow her down the corridor to room four.

Mary smiles and gestures for me to sit opposite her. We exchange the usual pleasantries, and I tell her I'm sorry about last time and I'm anxious now to hear how she can fix me. She nods.

'Tell me about your daughter,' she says, sitting back in her chair.

I know the script by heart – I've told the story to the concerned and the pretend-concerned for years now. She says, 'I see,' 'I understand,' 'Tell me about . . . She asks me questions, she clarifies, she nods, as if my words and my feelings and my thoughts are the most fascinating jewels.

'You seem to be very on top of the situation,' she says, after a long time. 'You're very practical.'

I smile, pleased. 'Yes, you have to be, don't you?'

'Do you?'

'Well, yes, of course.'

'Can you tell me about that?'

I'm not sure how to explain. No one ever asked me that before.

'Well, you have to get on with it. That's life. It's not easy, but no point complaining.' I smile. 'Who'd listen?'

'I'm listening now, Sally.'

Silence. I have to break it.

'Look, there's a pressure, you know, to cope well and do what you have to . . . and not bang on about it, you know? No one wants to hear about misery. It's not rocket science.'

She pours a glass of water for me. 'I'm curious to know where the pressure is coming from.'

I have to think about that one. More silence.

'I suppose it's what you believe. You don't want to be a victim, do you? A weak mother who can't cope? That'd be pathetic. You must be resilient. You have to overcome all the challenges – it's the only way.'

Surely it's obvious. I don't know why she's pursuing this. You have to be strong. It *is* the only way.

'When you say it's the only way, Sally . . . ?'

I take a gulp of water. Loosen my scarf. 'Look, what I mean is that you must overcome your challenges; you must fight back. Yes, it's sad. I'm not denying that. Very sad. Very distressing. A struggle. But you can't let the sadness rule your life; you can't wallow in it. It doesn't help to give in, does it? To the sadness, I mean.'

'And where does all that sadness go?'

The clock on the wall beats out the seconds. I can't answer her. How do you answer a silly, silly question like that?

She waits. The question sits on the air, suspended between us. Its arms folded.

I start to cry, very quietly. I must not cry. I must not come undone. I must maintain composure. Christ, why am I even crying? It's ridiculous.

I say, after a minute, 'I really don't know where it goes. But you can't let your feelings take over. You'd drown, wouldn't you, and that wouldn't help anyone, would it?'

She nods.

'Does it ever feel like you're drowning? Like it's too much? It's just that' – she puts a manicured finger on her chin – 'when you tell me your story, there are an awful lot of *should*s and *must*s and *have to*s. Where is that coming from, do you think?'

The minutes tick by. I feel safe, like I'm sinking into a soft blanket. I feel I don't have to be strong or hide or be cheerful. *Can I really just be me?*

'It's coming from myself. I believe it's important to be resilient. There's nothing wrong with that, is there? We mothers must cope well. Not just cope; it's important to learn and transcend, overcome your problems.'

'But it's a struggle? Being the perfect mother? At times?'

I can't trust myself to talk.

'What's going on for you now, Sally?'

I can't say the words.

'Take your time.'

Is the clock getting louder? The tick-tocking fills the room. I take some deep breaths. One, two, three, four, exhale. Hold for four.

When I talk, it's a whisper.

'It is. A struggle. Every day. Hard. Very hard. Sometimes . . . unbearable.'

Someone's tears are quietly pouring down my cheeks. They are not my tears. They arrive uninvited and decide for themselves to slide out of the corners of my eyes, one after another, free-falling. I am only vaguely aware of them. Their wetness. *Go away.* They drip off my chin onto my blue scarf. They run back, some of them into my hair, past my ear-lobes. They can't wait. It's like a race. I ignore them. Let them off. They don't concern me, and I have no power over them. The tears are crying themselves. Separate to me.

I'm discovering that words, spoken, can burst feelings awake. Feelings that might be manacled to some filthy prison wall for years will sit up and roar. *Who dared wake me from my slumber?* Tears are the damn bursting, flowing over words and feelings. Releasing me, an ointment for my heart.

We talk about Dan and the shadow between us. I let it all pour out. About how we only seem to talk to the edges of each other. Somehow the wound doesn't sting as much as I explore the bumps, bends, and bruises of our relationship. Compassion unravels the tangles in my head. Letting me let go.

After the session, I stroll along the waterfront. I feel light as a sunbeam. Slightly drunk. I can't explain it; it's like I've visited a quiet church, emerging tranquilised and soothed. Somehow, in the space of ninety minutes, the landscape has become a little more luminous. The sadness has leaked away for now. *I listened. I heard myself.* And I know I'll be going back next week.

On the journey home, I think about Doll. How she seems to be softening out, like a ball of cotton wool, fluffing out, expanding. Her scars are healing, and there are small things: half smiles, a glimmer of light in her eyes, some knowing I never saw before – if you look often enough, you'll notice these little changes. Gifts, really. These last weeks, it's like she's seeing the house for the very first time, and yesterday she even held Ruby's hand.

'Look, Doll's my friend. Quick, Mam, look.'

That's a first.

Small things. I'll take what I can get.

CHAPTER 53

ANDI

'I'll come in with you,' Stacey says as we both step off the pavement to let a woman with a buggy pass.

'No. I have to do this on my own,' I say, taking another piece of gum from my pocket. My mouth is dry, and the chewing will help. Might even make me look a bit braver than I actually feel.

After Doll came out of hospital, we were all on a high. We'd feared the worst, and then she turned a corner. Mom had decided to go and see a therapist, and it made such a difference. She was smiling again. Everything was coming up roses. Except it wasn't. The texts from Chelsea were getting nastier and more personal. Maybe she'd rearrange my face? Didn't I know Steve was using me? What time was my basketball practice again? I blocked her number, but that didn't stop her. So *I* have to.

I know she works part-time in Suzanne's Hair & Beauty Salon after school, and I've decided I'm going to march in there and confront her. See how she likes it when the tables are turned. I know what I'm taking on. Stacey says the Nolans have form, but fuck it, I can't live my life like this, and I'm not giving up Steve. Anyway, no one is going to push me around. Bullies are cowards behind it all.

Through the window of 23 Church Street, Suzanne's Hair & Beauty Salon is a dizzying swirl of pinks and purples. I push in the glass door and am hit by a heavenly cloud of perfume. Just inside, there's a slowly circling carousel of nail polish in every possible colour. Beyond it I can see Chelsea – kohl eyes, sweeping lashes, thick peach lips. Gross. She's chatting to a client who's getting her nails painted in a mesh of silver and gold.

A pretty girl with a blonde ponytail comes towards me. The name *Debbie* is pinned to her tunic. I'm conscious of my school uniform, but I think it suits how I want to come across today – bullied schoolgirl from St Mary's Academy.

'Hello, Debbie,' I say, peering at her lapel. 'I'm looking for Chelsea Nolan.'

Chelsea looks up when she hears her name and comes over to the reception area. Her face registers surprise.

'What do *you* want?' she hiss-pers, her lips barely moving. She looks vaguely uncomfortable. Here goes. I can't back away now, even though my heart is pounding so loudly I'm sure she can hear it.

'I want,' I say, raising my voice, 'for you to stop sending me those horrible texts.' The panic is a butterfly flapping its wings inside my head.

Chelsea's jaw drops a few inches in pure shock. In fairness, it nearly makes me laugh. There's a woman putting her coat on, and she looks up sharply. She glances from me to Chelsea, her face a question mark. She looks down then, arranging her scarf, rummaging in her handbag, determined not to miss the floor show. Chelsea's client is all ears too, craning her head around the side of the carousel to get a better view. A woman in a yellow sweater is sitting in the corner, pretend-reading her magazine. The silence lasts a few seconds but seems to stretch out like an elastic band.

Chelsea recovers fast. 'Keep your fucking voice down,' she whispers. 'You'll be kicked out.' More audibly she says, 'Excuse me? How dare you. I haven't a clue what you're talking about.' She glances around the salon. 'Please leave, or I'll call the manager.'

Debbie looks towards the door marked *Staff* at the back of the salon. 'Will I call Suzanne, Chelsea?'

Chelsea rolls her eyes. 'No, I'll handle her.' Her eyes narrow. 'You're confused, girl. You're mixing me up with someone else. I never sent you—'

'Call her down, Debbie,' I say loudly. 'Suzanne'll be very interested to see the texts this one is sending me.' I turn to Chelsea. 'You're a bully, Chelsea Nolan, and I want to hear you say you're sorry.'

Silence. Everyone is waiting. Debbie disappears to get Suzanne.

Chelsea propels me towards an annex. 'Call this off,' she says under her breath, her long lashes fluttering wildly. 'Don't embarrass yourself.' She gives an anxious glance over her shoulder.

'It's up to you,' I say sweetly. 'You can stop this right now.' I fold my arms to hide the tremble in my hands.

'Okay, okay, we're quits.' She chews her lip, nodding vigorously.

The door marked *Staff* opens, and Suzanne's voice is sharp and full of authority. Stacey was right —you wouldn't want to mess with Suzanne Fox. She marches towards us, her face grim. 'What's going on in my salon? Get in the back, both of you.'

'Actually, I've changed my mind. I'm leaving,' I say.

'You have no business coming in here making wild accusations,' Suzanne says crossly. 'I've a good mind—'

Chelsea and me exchange glances. 'I take it back,' I say. 'Chelsea explained.' Chelsea nods, relieved that the drama is about to end.

'You should apologise, miss,' Suzanne says, giving me a stern look.

'It's okay,' Chelsea says, looking at me. 'Leave her off. No harm done. She made a mistake.'

'That's very good of you, Chelsea,' Suzanne says, glowering at me. 'Off you go now.' I exit the salon, my legs wobbling like jelly sticks as I cross the road and walk through the shopping centre to Pizza Pizza.

I take the table in the corner by the window and take a few deep breaths to bring my heart back to normal. I text Stacey. Sorted. Talk ltr. I can't be sure it actually *is* sorted, but Chelsea Nolan now knows I'm not someone she can mess with and get away with it. Next time I *will* talk to Suzanne. Next time I *will* go to the guards. And next time she tries to jostle me off the pavement, I'll push back.

The adrenaline is still shooting through me. I'm not saying a word to Steve. This is strictly between me and Chelsea.

Through the window I can see him across the street at the pedestrian lights. In the late-afternoon dusk, he looks more gorgeous than ever. In about sixty seconds, he'll be here, sitting opposite me. A thrill runs up my spine. I know I am the happiest I've ever been, probably the happiest anyone has ever been.

He walks through the door and down to where I'm sitting.

'Hi, babe.' He leans over to kiss my cheek and takes the seat opposite.

I smile and try to unscramble my brain long enough to concentrate on the menu.

'Good news,' he says, as soon as we've ordered a triple pepperoni pizza to share. 'My ma's gone back to London.' There's no hint of regret in his voice, but I can see the pain behind his eyes.

289

'How do you feel about that?' I say.

He sighs heavily, stretching back in his chair. 'Relieved, to be honest. And my gran is too. She's promised us she'll get clean. Said she'd do it for me. She wanted me to be proud of her. But . . .' He shrugs his shoulders.

'You've probably heard it all before, Steve. Do you think she can do it this time?'

He shrugs again. 'Maybe. Maybe not. She might surprise us. I hope she will.' There's a soft edge to his voice. 'Gran said she was a fantastic girl growing up. She was sporty and she loved school . . . and then it all went sour for her.' His forehead furrows. 'That's life. You never can tell what sewer you might end up in.' His voice is flat.

'She'll come right, Steve,' I say, taking his hand. 'Things change. People change. I mean, I know it's completely different, but look at Doll. She's changed. She's not hurting herself anymore. She even smiles now, and she's definitely more chilled. Little miracles can happen. We never thought we'd see that. Your mum might turn her life around; you have to hope she will.'

He nods. 'I know. It's up to her, though. We're there for her, me and Gran, but it's up to her to take the first steps.'

The waitress brings our drinks.

'Maybe now we'll get some time to spend together,' he says, flashing me a smile. 'No hospitals, no long-lost mothers and jealous exes who aren't even exes to keep us apart.' He raises his Coke. 'To us,' he says.

'To us,' I say, clinking his glass.

'I had another word with Chelsea,' he says. 'She's harmless, really, and trust me, she won't bother you again.'

'Oh, I know she won't,' I say. 'I'm pretty sure she's gotten the message.'

'There's one more thing . . .'

Our pizzas arrive, and he waits as the plates are lowered in front of us.

'Well, come on, Steve?'

He looks at the food. 'It's not an ideal time, but . . .'

'But what, Steve? Don't freak me out.' I fidget with a strand of hair, nervous about what's coming next.

He leans in. 'Will you be my girlfriend? I mean, officially?' He hesitates. 'I know it hasn't been that long, but look . . .' He takes a tiny box from his pocket and moves it across the table. 'I can't stop thinking about you, Andi. I'm only happy when I'm with you . . .' He rolls his eyes. 'Am I making a mess of this?'

I laugh and open the box. It's a silver ring with a tiny blue stone. I slip it on. It's a perfect fit. I straighten my arm and spread my fingers, admiring how the stone catches the light.

'It's beautiful, Steve.'

'You didn't answer, babe.'

I look straight into his blue-and-amber eyes and trace my fingers across his lips.

'It's a triple yes,' I say, as my heart somersaults across the restaurant.

CHAPTER 54

DAN

Lorraine peers out over her glasses, the two grey suits sitting beside her a perfect foil for her mustard dress. She rests her arms on the polished mahogany and leans forward. On the other side of the table, I loosen my tie.

On the way to Dublin this morning, I rehearsed my defence. I thought about how I'd react if they told me I was fired. Some – usually the serious swindlers – brazen it out, refuse to resign, and get the big guns in, and you know, sometimes they get away with it.

More are grateful their misdemeanours won't hit the headlines and creep off quietly.

Me? I broke the rules. Hands up. But I won't go quietly. I decided that. There has to be perspective, and I'm not having my reputation destroyed because I let a client off the hook for a couple of grand in interest. A few weeks ago, the job was part of a life that was dragging me down; now I know I definitely do not want to lose it. I'm good at it. I've created a great team around me, and I'm not walking away from all that.

Lorraine clears her throat to speak.

'So we've listened, Dan, and we've examined the evidence,' she says, glancing at Frank McKenna on her left. 'And under the circumstances, and given that your actions resulted in no personal gain, we've agreed a written warning will suffice at this juncture.'

She purses her lips. 'We've taken your track record into account, your years of service, and the Colberts' particular circumstances. No further action will be taken.'

I take a moment to process the unexpected good news. *I'm off the hook.*

'You've a good reputation, Dan. The branch compliance overall is excellent. We see no reason to take' – she hesitates, fingering the pearl necklace at her throat – 'inappropriate measures on this occasion.'

The tension in the room drops a level. Frank swings his pen between his fingers, tapping it on the table.

'We found all regulations were followed in the branch, Dan. What we did was procedure; you know that. We have to follow our own policies.'

I nod. 'Sure, Frank. I understand that.' I like Frank, and I know his job isn't easy. I could argue about using a hammer to crack a nut and all that, but I just want to move on, case closed.

'We'll put all this in writing,' Lorraine says, closing the blue folder in front of her. 'Have you any questions, Dan?'

'I'm free to return to work?'

'Yes, absolutely.' She allows herself a smile for the first time, and it changes her entire face. She looks human, even approachable.

'And the Colbert account? Can you at least look at it, give Rob and his family a break?'

'We will; leave it to us. I'll be in touch about that.' She straightens up. 'And there's one more thing; you'll be getting a new financial advisor.'

'Oh? Shirley Lovett's not coming back?' Inside, I feel a flood of relief.

'No, I'm afraid not. She's about to be officially appointed wealth manager here in Dublin. She'll probably start pretty much straightaway.' Lorraine looks at Paul Gavan from HR on her left for confirmation.

He nods. 'Yeah, that's correct. We'll let you know the full details later today, Dan. We're in the process of appointing a new advisor for Glengarvan.'

'I'm happy for her.' It's the best I can manage.

There's an awkward pause, and Paul says, 'Thank you, Dan. Okay, I think we're done here.' He looks at his watch. Lorraine nods and reaches across to shake my hand.

'Best of luck and safe journey home.'

We all file out, exchanging goodbyes along with some stilted small talk.

In the basement car park, I take a minute before turning on the ignition. I think about Shirley, and how the throwaway remark about Joanne Colbert's MS started all this. Shirley had said *fair play* before reporting me a few days later. Am I glad she's moved on.

I punch 171 to listen to my messages. Claire wishing me luck, Sally saying to let her know how it went, and then Shirley's voicemail, soft and concerned, a little breathless. I can almost smell her perfume floating off the phone. 'Dan, hope all goes well. I wanted to let you know . . . I wanted to explain . . . for you to understand that, you know, I had to do the right thing; it wasn't an easy decision. I'll ring you again later. Or ring me when you get this . . . look, yes, ring me, Dan.'

She's priceless. Ever the sales-woman.

I text Sally and Claire with the news and pull out of the parking bay. Outside, the sun is trying to push through a duvet of cloud. The traffic is chaotic, and it keeps my attention focused till I get out beyond the Red Cow roundabout. Even from there, it's a long drive home.

On the M8, I set the car to cruise and think about my life and the debits and credits and the paybacks and what you can write off and what can be saved. At the end of the day, everything has a price.

Doll survived. I didn't expect her to, and it's brought some hope back into our lives, bringing her home and seeing some new spark kindling behind her eyes. And tomorrow, with this behind me, I'm looking forward to getting back to my office, back into the theatre of finance. Minus the love scenes with Shirley Lovett.

I take the fork for the M7, and it's a straight road now for the next two hundred plus kilometres. The sun is coming out, and the city suburbs give way to bright-green hills and fields of grazing cattle.

I settle back in my seat, grateful for the thinking time the journey home brings.

Home. I say the word out loud. *Home.* It sounds like a yoga mantra. And what is home? Where is home? I know the answer before it even forms. Sally is home. Wherever she is, that's home. And I realize now that I lost her, or certainly lost sight of her. She was there, somewhere nearby, sorting and solving and lately stumbling through, trying to keep the smile intact, some hope alive that Doll would turn a corner after years of Groundhog Day every day.

And I know she lost herself too, blurring inside those shapeless walls of Doll's misery. The question is – where was I?

The sun is hot through the windscreen, and I switch on the aircon and take off my tie. *Where was I?* I was off looking for some goddess, some fantasy woman whose perfume alone could make my head spin.

Shirley could read the sign I couldn't even see myself. *Available*. I might as well have put it on my lapel.

The Volvo swallows up the motorway, and I take each year like a ledger, poring over the memories and the hills and valleys. The past is a story we tell ourselves. And it tells us things, shows us patterns and trends.

By the time I get to Bluebell Grove, it's almost five o'clock. Sally's in the kitchen, taking off her coat. I stand in the doorway for a moment, inhaling the warmth and the cooking aromas.

She gives me a hug, and I fill her in on the meeting.

'You must be so relieved. *I'm* so relieved. We can put it behind us.'

She goes to put the kettle on and sits at the table. 'Audrey's put a roast chicken on, so we can eat when Andi gets in. We'll raise a glass to Lorraine and Co.' She looks at me. 'Sit down, Dan.'

'I've something I need to tell you, Sal.' I dig my hands in my pockets.

She looks up, alarmed, her hand cupping her chin. 'Go on.'

'There's a woman at work . . .'

Her eyes narrow.

'Shirley Lovett . . .'

'I know her. I've seen her around.' She hesitates, and there's a long silence. 'Are you having an affair?' Her face is expressionless, her voice flat.

'No!'

'So what is it, then?' She folds her arms, shivering slightly.

'I kissed her. Once. It was brief.'

She stares, and I can see the suspicion in her green eyes.

'I see. A kiss? When?'

'A few weeks ago.'

'Where?'

'At her flat.'

She nods slowly as she gets up to pour boiled water into a teapot. 'You were in her flat. Why?' She stares at the teapot.

'I went in for a drink after work. It just happened. Nothing else happened.'

She leans against the worktop. 'You expect me to believe that?'

'It's the truth. I swear on my life.'

'And why are you telling me this now?' She reaches for a mug and pours the tea. I can see the fine lines around her mouth slacken for a moment, like the muscles decided they needed a break.

'I'm telling you this, Sal, because . . . because I love you. I haven't said it in a while, and—'

'She's beautiful,' Sally says, her voice faltering. 'Shirley Lovett is a stunner.' Her shoulders sag, and she massages her temples in dainty little circles.

'Forget about Shirley Lovett. I got distracted. She came onto me . . .'

She snaps her head up. 'So it's her fault, is it? You couldn't resist, is that the story?' Her eyes are flashing now, and her voice is hard as jade.

'Something like that—'

She paces back and forth across the kitchen, and the pulleys and levers in her face have come alive.

'I trusted you.' She waves her hand angrily. 'It's not about the kiss, Dan. That's bad enough. It's more about you allowing it, you wanting it, you wanting her. That's the real betrayal.'

'I was the one who stopped it, Sally.'

'You were the one who's married, Dan!'

She bites the corner of her lip. 'I knew it. I knew there was something, but I couldn't put my finger on it.'

I come closer and lean against the table for support. 'Sally, it doesn't mean anything. You're the one for me. You always were, from day one.'

She doesn't reply.

'Look, I know I screwed up. I was drifting, and I admit that.'

She stops pacing and closes her eyes, and when she opens them again, she says, 'I know you've been drifting, Dan. I knew I'd lost you along the way.' Her face crumples. 'I just didn't know how to get you back.'

I reach out and wrap my arms around her. She doesn't resist. I can feel her breath against my shirt.

'Believe me, I'm back, Sal.' I tighten my hold, and she leans in.

'I want to believe you,' she whispers.

'Sally, I want a me-and-you again. Just us, no labels, a couple of lovers finding their way back.'

After a minute she says, 'I want that, Dan. More than anything.'

She winds her arms around my neck, and I can feel her muscles slacken like some weight has shifted off her.

I kiss her forehead. 'You know, that Winters woman? You said she's good?'

She looks up. 'Yes, she's been brilliant. Why?'

'She might be good for us. She might give us a space to talk to each other.'

Her green eyes widen. 'You'd come to the counsellor with me? You're serious, aren't you?' She bursts into tears, but she's smiling as she holds me at arm's length. 'You're willing to sit down and talk about us? How we'll come unstuck?'

I nod. 'A new start, Sal.' I can feel a warmth move through me.

She laughs and reaches up to kiss me. And I know now, and even she knows, I'm coming home.

CHAPTER 55

DOLL

Christmas Eve. The grass is coated white, and the sky is wide and blue. Mom and Audrey are drinking tea in the kitchen while I listen to a song on the radio. The singer is telling us to have ourselves a merry little Christmas. You almost believe it when he says that from here on our troubles will be far away . . . Could he put that in writing?

I look around the room. Lights wink. The fire is blazing, and you can see the flames reflected in the Christmas tree baubles. I hop off the armchair to touch one of them. My face is small and fat when I peer very close to the gold one. Like the brass doorknob in Nell's house.

Nell's house. It's like a dream.

It wasn't easy for me, coming back. I was gutted. But hugs and kisses from my family helped. To be loved. To be wanted. To matter. It made me see something I'd never seen before: that my heart had been trapped, slumped behind a woolly curtain. And I saw, when I came back, that all the love I could want was there, like a box of chocolates, for the taking. It had always been there; I just couldn't see it.

I couldn't wait to get out of that clammy hospital bed. I had five days of proving I would eat before they left me go, so I took everything they gave me. The nurses were kind. They kissed me goodbye and gave me lollies and said they'd miss me. How? I was out cold for most of my stay. But look, they meant well.

Now that I can't talk anymore and my head is fuzzy, I'm back to being special again. When I look at a magazine, I see squiggles instead of proper words, no matter how hard I squeeze my eyes. And my muscles aren't strong anymore.

But the thing is, I can remember my adventure. Like a video I can play in my head, again and again and again.

I wondered, at the start, if it was all just a dream. The first day home it was weird. I saw the tartan rug and the couch and remembered all the hours I lay there, shutting out the light. Nell said you can decline and decay or find a way to triumph. I was decaying, I can see that now. I was disgraceable, tearing my face open. My lovely face, Nan-Nan said. I'm not proud of that.

I sit now, instead, on one of the armchairs. Looking around me. At the familiar and yet the new. Remembering my barnacled life.

That first evening, Mom unpacked my bag.

'Where did this come from?' She was holding up a crumpled purple coat with silver buttons.

Andi inspected it, checked the pockets, and pulled out some orange peel and the tin of bubbles.

I gave a cry and tugged at the velvet. Andi laughed. 'Oh, Doll, let's try it on you.' She slips my arms in.

'It fits her, Mom. It's nice. The nurses must have thought it was hers. Look, quick, Mom. Doll's smiling.'

Mom looked at me. 'Doll, it fits you perfectly. Purple's your colour.'

I smiled back, hugging my memories to myself. Someday the bubbles might tell me another story. It was something, wasn't it, having the coat too? And even Nell's medal ended up under my hospital pillow.

'Happy Christmas, Ruby. Be good for Santa.' Mom says her goodbyes to Audrey. She comes and rubs my head, following my gaze. 'You admiring the Christmas tree, Doll?'

She sits by the fire and scoops me onto her lap. I lean my head against her chest.

ELO is playing 'Showdown' on the radio. In my head I see Valda rowing across the lake and the Headscarves in the sky, swooping and diving.

A thrilling memory. Break through – that's what Nell said. Break through the skin of despair. Maybe that's what memories are for. When despair gets too much, you can escape into yesterday's adventure.

I tap my hand against my leg to the beat. Mom smiles down at me, and I smile back at her.

My granny didn't let me down in the end. She promised she'd protect me, and she did. I know now that there's more than this stony life – it's a huge forever universe, and Granny is still living in some other corner of it. And Major Tom too. I hope they've met. I'd say they'd be friends. She always liked a rebel, she said. And a man in a uniform.

Will is home for the holidays. Later, after my bath, he tucks me into bed. As he turns to leave the room, he bends down. 'Jesus, is that your doll behind the locker?'

I open one eye.

He's picking something off the floor, dusting it down. He fires it at my bed, laughing.

'Ah, Doll. You can't be buckarooing your toys out of the bed.' He blows me a kiss and closes the door.

I sit up straight. The curtains are open, and the moonlight pools in. Nan-Nan! I pick her up and kiss her face. Where did she come from?

Under my window, I can hear carol singers singing 'O Holy Night'.

The voices float up. I hold Nan-Nan close and listen in the stillness. Her lashes flutter.

'How are you, sweetheart?'

I gasp. 'Oh my God, Nan-Nan, you're back.'

'Yes, honey. I just wanted to say hello before I return to Almazova.'

My mouth falls open; I don't know what to say. I tuck the duvet up around her and kiss her face.

She smiles. 'I had another mission here.' She waves her hand in a circle. 'And I wanted to see how you're doing.'

My body is tingling head to foot.

'How *are* you doing, Doll?'

'Good, Nan-Nan.'

'Your face is perfect. I'll tell Nell. She will be so proud of you.'

'How's Tiger?'

'She's still grieving for her father, but she's got a good family. Just like you, Doll.'

'I know, and that's why I'm trying, you know, to break through . . . like Nell said.'

She traces a line around my cheekbone. 'It's the little things that transform us, Doll. Like realising we're not helpless. We can open out our heart. Let it breathe. Let the light in.'

I nod. I get it. 'And the Orb?'

'Shining and safe in the cathedral. Equilibrium restored. Thanks to you, Doll.' She presses my eyelids closed. 'I must go, child. Tomorrow is a big day. Get some sleep now.'

'Will you be back for me someday?'

'You know I will.'

'Happy Christmas, Nan-Nan.'

She ruffles my hair. 'Happy Christmas, Doll.'

She steps across the bed, takes off her hat, raises her arms towards the white moon. Even as I watch, she replaces her hat firmly, steps up to the window, and releases the catch. She turns for a moment to wink at me. Then, like a bird, she swoops upwards, across the rooftops into the sky. I kneel, resting my chin on the windowsill as she floats up into the night.

I stay there long after Nan-Nan's disappeared from view. A shooting star fires across the sky. Below on the footpath, the carol singers are singing softly.

Silent night, holy night,
All is calm, all is bright . . .

The End

Coming Soon

The Girl with Stars in Her Eyes

Dan

'Good trip?' It's the way she says it. Pursing her lips and avoiding my eyes. It's like she knows. But she couldn't possibly know, how could she? 'The usual . . .' I nod, unzipping my bag, folding a sweater, hanging my suit in the closet. Avoiding her gaze. I snap the suitcase shut and shove it under the bed.

'Traffic was murder, though. Even for a Friday.'

She nods. 'Yeah, that's Dublin for you.'

I pull a sweatshirt over my head. There's an awkward silence. She folds her arms, looks out the window.

I'm going for a run,' I say, lacing up my trainers. 'I won't be long.'

She shrugs. 'It's starting to drizzle, bring a rainproof.'

'Is there something wrong, Sally?' I can't stand the tension.

'No. Why are you asking me that?'

'Well, you're very quiet, it's not like you.'

She sighs and rubs her palms over her face. 'It's Doll.'

I don't say it but I'm thinking: here we go again. 'What now?'

She looks up sharply, reading my impatience. 'What now? Are you blind? Don't you see the change in her?' She stops. Straightens the blue throw on the bed, smoothing out imaginary creases. 'Doll's falling back, shutting herself off.'

She looks up, folds her arms again. 'Or are you too busy at work to notice what's going on under your nose?'

She switches her hands to her hips – it's what she does when she's ready to erupt and looking for someone to blame – and I'm not in the bloody mood.

'You know what, Sally?'

I zip up my windcheater. 'Maybe you need to get out for a run yourself. Get rid of some of that stress . . . and then we'll talk. When you're calmer.'

303

She brushes past me. Her eyes flash. 'I'm not even going to answer that.' The door slams behind her. She opens it a fraction. 'By the way, I'd love to go for a run, but someone has to mind Doll. Enjoy yourself though.' She disappears down the stairs and I can hear saucepans banging loudly in the kitchen.

Do I need this? As if I hadn't noticed Doll's form. Her wails in the early hours. As if I couldn't see the way she stares out the window, the light switched off inside her head, the invisible sign saying: there's no one home. For Chrissake. I'm not blind.

I bang the front door shut and jog down the avenue, out onto the Mill Road and right again onto the river path. The rain is hammering down now but it's good to get out into the summer evening and let the hassles of the day behind you. I quicken my pace seeing if I can out-run the bastards. I decide to take the longer route; who'd want to go home to that?

I cut across the school grounds, exit onto Monastery Road heading for the path that cuts through Glengarvan wood, a good hour's run. The rain is warm against my face, and I can feel the layers of mental grime peel away as I fall into a steady rhythm.

She knows something. The way she wouldn't meet my eye. And not just this evening, she's been in strange form for the last few weeks. She's concerned about Doll – I wouldn't blame her for that – but there's something else. Something she's not saying. She suspects something.

I hop over the wooden gate onto the path that criss-crosses the wood. The rain is a soft drizzle now and there's a rainbow arching through the beech trees on my right. I stop for a second to admire the hazy blues and pinks and yellows filtering through the dripping leaves. For some strange reason, I feel like crying, how dumb is that? I must be getting soft in the head.

I push on but I can't escape the band of unease across my chest, squeezing tight like a too-small shirt. Guilt? Shame? Is there a difference, no doubt someone could tell me, but would it matter? They were only labels anyway at the end of the day, names for feelings that filled you up with regret. But there was excitement too. And joy. Last night in the Gibson Hotel he'd felt joy. Joy and guilt. Mary Winters at the Counselling Centre said feelings need to be expressed. Not suppressed. There's something in that. Still…certain stories are best left untold.

Deeper in the woods now, I can smell honeysuckle, wild jasmine, nettle, the deep earthy scents released by the drenched grass underfoot. The world being washed clean. Wish I could be washed clean.

I hate lies. Secrets and lies. You hear a lot of secrets in my job at the bank, stories unfolding in the back offices. Confessions whispered across the desk over cold cups of coffee.

I slow my pace, get my breath back. What would Sally say? Would she understand? Would she forgive me? Would she say it's the last straw, Dan?

Back home, I take the stairs two at a time. Tomorrow, I'll do it. I'll tell her.

I turn the water to hot and step into the steaming shower. I'll say, Sally, there's something you should know. I close my eyes, let the hot water sting my face, like a slap. And I can't help thinking that this is the calm before the storm.

Acknowledgements

They say it takes a village to raise a child. I reckon it takes a village to write a book too.

To my husband Derek, thank you for letting me disappear, yet again, to 'get some writing done' and for the endless cups of tea and support.

Thank you to my sister, Rosemary, for sparking the idea in the first place and to Margaret O'Connor at Sherkin North Shore Writing Workshop where I wrote the very first page of this novel.

A huge thank you to my beta readers for taking time out to read my first draft: Nicola Garrett-Elovsson, Aileen Quirke, Rosaleen O'Leary, Anne Riordan Connolly, Rosemary Sexton, Anita McKenna, Terry McKenna, John Gilroy, Colette Doonan, Ciara Gallogly, Lorraine Crowley, Shauna McSweeney, Alannah O'Kelly-Lynch, Aileen Lyons, Paul O'Kelly-Lynch, Eithne Griffin. Without your support and enthusiasm, I couldn't have done it; I learned so much from your comments and feedback; your time and efforts were a gift to me on this journey. A special thank you to Miriam Nash, so glad you're in my corner.

A big thank you to Dr Mary Murphy and Hugh Griffin who generously gave of their time and expertise. When I needed to know about horses Caoimhleann O'Leary came to the rescue and thank you, Orla Kenneally for filling me in on teenage romance. Joan Cronin, I so appreciated your words of support and encouragement.

I needed a professional eye along the way and thank you to Niamh Boyce from the Writer's Centre for your helpful and generous feedback and to editors Brian Langan and Richard Bradburn for your constructive insights.

To Rachel Keith in Oklahoma – thank you so much for your enormous skill and precision in copyediting and proofing the final manuscript. I am in awe of your eagle eye.

Writing can be a lonely furrow and you need allies – so a debt of gratitude to my Listowel writers' gang: Hillary Mullane, Anne-Marie

McCallion, Brenda O'Donoghue, Elaine Ruby, Anne Lynch, Imelda McDonagh – thank you for your friendship, support and encouragement. And I am so grateful to my Write Night band of writers who cheer me on and give me energy and inspiration – so thank you Rosemary McSweeney, Amanda Leahy, Mona Lynch, Dorothy Ahern, Shree Krishamoorthy, Tony Ryan, Ann Heffernan, Eileen McNeela, Mary Galvin and Michelle McLaughlin.

As a child, my aunt, Maureen O'Herlihy introduced me to the magic of words. In latter years, Maire O'Donoghue, AWA writing coach has encouraged so many fledgling writers in her Blackrock classes, including me, so a huge thank you Maire. Dr Ann Rath, you are an inspiring coach and thank you and all the wonderful writers in your Lismore writing workshops – so much encouragement.

Thanks to Orla Kelly Publishing for so skilfully and patiently getting the book to publication and to Charlie Neville of Charlie Neville Design for your expertise and creativity. And to Terri Murphy and Mary Buckley, Creative Concepts, thank you for your ideas, boundless enthusiasm and love. You are the business! Take a bow too, Stephen Ryan and his team at Narration, Fiona, David, Eoin and Rachel, you were fabulous to work with.

A final thank you to the English Folk Dance & Song Society and the McPeake Family for their kind permission to reproduce the lyrics of "Will ye go, Lassie go."

About the Author

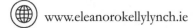 www.eleanorokellylynch.ie

eleanorokellylynch@gmail.com

 eleanoroklynch

@eleanoroklynch

 Eleanor O'Kelly Lynch

Please Review

Dear reader,

Thank you for taking the time to read my book. As a first time author, I would really appreciate if you could tell others about it if you think it is somethign they would enjoy to read. Also if you could leave a review of the book on Goodreads or if you purchased the book online, if you could leave an honest review there.

This matters because most potential readers first judge a book by what others have to say.

Thanking you in advance.
Eleanor